CASE RESEARCH IN
PUBLIC MANAGEMENT

CASE RESEARCH IN PUBLIC MANAGEMENT

DAVID E. McNABB

M.E.Sharpe
Armonk, New York
London, England

This book is dedicated to my longtime friend and
mentor, Professor and Dean Emeritus,
Dr. Gundar J. King

Library of Congress Cataloging-in-Publication Data

McNabb, David E.
  Case research in public management / by David E. McNabb.
    p. cm.
  Includes bibliographical references and index.
  ISBN 978-0-7656-2336-2 (cloth : alk. paper) — ISBN 978-0-7656-2337-9 (pbk. : alk. paper)
  1. Public administration—Research. 2. Public administration—Case studies. 3. Qualitative
research. I. Title.

  JF1338.A2M378 2010
  351.072'2—dc22   2009018629

Printed in the United States of America

The paper used in this publication meets the minimum requirements of
American National Standard for Information Sciences
Permanence of Paper for Printed Library Materials,
ANSI Z 39.48-1984.

∞

CW (c)	10	9	8	7	6	5	4	3	2	1
CW (p)	10	9	8	7	6	5	4	3	2	1

Brief Table of Contents

Detailed Table of Contents

Introduction

The essence of a case study is that its aim is to illuminate a decision or set of decisions and to understand why they were taken, and how they were implemented and with what result.
—Sally A. Kydd, 1999

The once strong belief in the relevance of public administration and its ability to make a significant contribution toward the resolution of increasingly complex, often global in scope, problems of governance has come into question among scholars and practitioners. One of the reasons for this is that public administration has historically focused on domestic governance issues. This meant it dealt with problems of management in organizations from the smallest special noxious-weed or mosquito-abatement district to very large national agencies like the Department of Defense and global organizations such as NATO or the United Nations.

A fundamental goal for research in public administration has been to make local government more effective and national government more efficient, regardless of the nation within which the government is located. The literature of the discipline clearly supports this view. However, the very nature of the globalization of governance has made it necessary for the discipline to expand its focus to include greater attention upon challenges and issues that extend across national borders and which require cross-border cooperation and collaboration (Brinkerhoff 2002). The case research method may be ideally suited to the study and analysis of these situations.

The case study has a long history of use in research in applied public organization and management. However, for some researchers in the social and administrative sciences (including public administration and political science), the case research method long remained somewhat a subject of derision. The method was discounted as inappropriate for serious research or simply ignored, or often shrugged off as "not real science." This may be because not everyone understands what case research is, what it is good for—and what it is not. Despite the belief that case research survives in what Gerring (2004, 341) described as "a curious methodological limbo," it is clearly thriving in public management and political science research.

This book was written to help bring the case method out of the limbo to which it was mistakenly assigned and into the mainstream of research in public management. It is hoped that the discussion and case examples repeated here help researchers and public managers understand the *what, why,* and *how* of this increasingly important research method. In contrast to researchers such as Yin (1994) and others who consider the case study approach not a research *method* but rather a research *strategy*, in this book I have adopted the method model. I have also done so in my other studies of research methods.

Cases as Applied Research

Some confusion may arise as to whether the book is about case research on management topics in public organizations, or whether is it about case research on the administration of public programs. It is neither—and it is both. I have intentionally tried to select examples of case research on applied rather than theoretical issues. In my mind, the men and women who work in government administer and manage—often at the same time. Therefore, the terms public management and public administration are used interchangeably throughout the book.

Lan and Anders (2000) reviewed more than 600 research papers published in eight academic and professional public administration journals over a three-year period in the 1900s. Most of that research dealt with managerial issues in federal, state, or local government agencies, with particular emphasis on issues of concern to executives. This means that most research in public administration has been applied rather than theoretical. The purpose of applied research is to help practicing public managers solve practical problems of implementing policies and programs. Research in public management tends to focus rather heavily on ways to improve the practice of managing government organizations. Thus, the case method is particularly appropriate in public administration and management.

Typical management issues addressed by researchers at the start of the current century were human resources, finance and budgeting, policy, planning, performance measurements, and similar management concerns. Less than 2 percent of the papers looked at ethical issues in government. In addition to management topics, major research topics included current international issues, government, and governance in general, with a small number on research methods.

While no single approach dominated the papers examined, a small majority (59 percent) favored qualitative research over quantitative methods, and the case research method was the most popular approach among all qualitative methods. No distinction was made between single-case and multicase studies. Other qualitative approaches included ethnographic methods, literature reviews, and reportorial narratives.

Case Research: Qualitative or Quantitative?

One of the reasons for the case method controversy in the past is that many researchers were long taught that quantitative research based on behavioralist research principles was the only appropriate approach for research and analysis. In this approach researchers establish tentative hypotheses prior to their data gathering and often revise these as their analysis progresses; they identify as variables the key constructs proposed in their hypotheses. Their research is designed to test hypotheses. Searching for cause-and-effect relationships between defined variables that can be measured is a hallmark of quantitative research studies.

Case researchers, on the other hand, seek greater *understanding* of interactions and processes in the social situations that they observe—or are told about—taking place in groups and organizations. Thus, a goal of case research is to describe what is happening, why it is happening, and how it happens in an organization. Case research is qualitative research, and qualitative researchers develop concepts, insights, and understandings from patterns they see in their collected data rather than collecting data to assess preconceived models, hypotheses, or theories (Taylor and Bogdan 1998; Bryman and Burgess 1999).

Case research seldom employs statistical analysis of its collected data. This is because case research is most often carried out to produce deeper knowledge about a single unit or a small number of units on an issue of interest. It is usually inappropriate to apply statistical analysis in a case research design, although some case studies do include both interpretive and causal data analysis techniques.

When more than one case is included in a research study—the multicase approach—the researcher often compares examples of a program, policy, or application in different but similar jurisdictions. The researcher then reports the differences and similarities and often adds suggestions on implications of the differences for other similar organizations. Survey studies, on the other hand, involve measuring some phenomenon (such as an attitude, an opinion, a belief, or acceptance of an idea) in larger samples in order to predict future events and behaviors based on their findings. The objective is to identify cause-and-effect relationships by applying inferential statistical analyses to measurements taken from a sample of subjects drawn from a population of interest (subjects can be individual units, groups, or organizations).

Case researchers typically approach a topic with little or no preconceived assumptions; rather, such interpretations are expected to appear out of the data collected from the case. While behavioralist researchers are often guided by a strict set of rules and processes, case researchers are more likely to be investigating a situation or event within an organizational context for which no causal thesis is warranted. Case researchers approach their research situation with a willingness to be *flexible*; this enables them to follow where the data lead.

Objectives for the Book

This book grew out of several decades of teaching research methods to under-graduate and graduate public- and private-sector management students at several universities in the United States and Europe. During those years, the prevailing research philosophy emphasized the use of quantitative methods that followed behavioralist principles. Only lately have qualitative methods achieved broad acceptance in these academic fields of inquiry and the professional literature of those disciplines; most research methods texts have continued to emphasize quantitative research designs. However, this is changing rapidly as many research methods texts now include discussions on both qualitative and quantitative methods. This book was written to serve as an expanded guide to what has become a mainstream research approach in public sector and nonprofit organization management: the case research method.

The book is organized into two sections of ten chapters each. The first section focuses on the methods and procedures for doing case research, regardless of the topic of interest. The second section reviews a variety of cases on federal, state, and local government organizations. The cases were selected from the public administration and government documents literature because they focus on some area of interest in public management. None of the cases are meant to serve as teaching cases. They are meant to serve as examples of how other researchers have used case study research on the topic; they are intended as *method* examples, not *topic* examples. A smaller number of international case studies are also included for the same purpose. The example cases have been included because they represent models of the method as it is actually used in research in public management.

Acknowledgments

I wish to first acknowledge the great debt of gratitude I owe to Harry M. Briggs, executive editor at M.E. Sharpe, and to the many highly supportive and helpful members of the M.E. Sharpe editorial staff. The entire M.E. Sharpe team has continued to provide welcome support throughout the proposal and writing phase of this and earlier books. You all have my thanks. I am particularly indebted to Managing Editor Angela Piliouras, who has been a tower of strength throughout the production of this and my earlier M.E. Sharpe books; she deserves more thanks than I can every give.

I also wish to give full credit—and my thanks—to the authors of the cases I have reviewed or mentioned in this text. I apologize in advance for any errors that may have crept into my reviews of your work, and for those times where I may have stressed elements other than those that you might have selected. My purpose for including your work was purely instructional and supportive. And, if I have not included examples that other readers might feel are more representative of the case method, it is only because I picked the cases that interested me. Lucky for all of us, there are hundreds if not thousands of good examples of case research from which each of us can choose. As authors Streib, Slotkin, and Rivera reported in their 2001 study of practitioner-related articles in *Public Administration Review,* the case method is today second in preference only to the survey method.

I also wish to thank three colleagues to whom I owe a debt that can never be fully repaid: Professors Cheryl S. King, Larry Geri, and Don Bantz of the MPA program at The Evergreen State College in Olympia, Washington. They gave me my start in public administration education, and for that I will always be grateful.

Finally, I must again thank my family: Janet, Meghan, Michael, and Sara. Your encouragement and support has helped me through many trying moments.

Part I

The What and How of Case Research

The first section in this book is a complete-in-itself manual for students and practitioners of public management who are planning to conduct a case research project. The first of the ten chapters in this section begins with a detailed overview of the case research process. The second chapter explains the several different purposes for which case research is used, and describes the types of research designs that have been developed to meet those research requirements.

The third chapter is an overview of some of the ways that case research is classified. Chapter 4 is a more detailed focus on single-case designs; chapter 5 does the same for multicase designs. Chapter 6 includes step-by-step guidelines for getting started in either a single- or a multicase research project. Chapter 7 is a description of meta-analysis of case research; it includes an overview of the meta-analysis process.

Chapters 8 and 9 go into some detail on how researchers analyze primary data in case research and how textual data can be used in case research. The final chapter in this section is a brief guide to help in the writing and publishing of the results of a case research project.

> 1 <

What Is Case Research?

*Case study research consists of a detailed investigation, often
with data collected over a period of time, of one or more
organizations, or groups within organizations, with a
view to providing an analysis of the context and processes involved
in the phenomenon under study. The phenomenon is not
isolated from its context (as in, say, laboratory research) but
is of interest precisely because it is in relation to its context.*
—Jean F. Hartley (1994)

Following a pattern established in research in the social and administrative sciences, case research in public management has proven to be an effective way of identifying and disseminating knowledge on the successes and failures of public managers in government organizations. Case research involves a detailed investigation of one or more organizations or groups within organizations (Stokes and Perry 2007). The investigators then report on the findings of an analysis of the content or processes related to the phenomenon being examined (Hartley 1994). Also, the teaching and learning approach that involves the analysis of case studies is now regularly accepted in many graduate public management programs as a method for exposing students of public management to problem solving and decision making in real-life situations. This has resulted in the case research method becoming an important alternative to traditional behavioralist research methods.

The History of Case Research

Case research has been one of the most popular research approaches in public administration since its appearance during the middle years of the twentieth century. Whelan (1989) traced the early applications of the case approach to 1948, when a planning committee was formed at Harvard University to develop guidelines for applying the method to research in public administration. Under the leadership of Harold Stein, the original Harvard program was renamed the Inter-University Case Program (IUCP). The IUCP published a text with twenty-six cases in 1949, just a year after their first meeting. In the introduction to that casebook, the public administration case was described as "a narrative of the events that constitute or lead to a decision or group of related decisions by a public administrator or group of public administrators" (Stein 1952, xxvii).

A number of now-classic case studies were published beginning about the same time as the method was evolving at Harvard. Philip Selznick's *TVA and the Grass Roots* appeared in 1949; Herbert Kaufman's study of the forest service, *The Forest Ranger*, was published in 1960. A third classic case study, Michael Lipsky's (1980) study of city bureaucracies, *Street-Level Bureaucracy*, has helped the case approach to achieve recognition as a valid and important research methodology.

These larger case studies have been mirrored in miniature by acceptance of the approach in the discipline's professional literature. For example, in his detailed overview of the state of public administration research methods, Yeager (1989) found that one or more case studies had appeared in every issue of *Public Administration Review* (PAR) for more than forty years. If their continuing appearance in PAR—the discipline's leading publication—and other public administration journals is any indication, case studies are just as popular today as they were when Yeager examined the field in the late 1980s. PAR has accepted the case method as a mainstream research approach.

The key to the popularity of the case study approach lies in its great flexibility (Masoner 1988). Case studies can be written to serve as examples of what a public administrator ought not to do, as well as what should be done. However, their primary purpose is to teach practicing public managers about the decisions, problems, and programs of other public managers. Case reports serve to inform administrators about the latest developments and thinking going on in their field. Moreover, published international case research means that government managers are able to learn from the managerial and administrative experiences of agencies, locations, and levels of government around the globe, thus avoiding the need to "reinvent the wheel."

The Meaning of Case Research

Many authors have proposed definitions for the terms *case, case research, case studies,* and the *case study method.* A case is a description of an organization or a phenomenon of special interest. Thus, a case may be the story of an application of a particular public management tool in a government or nonprofit agency or organization. Further definitions are displayed in Box 1.1.

In this text, case research is considered to be a research method, in which qualitative or descriptive data collection and analysis techniques are used to enable a researcher or researchers to add to the knowledge base of a discipline. A case study is a case that is studied using the case research method for some special, often instructional, purpose.

Box 1.1

Defining Case Research

Definitional instances to which case research has been applied:

- The case method is used when the research is qualitative with one or a few subjects in the sample.
- When the research is ethnographic, involving field observational data gathering, it is probably a case study.
- When the study is done to trace a process across more than one unit, it is a case study.
- It is a case when the research is done to describe in depth the properties of a single organization or unit.
- When the researcher studies one phenomenon, event, or example (such as performance measurement), the case method is the most appropriate method.

Source: Gerring (2004).

The case study method is also a pedagogical approach to teaching in which students study applications of conceptual models and/or theories through the study of case studies.

The Case in Public Administration Research

Yeager traced the application of case research to Harold Stein, who, in an article published in 1952, was one of the first to promote the method as a way to do public administration research. Crediting Stein, Yeager (1989, 685) offered this definition for a public administration case:

> A public administration case [is] a narrative of the events that lead to a decision or group of related decisions by a public administrator or group of public administrators.

Another definition of the case referred to by Yeager was proposed by the business administration scholar T.V. Bonoma in a 1985 *Journal of Marketing Research* article. Rather than focusing on cases in public management, Bonoma's definition has more of a general management focus:

> A case is a description of a management situation based on interview, archival, naturalistic observation, and other data, constructed to be sensitive to the context in which management behavior takes place and to its temporal restraints. These are characteristics shared by all cases. (Bonoma 1985, 199)

Harry Eckstein (2002) defined the case technically as "a phenomenon for which we report and interpret only a single measure on any pertinent variable." The term *measure* refers to the concept that the description either refers to the case in question or does not. It does not mean quantitative measures such as measures of central tendency, association, correlation, variance, or others.

Many researchers consider the several editions of Robert K. Yin's *Case Study Reseearch* to be the seminal works in the methodology of the case study. In the first edition of his important series, Yin (1994) stated that the distinguishing characteristic of the case is that it attempts to examine (1) a phenomenon in its real-life context, when (2) the boundaries between phenomenon and its context are not clear. In the second (1994) edition, Yin added that the case study is "an empirical inquiry" that (1) investigates a contemporary phenomenon within its real-life context, particularly when "the boundaries between phenomenon and context are not clearly evident" (p. 13).

Gillham (2000, 1) expanded on Yin's (1994) concepts, adding that a case under study has four fundamental principles:

1. It is a unit of human activity taking place in the real world.
2. A case can only be studied—and understood—in the context of the activity in which it is embedded.
3. Context exists at the time of the case analysis (thus supporting the "snapshot" idea of the case).
4. The case and its context are merged in such a manner that it is difficult to identify distinct boundaries between the two.

Recognizing that the researchers who proposed these definitions had different things in mind when talking about case research, Gerring (2004) found flaws in all of the definitions. Instead, he defined case research as *"an intensive study of a single unit for the purpose of understanding a larger class of (similar) units"* (emphasis in the original). He further defined a unit as "a spatially bounded phenomenon—e.g., a nation-state, revolution, political party, election, or person—observed at a single point in time or over some delimited period of time."

Teaching Cases

Some might say that all case research is conducted with the underlying purpose of instruction. However, in practice, teaching cases are generally treated as a separate species of the genus *case research*. Teaching cases are designed for use as the principal tool in the case study instructional method. This is the dominant instructional approach in graduate business administration and, increasingly, in public management courses. The teaching case is described in more detail here, but will only be marginally addressed in later chapters.

Teaching cases tend to be detailed descriptions of an organization and an existing or a (correctly or questionably) solved management problem or situation in that organization. Typically, students are required to analyze the case in order to identify and separate symptoms of the management problem and propose alternative solutions based on the students' interpretation of the case and current management concepts. The cases may be written as an analyst's evaluation of an organization, with little or no guidance for students. Or they may include such guiding principles as brief descriptions of competing theories or a list of questions either on the case itself or as guides for student analysis of the material.

There are a number of different subspecies within the broad family of teaching cases. At the most basic level, all cases fall into one of three major classes: problem cases, decision cases, and evaluation cases. However, Lundberg et al. (2001) dissected these three broad classes into as many as nine different subcategories:

1. *Iceberg cases:* As the name suggests, iceberg cases require students to apply conceptual models as they analyze what lies "below the surface" of the described organization. The learning objectives are building problem identification skills, information gathering, assessment skills, and understanding of the relevance and application of models and theories.

2. *Incident cases:* These are the shorter cases often included at the end of a chapter. Little information on the organization is provided. Incident cases usually describe a specific incident or application and are designed to generate discussion of a concept or concepts presented in the chapter.

3. *Illustrative cases:* These cases are similar in scope to the cases found in the professional literature. They tend to follow an accepted structural format. The purpose of illustrative cases is to provide readers—students or practitioners—with a detailed description of a management practice as it occurs in a real-life situation. If used in a classroom, they are intended to bring reality into the discussion and illustrate how existing applications do or do not fit their ideal theoretical stereotypes. Most of the cases described in this text fall into this category.

4. *Head cases:* Similar to human relations cases, head cases are designed to illustrate actors' interactions, thoughts, and feelings about a situation or a decision. Their underlying objective is to show students the human side of theoretical or real-life management activities by allowing students to "get into the actors' heads." Often loosely structured, head cases allow students to use their imagination and make broad assumptions.

5. *Dialogue cases:* Similar to head cases, dialogue cases focus on the interpersonal relations of two or more people. The reactions of the individuals are often written as dialogue between the parties. Students are often asked to take the part of one of the actors and describe what the actor would do or say after the dialogue. These cases may also focus on such interpersonal concepts as assumptions, stereotyping, diversity, beliefs. values, and leadership styles.

6. *Application cases:* Similar to illustrative cases, application cases describe an organizational situation in which either a management technique or a theory has been applied. In this case, the large amount of information provided is presented in a format that is far less structured than in the illustrative case. Students analyze the situation to determine the effectiveness of the application and to determine whether one or more alternative applications might have been more appropriate or effective.

7. *Data cases:* These cases are more suited for use in the classroom than as guides for practitioners. They present a large amount of information in an unstructured or informal way, with students required to sort through the material to identify the relevant facts. Data cases are also a good tool for teaching how data can be organized and classified into relevant groups. Another objective of using data cases is to teach students how to discern the differences between problems and symptoms.

8. *Issue cases:* These dual-purpose cases—useful for teaching and illustrating practical applications—are designed to show readers the dilemmas that public managers face in their careers. As such, they are often used to illustrate ethical dilemmas.

9. *Prediction cases:* Often used in graduate management education, prediction cases are usually written in two or more parts. Students are required to predict the outcomes they expect will occur from the information in the first part and then compare their first evaluation with the information presented in the second or later parts of the case. Their predictions are supposed to be based on a conceptual model discussed earlier in the classroom. This model helps students evaluate the accuracy of their predictions.

For more information about writing, analyzing, and using teaching cases, see Barnes, Christensen, and Hansen (1994); Lundberg et al. (2001); Ellet (2007); and Shapiro (2007); among others.

When a Case Study Is *Not* Case Research

Case research refers to a specific type of research design. A case study, however, can be the product of exploratory research, survey research, experimental research, action research, or any other research method. How the data are collected and analyzed in a case study is not restricted to any single research methodology. A case study is usually the report of some examination of an individual organization, a unit, one or more individuals as a group, or a phenomenon such as a new managerial task—or of a small number of such units or phenomena.

If the case is on a management task, such as a new approach to performance measurement, for example, the case researcher studies the phenomenon within a unit or compares its application across a small number of units. In the administrative sciences such as public and business management, the purpose for examining a phenomenon in a case study is often to provide instructions for others who might wish to apply the same new approach.

Often the label "case study" is attached to a research report because the study focuses on a single agency or subunit, but the report really describes a research project in which data were collected in something other than the classic definition of case methodology. An often-seen example is the *survey research* report. In survey research, a sample of individuals in a study unit is asked to respond to fixed-response items on a questionnaire. A typical purpose of studies of this type is to measure the subjects' attitudes or opinions on some topic of interest at the time the survey is conducted.

An example of such a study is the survey of federal employees in a regional office of the U.S. Environmental Protection Agency (Soni 2000), which described a survey to establish the extent to which workers valued diversity in the workplace and their support of diversity-management activities in their organization. The sample consisted of 160 supervisors and 350 nonsupervisory workers. A stratified random-sampling approach was used to ensure representation by white males, white females, minority males, and minority females. The survey instrument used Likert-type statements in an agree/disagree distribution. The author concluded that the research did produce some insights into what factors might have influenced employee support for diversity in an organization. Not to take anything away from the research or the finding, this article described what might more appropriately be considered a *quantitative survey research design* rather than a case research design.

A similar study—also not a case in the classical sense—was conducted among the employees of five separate units of a regional office of the General Services Administration (McNabb and Sepic 1995). In that study, a survey questionnaire was administered to measure the attitudes of employees toward a proposed implementation of a total quality management program. The study did not investigate the organization in depth, nor did it examine employee attitudes or opinions beyond the single question: Was the organization ready for a change?

Public Administration Examples

Additional illustrations of this question can be found in a 2008 issue of *Public Administration Review*. Three articles in the January/February 2008 issue include some aspects of the case study method: Schachter's "Lillian Borrone: Weaving a Web to Revitalize Port Commerce in New York and New Jersey"; Handley's "Strengthening the Intergovernmental Grant System: Long-Term Lessons for the Federal-Local Relationship"; and Prager's "Contract City Redux: Weston, Florida, as the Ultimate New Public Management Model City."

The Schachter (2008) article is an entertaining and enlightening report of one administrator's life story, focusing on the steps taken on the path to becoming the first woman to achieve a position as the chief administrator of one of the largest port authorities in the world: New York/New Jersey. Although the article does offer

9

some advice on the importance in a career of establishing networks, it is not a case study; it is a life history. This in no way takes away from the importance or relevance of the story described in the article. The story highlights—without describing in detail—the "glass ceiling" barriers that have unfairly limited the advancement of women in many organizations. However, the purpose of this life story is not to function as an action guide for other women or minority public managers to follow when faced with the same or similar problems.

Handley's important essay (2008) on relationships between the federal and local governments comes much closer to being a true case study. It is largely a historical report of the problems that have characterized implementation of the federal grants-in-aid programs, with a focus on the Community Development Block Grant program. It describes the program from its beginning in 1974 until the time of writing the article.

Four Primary Challenges

The article identifies four primary challenges associated with federal grants-in-aid: (1) the politics of decentralization, (2) the inability of smaller units of government to maintain required capacity to benefit from national programs, (3) program accountability issues, and (4) the problems of limited program adaptability. Handley (2008) concluded that these difficulties often contributed to less than optimal intergovernmental cooperative implementation of grants-in-aid programs, and that without changes the difficulties are likely to continue.

Of these three research articles, Prager's (2008) paper on privatization and outsourcing may be closest to the classic case study research model. The article begins with a brief comparison of two outsourcing models. The first is a partial outsourcing model followed by Lakewood, California, and second is the more or less completely outsourced model followed by the city of Weston, Florida. The focus of the study is the experiences of the city of Weston.

Weston is located a little more than 30 miles north of Miami, has a population of nearly 62,000, and covers 25.8 square miles. It is one of the few cities in the world that outsources all city services except the few that can be handled by its three employees.

Prager (2008) pointed out that while Weston contracts out almost everything, it is, however, committed to doing so in principle, something that cities that follow the Lakewood plan are not. This case explores the Weston model in order to determine whether circumstances that led to it being adopted in that city were unique, or whether it can be adopted as a model of municipal management applicable in other places as well.

The case concludes with answers to two questions that serve as suggested lessons for other municipalities considering adopting the Weston model: First, does Weston's experience suggest that smaller cities can avoid the pitfalls associated with outsourcing services? Prager's (2008) answer is, possibly, but those considering adopting this approach should look at other alternative models first. Second, is the Weston model applicable elsewhere? Prager concludes that, yes it is, but making it happen won't be easy. The Weston experience may work best for cities that are not committed to civil service or that have an organized labor force.

Is the Weston model a harbinger of the wave of new public management? Prager's (2008) answer is a qualified yes. Cities that meet the Weston conditions—no history of government employees, the existence of supporting governments (e.g., county and state that already have a history of providing services to residents), and affluence—would do well to look closely at the Weston model. It is also a good example of a comparative case study model.

The Focus of Case Research

So far, we have looked at what cases are, what they are not, and how different data collection methods may be used in case research. Possibly the most important issue concerning the nature of a case study is establishing the focus of the study—the topic or issue that is being examined. Case studies are typically intensive studies of one or a few exemplary individuals, families, events, decisions, processes, programs, institutions, organizations, groups, even entire communities, or any other social phenomenon (Lang and Heiss 1994; Arneson 1993; Lan and Anders 2000.). Thus, they tend to be narrow but deep in scope.

Discussing the case method as one of three qualitative approaches for research in organizational communications, Arneson (1993) saw this narrow but deep scope of the case method as an appropriate research approach to follow when some noteworthy success or failure in an organization is present. He added that qualitative case studies are an appropriate approach when evaluating programs that are directed toward *individualized* outcomes.

The Question of Causality in Case Research

The case is thus a descriptive study of one or a few particular entities and, therefore, is only minimally appropriate when the research objective is to make inferences of causality. Case studies should not be considered typical or representative, nor should they be considered to have external validity. Because each case study is unique, it must be considered as a description and not typical of a larger set. However, the topic of the case study may be selected and described as a way of identifying a *theoretical* relationship between antecedents and events or conclusions (Roberts 2005).

Case Research as Interpretive Research

It is also important to keep in mind that the case study method is considered to be primarily a qualitative or interpretive approach to research, although as noted earlier with methods of collecting case data, case reports often include elements of both qualitative and quantitative methods (Roberts 2005; Gillham 2000; Pennings, Keman, and Kleinnijenhuis 1999). Thus, all evidence can be gist for the case researcher's mill, just as many different data-gathering methods may be used.

Case research typically emphasizes nonstatistical, ethnographic research techniques to produce greater understanding of a phenomenon. The data collected in the research of the case may be a collection of words, symbols, pictures, or other nonnumeric records, materials, or artifacts that are collected by researchers. The data are gathered to describe events, programs, activities, and other circumstances in which some aspect of human behavior is involved. For us, that is the behavior of managers and workers in public organizations and the decisions made in the act of governing. This leaves the door open for case study research of all activities in all levels of government and its partners, collaborators, and network participants.

Causation in Social Science Research

According to Lawrence Mohr (1992), case research in the social sciences has two aims. First, it wants to explain or describe behavior as it occurs in observed situations. Second, the findings should be widely relevant—that is, they should be valid enough for application in similar but unobserved situations. Validity of this type is necessary to validate the research as "a genuine contribution to knowledge rather than a bit of gossip." The single-case study, even if an in-depth and detailed examination of the situation, was for many years considered to be inferior to large-sample quantitative research for achieving either or both of these aims. Mohr, however, disagreed strongly with that assumption, adding that most methods in social science research have weaknesses and that the case method is neither weaker nor stronger than any other research approach.

Mohr (1992) believed that the perceived limitations of the case study as a research design were both superficial and exaggerated. He thought it was extremely important to recognize that there are no designs in social science that will accomplish both of the aims of research with high assurance and reliability. Rather, all designs have serious limitations. He was convinced that the case method has great potential as a tool for achieving both of the goals and, therefore, should not *in principle* be considered inferior to large-sample research of any description. He emphasized "in principle" because much depends on whether the case study design is used well or poorly and whether it is a good fit to the requirements of the research question in a particular study.

Mohr (1992) resolved the question of whether case studies can or should be used to explain causation by claiming that there is more than one type of causality in social science: *physical* causality and *logical* causation. Physical causation is explained by the reaction between a force and a motion, as in the example of billiard balls moving after being struck by a cue ball: A causes B. The point of physical causality research is to bring out the relationship between force and motion, between a reason and a responding behavior. Mohr noted that physical causal reasoning is common in the social sciences, and that case research in which physical causality is identified is often appropriate and valid.

Logical Causation

Logical causation follows a conditional response model: say, a ball is thrown at a thickly shuttered window. Before the ball strikes, the shutter is opened by someone. The ball, which would have bounced off the shutter causing no damage, strikes and breaks the glass that is behind the shutter. In this model, opening the shutter logically "caused" the glass to break. Thus, for event A (the ball in motion) to "cause" event B (the broken window) to happen, condition C (the intervening opening of the shutter) has to occur. Case research is less likely to establish an A–B connection because of the unknown effect of unexpected C. Mohr (1992, 88) concluded that "the true criticism of the case study . . . is not that it's a design by which it is difficult to establish causality, but that it is a design by which it is difficult to establish causality through logical causal reasoning."

Although conceding that the case method has a role in political science—and hence, public management—Jasjeet Sekhon was less sanguine on the inferential role for the method (emphasis Sekhon's):

> Case studies have their own role in the progress of political science [and its sister discipline, public administration/public management]. They permit the discovery of causal mechanisms and new phenomena, and can help draw attention to unexpected results. They should *complement* statistics. Unfortunately, however, case study research methods often assume deterministic relationships among the variables of interest; and failure to heed the lessons of statistical inference often leads to serious inferential errors, some of which are easy to avoid. (Sekhon 2004, 281)

Cases and Causal Inference

Case research is seldom used as a means of extrapolating small sample findings to a larger sample or population. In fact, the chief criticism of case research in general has been that is usually intended to be descriptive and therefore not usually valid for making causal inferences. Hersen and Barlow (1976) dispute this criticism; some single-case designs have been framed as controlled experiments from which some limited causal inferences may be made.

Although most authors writing on the case study method have concluded that it is not appropriate for making inferences to other, similar subject cases or for establishing causality, many others have concluded the opposite. They assert that the case method—albeit only in certain circumstances—is appropriate for inferring causality (Blampied 2000; Gerring 2004; Mohr 1992; Pennings, Keman, and Kleinnijenhuis 1999). It has also been suggested that, again in certain applications, single-case research (1) is based on the positivist tradition of null hypothesis testing; (2) it emphasizes the visual analysis of data discovered during the case analysis, which is then presented in tables and graphs; and (3) it relies on replication for verification. Gerring made the point, however, that the inferences made from case research are *exploratory* and *descriptive* rather than causal and probabilistic.

An Answer to the Causation Question?

Pennings, Keman, and Kleinnijenhuis (1999) blended the qualitative and quantitative approaches in their discussion of causality in the political science case study. Their approach is similar to the logical causation model discussed by Mohr (1992). They identified two methods of data analysis in causal inference studies: case-oriented research and variable-oriented research. Case-oriented research is exploratory research, whereas variable-oriented research is the hypothesis-testing model. The objective of case-oriented research is a full understanding of one or a few cases using as many variables as appropriate. The objective of variable-oriented research is the understanding of variables, using as many cases as appropriate.

The preferred method of data analysis in the case-oriented approach is in-depth analysis and an interpretive, descriptive narrative approach. However, in variable-oriented research, the preferred methods of analysis include such quantitative analysis techniques as frequency distributions, discriminant analysis, analysis of variance (ANOVA), and regression analysis. The choice of technique depends upon the level of measurement (nominal, ordinal, or interval). Multicase studies may involve either the descriptive approach or the statistical analysis approach.

In establishing causality in a small number of cases in a multicase design, the variables used to explain the occurrence of an event or phenomenon are treated as dichotomous—with (1) representing the presence of a condition or event and (0) representing its absence. The phenomena can be the conditions or preconditions that led up to an event or condition.

In this way, both qualitative and quantitative approaches can be used in case-oriented research. However, Pennings, Keman, and Kleinnijenhuis (1999) focused on the quantitative technique of *qualitative comparative analysis* (QCA) developed by Charles Ragin in 1987. In that model, causality is inferred through an analysis of the existence or absence of one or more variables in a majority of the cases studied.

Summary

Since its appearance during the middle years of the last century, case research has become a widely accepted alternative approach to research in public administration, political science, and the administrative sciences. The case study was developed originally in the life sciences as a tool for the study of people or small groups.

Thus, the method has particular value when the research objective is an in-depth analysis of one or a few similar organizations in which a particular phenomenon of interest has been applied.

Case studies serve several purposes. First, case studies are valuable for helping public administrators learn how other administrators and managers have accepted and applied new management techniques, policies, and practices. Second, they provide feedback and professional analysis and recommendations for the individuals and managers in the cases under study. These two applications are the focus of this book. A third important application comprises the teaching cases used to help build knowledge and develop management decision skills in higher education programs in public administration, political science, and public and nonprofit organization management. This approach, which was briefly described in this chapter, is not examined in any further detail.

➤ 2 ◀

When to Do Case Research and How to Pick Cases

The most important (and difficult) stage in . . . case study research is the selection of cases. Cases can, of course, be drawn randomly from a population to eliminate the danger of selection bias. Yet drawing a random sample is often not possible because the universe of cases is not known or is not accessible.
—Juliet Kaarbo and Ryan K. Beasley (1999)

This chapter examines two elementary questions in research design. The first seeks to answer why researchers choose to do case research in the first place. The second focuses on what may be the most important question in case research—how to select the case or cases to study. The case method is typically chosen when the researcher wants to delve deeply into or produce a richer description of a phenomenon than survey or experimental research designs would be able to achieve.

The case selection question is approached from two different points: (1) how to select the case in a single-case design and (2) how to pick cases when selecting two or more cases in a multicase design. Case selection for meta-analysis case research is addressed in chapter 7.

Many different approaches and sets of rules or steps have been suggested for doing case research; two are presented in this chapter. The first approach describes a set of steps to follow when conducting single, representative-case research; the second is a more detailed set of steps that are typically followed in multicase studies. The chapter begins with a discussion on how researchers go about selecting a subject for their research—an activity common to all case research.

Why Researchers Choose the Case Research Method

The subjects selected for a public management case study are typically selected because they point out some underlying problem within an organization or among

---

Box 2.1

Addressing Case Research Issues

Netherlands researcher B. J. Oosterman chose a single-case research design to call attention to the importance of concurrent engineering to organizational success. In describing his research design, he highlighted some of the issues that must be addressed when opting for a case study research design. First, he warned that "critics of case study research believe that single-case studies can offer no grounds for achieving reliability or generality in respect of the findings. Others feel that case studies bias findings or are only useful as an explorative tool."

However, Oosterman noted, "Other scholars have stressed the enormous potential of case studies and introduced procedures that offer the opportunity to establish 'good' research. In general terms, if the case design is sound, and the researcher is explicit about the phenomenon and context of the study, the results of case study research cannot be dismissed out of hand."

Oosterman concluded with the following recommendations:

- Conducting case study research involves considerable preparation and a careful approach.
- It is necessary to have a clear research design that connects the data to be collected to the initial research question.
- The case research design should have a strong theoretical foundation; proper use of theory will aid the design by providing better focus and greater weight for the collected data.

Source: Oosterman (2001, 7).

---

groups of individuals in an organization, or because they represent a successful solution to a problem. The researcher and individuals involved in the case often hope that publishing a narrative of a successful experience will provide a model for others to emulate.

Because public administration researchers have used the case study for so long and in so many different ways, it is not surprising that so many different purposes for the method have surfaced. However, most authors agree with Lang and Heiss, who wrote that this one fundamental principle underlies all case studies:

> The basic rationale for a case study is that there are processes and interactions . . . which cannot be studied effectively except as they interact and function within the entity itself. Thus, if we learn how these processes interact in one person or organization, we will know more about . . . factors themselves and perhaps apply these (what we have learned) to other similar type persons or organizations. (1994, 86)

Figure 2.1 **Purposes for Selecting the Case Research Method**

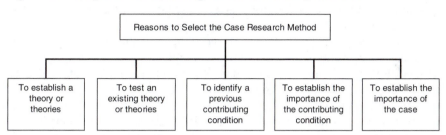

Other researchers have described a variety of different scenarios that make the case study method a particularly appropriate design. Bailey (1994), for example, identified a number of different designs for case studies in public administration: (1) They can be descriptive, interpretive, or critical; (2) they can be carried out with the idea of solving administrative problems or for the purpose of forming a theory; (3) they can have a purely practitioner-oriented focus; or (4) they can be "esoteric scholarly studies." For maximum value, however, Bailey concluded that, regardless of the underlying purpose for doing the case research, the ideal case study was one that had value for *both* practitioners and academics.

Van Evera (1997) was more focused in his determination of the purposes for case studies, identifying five purposes for which they can be used: (1) to establish a theory or theories, (2) to test an existing theory or theories, (3) to identify a previous condition or conditions (the *antecedents*) that lead or contribute to a phenomenon, (4) to establish the relative importance of those contributing conditions, or (5) to establish the fundamental importance of the case with regard to other potential examples (Figure 2.1). Each of these purposes is discussed in greater detail in the following sections.

Developing Theory from Cases

Establishing a theory upon which to base predictions of future events is an important reason for much of the published research in the administrative and social sciences (Eisenhardt 1999; George and Bennett 2005). In a review of works that used the case study method to examine city planning and planners, Fischler (2000) noted that case studies are uniquely suited for exploring the interaction of personal behavior and collective institutions, and for discovering and explaining the interplay of agency and structure.

In the Fischler approach, developing theory from case studies occurs through a four-phase process: (1) formulation of research questions and hypotheses, (2) selection of the case and definition of units of analysis, (3) data gathering and presentation, and (4) analysis of the findings and building subsequent theory. The content produced in one or more case studies might serve as contributions to a theory of government planning practices, for example. Used in this way, he concluded that cases are "the most essential tools" in theory development.

Finally, Fischler (2000, 194) recommended that case studies should remain an important research approach: "Case studies that explore the behavior and experience of innovative practitioners and innovative organizations, be they public, private, or not-for-profit, should therefore be placed high on our agenda."

Developing new ideas, concepts, and theories requires that a researcher first have a thorough grounding in *existing* theory. This can come from a comprehensive review of the literature on the topic or extensive practical experience in a public management situation. Sources may be personal interviews conducted with experts. Sources may come from the extensive body of domestic and international professional or occupational literature, or from current and past textbooks. Or they may be from other published materials such as newspapers, encyclopedias, yearbooks, unpublished papers, opinion pieces by other scholars, or material prepared expressly for and existing only on the Internet.

Testing Theories That Already Exist

Case studies may be used for both testing existing theories and developing new theories (Van Evera 1997; George and Bennett 2005). Several different objectives can underlie theory testing: to strengthen or refute support for an existing theory, to focus or expand conditions for a theory, to establish which of two or more theories are best for illustrating a theory, or to explain a category or an observed situation or circumstance. A number of case study reports are discussed in detail in the following pages to show how researchers choose cases for specific design objectives.

Benbasat, Goldstein, and Mead (1987), writing about research in information systems applications, found the case approach to be particularly appropriate for research on problems in which theory and research are in their early, formative stages. Because of the constant and rapid changes and innovation in technology, researchers are often behind in proposing changes or evaluating theory and development of new systems. In these situations, researchers learn by studying the innovations implemented by users of these and similar systems. By studying the theories that are shaping developments in the field and comparing reports of what other practitioners are doing, researchers are able test existing theories against the changes that are taking place in practice.

A case study of the Federal Emergency Management Administration (FEMA) prior to its inclusion in the new Department of Homeland Security after September 11, 2001, is an example of how a case can be used to test an existing theory (Ward et al., 2000). In this case, the researchers described operations in FEMA from 1980 to 1992 and again from 1992 to 2000. The FEMA case study evaluated a then-current theory that the adoption of information technology (IT) in an organization will result in major changes in the internal and external management structures of an organization.

> If such changes did occur, the changes should be of a type that a "reasonable" person would likely find to be positive or beneficent. Specifically, changes should occur in the following areas: the nature of work and work processes, organizational hierarchy and authority allocation, and internal and external control structures. If, on the other hand, the findings from organizational research are correct, then FEMA's work processes within the organization may change superficially, but still maintain the existing management systems of authority and control. Given FEMA's problematic history . . . such superficial changes would lead a "reasonable" person to conclude that the organization had attained either a neutral or a negative outcome. (Ward et al. 2000, 1020)

FEMA was established in 1979 by executive order of President Jimmy Carter (FEMA 2008). Originally intended by Congress to coordinate recovery efforts after natural disasters, the agency was expanded by President Carter to also manage Cold War civil defense preparedness and response activities. Under President Ronald Reagan, the chief focus of FEMA became assuring the continuity of the U.S. government after a nuclear attack by the Soviet Union. All purchases and installation of government information technology came under the control of its Office of Information Resources Management (IRM).

Because of its emphasis on the continuity of government, the IRM did not develop or support a flexible approach to overall agency systems building. Potentially more damaging, IRM did not invest in IT support for natural disaster response. Instead, it developed hardware and software under Department of Defense network standards. Without coordination or guidance from within, FEMA's various divisions developed their own IT solutions to meet their individual needs. This resulted in a number of stovepipe systems unable to communicate with one another; by 1992, more than 100 different systems existed within FEMA's divisions.

The problems came to a head on August 24, 1992, when FEMA was unable to respond to the aftermath of Hurricane Andrew in southern Florida. More than 250,000 people were affected by the hurricane. FEMA's response to the disaster was, according to Ward et al. (2000), "disgraceful" and the agency's "worse response [ever] to a natural disaster." With no IT support from its own IRM, field workers had to purchase 300 personal computers on the local market. Even then, a training program had to be set up to train FEMA personnel in their use.

The end of the Cold War in 1989 freed up FEMA funds from spending on civil defense and continuity programs and allowed greater emphasis on natural disaster recovery programs. The inability of FEMA to respond effectively to natural disasters such as Hurricane Andrew reinforced the plan for restructuring the agency and the shift in emphasis, including improving IT support for natural disaster relief.

President Bill Clinton appointed a new director shortly after taking office in 1992. By June 1993, a prototype disaster management information system was in place in

Salt Lake City, Utah. The new system linked laptop computers with microwave and satellite data links. Additional system developments followed, so that by the end of the Clinton presidency, FEMA felt that it had a network in place that was able to "provide information on everything from weather forecasts to the location of small businesses and schools in affected area."

The agency's ability to respond to disasters would be put to the test twice in the first decade of the new century by events of 9/11 and Hurricane Katrina—events that brought to light failures in communications coordination, disaster prevention, and emergency response.

Identifying a Previous Condition

Case studies that identify a previous condition are analogous to a medical checkup, in which a doctor or team of specialists diagnose a condition in order to develop a treatment regimen. Case studies are often written by practitioners, in which they describe their experiences with some problem and the solution they used or the application of some technical or managerial process. The case can focus on the successful or unsuccessful solution, providing a list of steps for other managers to follow or avoid.

An example of a case study that describes in detail the conditions and extent of homelessness, substance abuse, and poverty is the Fox and Roth (1989) report on homeless families and their children in the City of Philadelphia. The authors wrote about the deplorable social situation that existed in the city during the last half of the 1980s. They also identified drastic federal, state, and local cuts in spending for social services as a major contributor to the growth in poverty and homelessness in Philadelphia.

Their study concluded with a number of broad policy-level steps needed to address the growing homelessness problem nationally. First, the federal government must provide greater support for low-income housing and drug and alcohol problems. Second, the city's substance-abuse epidemic must be addressed. Third, given that homeless families face multiple problems, reducing the number of homeless families requires providing access to permanent housing and a full range of services. And fourth, "immediate and intensive interventions to treat the serious deficits that homeless children face in the area of developmental delays, educational delays and psychological trauma—all traceable living as a homeless child—must be addressed" (Fox and Roth 1989, 149).

This case study was an excellent description of a tragic social problem. However, it did not provide much in the way of theory building or testing. Nor did it provide specific suggestions that other public managers could use to deal with the same problems. Instead, it outlined several desired shifts in social service policy.

Establishing the Importance of Contributing Conditions

By studying practitioners' experiences with new technology and innovations in managerial and organizational structures, case researchers find answers to the *how* and *why* of management and organizational issues. These involve case studies of an actual organization and the results of managers' actions. By reviewing cases that identify the antecedents of situations in which a management decision is required, researchers can compare them with the circumstances in their organizations. Finally, examining previous case studies involving similar issues may bring to light flaws in earlier solutions, making it possible for administrators to avoid having to deal with similar problems for which corrections have already been found.

Establishing the Importance of the Case to Other Examples

A good place to find case studies that fit this design is the collection of research reports sponsored by the IBM Center for the Business of Government. A list of these cases and copies of the cases are available at the center's Web site: www .businessofgovernment.org.

Three examples of cases that illustrate how to compare the importance of the case to other examples are the (1) O'Connell (2001) case of the CompStat for use of performance data by the New York City Police Department; (2) the Henderson (2003) case describing how the CompStat model evolved into the CitiStat approach, which was implemented by the mayor of Baltimore, Maryland, for managing performance and results with the system in Baltimore (a Baltimore CitiStat follow-up case by Behn [2007] established a set of guidelines for use by other mayors); and (3) a similar case in which the CitiStat approach was transformed into a SchoolStat model and implemented in the Philadelphia, Pennsylvania, School District (Patusky, Botwinik, and Shelley 2007).

Each of these examples illustrates the importance of these innovative approaches as models for public managers to implement performance management systems and programs. The Philadelphia SchoolStat model was the latest in this series of cases on the "Stat" performance management approach. The Philadelphia model is an adaptation of the New York City Police Department CompStat and Baltimore CitiStat programs for use in the public schools. The chief goal of the program was to incorporate data-driven Stat practices into an integrated management system focusing management efforts on achieving measurable results.

These performance management systems have two main components: Stat practices and regular meetings with group senior managers to analyze measured performance and jointly plan improvement strategies. The term *Stat practices* refers to the use of statistical data to analyze past performance and form future performance objectives and strategies. In this way, it is similar to the use of statistical data in traditional total quality management and continuous process or product improvement programs. The data are presented and discussed at monthly meetings in which managers explain progress and failures to meet goals and objectives, and new strategies and tactics are formulated.

23

How and Why Researchers Pick the Cases They Study

Selecting which cases to study is usually a simple matter in single-case designs; researchers study the case that they are most familiar with or one that they have access to and holds the promise of providing an interesting and rewarding research experience. Selecting cases for a multicase study, however, is far more demanding. Here, the cases must all meet the requirement of addressing the same issue, phenomenon, or other research question. This requirement is particularly critical in comparative case study designs.

The key to success in the multicase design selection is first to clearly specify research objectives; examples of objectives include whether the study will involve identification, testing, or development of a theory; solving a problem; or gaining greater understanding of an issue or phenomenon. If the cases selected do not contribute to the selected objectives, they should not be included (George and Bennett 2005).

Kaarbo and Beasley (1999) identified three tasks in case selection: choosing comparable cases, selecting cases that vary on the study issue or question (the dependent variable), and selecting cases that reflect the various subgroups of the population in order to identify alternative explanations.

Choosing Comparable Cases

The key reason for selecting comparable cases is that without comparability the researcher cannot know whether the variation in the cases is due to the study variable or whether other factors influence the change across variables. Cases do not have to be comparable on variables other than the study question; researchers do not need to be concerned with irrelevant differences. Kaarbo and Beasley (1999) warned that cases should be chosen to control for alternative causes of a hypothesized relationship, and not for comparability on nontheoretically derived properties.

Choosing Cases with Variability

Variation in the values of the dependent variable is the second important criterion for deciding which cases to select. Without this variation, the researcher will not be able to make inferences about the phenomenon under study. The explanatory variables can exist in cases that are not about the phenomenon. To ensure that this variability is present, researchers have two choices: pick the cases based on variation in the values of an explanatory variable, or pick cases based on variation in the dependent variable.

For example, a dependent variable might be citizen participation in local government planning issues. Explanatory variables might be demographic variables, such as age, gender, or ethnicity; socioeconomic variables; ease of access; and the like. Selecting cases based on variation in the dependent variable gives researchers the opportunity to comment on this variable upon completion of the data-gathering phase.

Choosing Cases with Variation across Subgroups

Selecting cases with variation across subgroups has the advantage of making it possible for the researcher to choose cases with an alternative explanation in mind. Selecting cases that vary across subgroups has an added dimension over limiting the selection to cases that meet the comparable cases criterion. Finally, in selecting comparable cases, the researcher should keep the following cautionary statement in mind:

> In choosing comparable cases, the researcher is recognizing the limits of the hypothesis, arguing that it only applies to cases that are comparable on a certain number of theoretically derived dimensions. In choosing cases across subgroups, the researcher is purposefully stretching the investigation of the hypothesis across a variable derived from an alternative solution. (Kaarbo and Beasley 1999, 383)

Summary

Case study research can be used for five purposes: (1) to establish a theory or theories, (2) to test a theory or theories that already exist, (3) to identify a previous condition or conditions that lead or contribute to a phenomenon of interest, (4) to establish the importance of those conditions, and (5) to establish the fundamental importance of the case with regard to other potential examples.

Cases can be chosen using three different criteria: (1) based on the comparability of the case with the study phenomenon or issue, (2) based on the variability cases display in the study phenomenon, and (3) making the final choice so that all subgroups are present in the final group of cases studied.

➤ 3 ◄

The Range of Case
Research Designs

Case study research is a heterogeneous activity covering a range
of research methods and techniques, a range of coverage from the
single-case study through carefully matched pairs to up to a dozen
cases, differing lengths and levels of involvement in organizational
functioning and a range of different types of data (including both
quantitative and qualitative designs). Reaching conclusions about it
as a research strategy is inevitably difficult.
—Jean F. Hartley (1994)

The case method focuses on the in-depth study of one or, at most, a very few cases; this approach is generally considered to be qualitative research, although quantitative methods are also applicable and appropriate. The in-depth study model was developed and honed through decades of case analyses by anthropologists, sociologists, and organizational behavioral researchers, among others.

The ability to achieve an in-depth analysis of a unit, organization, or process is recognized as one of the chief advantages of the case research method. In-depth analysis makes it possible to achieve greater understanding from a case study. This comes from the possible collection of high quality and quantity in detail, richness in description, completeness of explanation and understanding, and wholeness in a final explanation (Gerring 2004). However, it is important not to overemphasize the importance of rich description and ability to conduct in-depth analysis in the case approach (Hartley 1994).

Classes of Case Research

It is possible to group qualitative case studies into three broad classes of research strategies: *explanatory, interpretive,* and *critical* (Figure 3.1). Although found in all three types of studies, case research is more appropriate for explanatory and interpretive research studies. Therefore, these two research strategies are discussed in greater detail in this chapter, beginning with the explanatory model.

Figure 3.1 **Case Research Designs in Public Management**

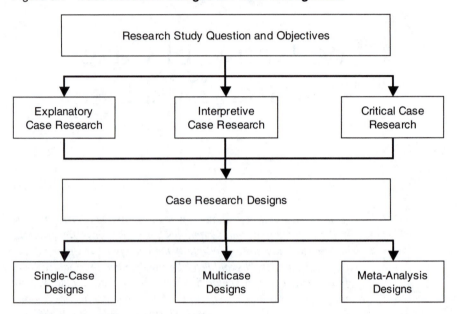

Explanatory Case Research

Explanatory research studies are conducted to develop a *causal explanation* of some social phenomenon (Schwandt 1997). In these studies, a researcher (1) identifies a specific social event, circumstance, or consequence—such as crime in the inner city—important enough to be investigated and (2) proceeds to identify the social, economic, climate, practice, or other such characteristic or event in the social environment that might be explained as a potential *cause* of the consequence of interest.

One of the major objectives of explanatory case research is to build *theories* that may be used to explain a phenomenon. The theory can then be used to predict future behavior or events given the same or similar circumstances. The ability to predict future outcomes gives administrators a measure of control over events. Therefore, the ultimate goal of explanatory research is the *control of natural and social events* (White 1999). Explanatory research is the easiest approach to understand and apply, and is often used simply for this reason (see Box 3.1).

In addition to the controlling aspect of explanatory research, this strategy is seen by many as the fastest way to produce a cumulative stream of knowledge in a field or a discipline. Possibly because of this, explanatory studies are still seen most often in public administration research. Explanatory research may also fulfill much the same role in qualitative studies as exploratory research does in quantitative studies; it is used for gathering fundamental information about a topic, its contributing factors, and the

---

Box 3.1

When to Use an Explanatory Design

The following description of when to use an explanatory research design is available online at the *Sociology Guide*, http://www.sociologyguide.com/research-methods&statistics/research-design.php: "When the purpose of the study is to explore a new universe, one that has not been studied earlier, the research design is called explanatory. The research purpose in this case is to gain familiarity in unknown areas."

The explanatory research design is used to frame a research problem so that a precise investigation can follow. When the universe of study is unknown, an explanatory design form is often the first step in a broader research program—in these situations, the explanatory design is often referred to as an exploratory design. Other types of research designs are used after the initial study establishes parameters and suggests variables, often resulting in an exploratory-descriptive-causal progression of study designs. In case research, however, the causal design is seldom used.

When carrying out an explanatory case study, instead of concentrating on nonspecific areas and selecting a few aspects for consideration (as may be the case in descriptive research design), researchers are eclectic in their data gathering, often collecting a great variety of data. In gathering data through an observation method, according to the *Sociology Guide*, researchers "are able to see the actors in their total life situation."

The authors of the *Sociology Guide* also noted that explanatory studies are not the same as "raw empiricism"; that is, they do not involve "fact gathering that is unrelated to sociological theory. The explanatory study always carries with it a set of concepts that guide the researcher to look for the facts."

Source: Sociology Guide (2006).

---

influences it might have on various outcomes. Such studies are sometimes conducted as preliminaries to follow-up research.

An Explanatory Case Example

An example of what may be considered an explanatory case is the study of the responses of the government to the catastrophic destruction of the World Trade Center in New York City. Cohen, Eimicke, and Horan (2002) described the response of the thousands of city workers, elected and appointed officials, and other persons in the public service "as government and public service at its finest." As New York City residents, the authors of this case were in a position to evaluate the intergovernmental response and the quick thinking of city officials on the scene as the disaster unfolded. They described the cause of the many organizational successes as the emphasis on safety preparedness pushed by then-mayor Rudolph Giuliani and the readiness of government managers to make tough decisions on the spot:

> What is most striking is the skill and intensity of government's response to the emergency: The quick thinking of the PATH [Port Authority Trans-Hudson, a commuter rail service] officials sending a train of passengers back to New Jersey and an empty train to Manhattan to facilitate evacuation [thereby saving more than 3,000 potential victims]. The decision in the local schools near the World Trade Center to evacuate and for the rest of the city's schools to remain in session, taking particular care in ensuring that all children were met by adults at the end of the day. Decisions to close the bridges, ports, and airports, and of course the mayor's inspiring personal leadership in the first hours and then first weeks after the attack. (Cohen, Eimicke, and Horan 2002, 29)

The authors of this case concluded their analysis of the events after the terrorist attack with the following lessons that other cities might learn from the way the many city, state, and federal agencies cooperated in the aftermath of the disaster:

- Planning for emergency response in advance is essential.
- Organizations involved in emergency response, response procedures, and resources must be retained and available, even when the threat seems distant. The unexpected can occur in a heartbeat.
- Greater redundancy in emergency communications systems is absolutely critical (many systems either failed or became overloaded during the emergency response). Cellular and hard-wired communications should have two levels of redundancy.
- Emergency response personnel need to expect communications breakdowns and the need to assume decentralized decision making. Contingency planning for such breakdowns is critical.
- Nothing can substitute for the presence of inspiring leadership during a crisis.
- Finally, the most profound lesson to be taken from the events of September 11, 2001, and immediately afterward is that the ethos of public services is alive and well, and is as important to society as ever. As a reflection of the loyalty and dedication of government workers, public servants died in the hundreds in the performance of their duties during this tragic emergency.

Explanatory Cases on Additional Topics

State and local governments have had to learn how to function through recurring cycles of boom or bust. The following comments by Wheeler (1993) established the framework for his book on innovation in state and local government, which was published more than fifteen years ago. However, it clearly describes the position in which most state and local governments find themselves as the first decade of the twenty-first century approaches its close:

> In the wake of the federal budget crisis in Washington and the subsequent elimination or downsizing of many federal programs, much of the burden for addressing contemporary issues will rest with state and local governments. They will be required to assume more responsibility for the development and implementation of social programs. (Wheeler 1993, 1)

Wheeler was describing how a wide variety of innovative solutions to civic problems were evolving at the state and local government levels. He included case research in such public sector service areas as education, health care and drug abuse, environmental management, housing, and economic development. As an illustration of the focus of the studies, the following cases on topics in health care and drug abuse were described in some detail:

- Medical Care for Children Project
- Health Care Access Project
- Meeting the Obstetrical Needs of Low-Income Women
- Child Abuse Prevention Project

Each of the cases followed the same format: (1) a brief description of events and circumstances that made the public service program necessary, (2) a detailed description of the program that emerged from information gathering and planning sessions, (3) obstacles planners encountered and overcame in implementing the program, (4) future plans for the program, (5) notes on how the program might be replicated in other locations, and (6) key lessons learned from the implementation of the program. A few notes and afterthoughts were included at the end of some of the cases.

Interpretive Case Research

Not all human events or actions can be defined by the causal explanations found in explanatory research. Additional insight is needed if human action is to be understood, let alone explained; understanding can be achieved only by studies that follow the second approach in the triad of qualitative research objectives: interpretive research.

Interpretive research helps administrators understand the actions of people in social circumstances. An explanatory case study of a failed job-enrichment program to see why it is not working might identify personal motivation and job design as leading contributors of the failed program. An interpretive case study would go beyond this explanation. To do so, the researcher might circulate among employees in their job setting and ask them what they think about the enrichment program; what meaning it has for them; and how it conflicts or reinforces their existing attitudes, opinions, and behaviors. In this way, the research seeks to discover the meaning of the program, in this case, how it fits with workers' prior norms, rules, values, and social practice factors in the culture of the organization (White 1999). Thus, in the interpretive approach the case researcher seeks to achieve "a classification, explication, or explanation of the meaning of some phenomenon" (Schwandt 1997, 73).

Interpretive case studies require the researcher to go beyond simply describing or explaining a phenomenon. The researcher seeks also to interpret the phenomenon for the reader. This entails interpreting what it *means* as well as what it *is*. Research can be classified as interpretive when it is builds on the assumption that humans learn about reality from the meanings they assign to social phenomena such as language, consciousness, shared experiences, publications, tools, and other artifacts.

The task is made difficult because a fundamental tenet of interpretive theory is that social phenomena are constantly changing. Thus, the meanings that people assign are in a state of constant change. At the same time, interpretive case studies are always context laden. Because things are always changing, conducting an interpretative case study is like shooting at a constantly moving target.

Context laden means that the case cannot be understood without a complete description of the context of the subject. A primary goal of the interpretive research approach is to provide multilayered descriptions and interpretations of human experiences (Meacham 1998). To achieve this goal, interpretive research looks at the way humans make sense out of events in their lives—as they happen, not as they are planned. Therefore, to thoroughly understand an event or an organization, the researcher must also understand its historical context.

Interpretive research is important for the study of government organizations and agencies. The fundamental objective for interpretive research makes this approach particularly relevant in applications such as these:

> The basic aim of the interpretive model is to develop a more complete understanding of social relationships and to discover human possibilities. Recent studies of organizational culture demonstrate the importance of interpretive methods for properly understanding norms, values, and belief systems in organizations. (White and Adams 1994, 45)

Principles of Interpretive Case Research

Klein and Meyers (1999) developed a set of seven fundamental principles to help researchers conduct and evaluate interpretive case studies: the hermeneutic circle, contextual nature, interrelationships, abstraction and generalization, dialogical reasoning, multiple interpretations, and suspicion. Some of the key elements of these concepts are discussed in the following sections.

Hermeneutic Circle

The first and most fundamental of these principles, the hermeneutic circle, is derived from document and literary analysis. The hermeneutic circle was devised to illustrate a phenomenon of the learning and understanding process. People develop understanding about complex concepts from the meanings they bring to its parts, such as words, and the way that these parts relate to one another. Interpretation of the larger whole moves from a preliminary understanding of the parts to an understanding of the whole—and then back again to a better understanding of the parts, and so on. The process of developing understanding thus moves continuously in an expanding circle of greater and greater understanding.

Contextual Nature

The second principle of interpretive research is the contextual nature of the studied case phenomenon or organization. The researcher's meaning is mined out of the particular social and historical context of the phenomenon; all patterns discovered within this embedded context are constantly changing. The organizations or phenomena that are interpreted are thus time and situation specific.

Interrelationships

The interactions between researchers and the subjects they study constitute the third of the seven principles of interpretive case research. The interpretation is not inherent in the case under study. Rather, it is developed from the interrelationships that take place between case subjects and researcher. Gummesson (1987) saw this as similar to the interaction that often results in the researcher metamorphosing into an "internal consultant" role during the case study research project. The researcher, by interacting with participants, becomes one with the members of the group under study.

Abstraction and Generalization

Together, abstraction and generalization make up the fourth principle of interpretive case research. The case researcher must deal with abstractions when attempting to bring order to disunited parts. Order is achieved by categorizing phenomena into generalizations and concepts. Any inferences drawn by the research based on a subjective interpretation of a single case must be seen as theoretical generalizations and not as inferences to a wider body of groups, events, or circumstances.

Dialogical Reasoning

Reasoning that is based on a dialog with case subjects is the fifth principle of interpretive research. In this intellectual process, the case investigator identifies all the preconceptions or biases brought to the planned case research activity. These are then weighed against the information that actually emerges from the case data-gathering process. The dialogical reasoning principle forces the case researcher to begin by defining the underlying assumptions that guide the research and the research paradigm upon which the study is based. By carrying out a dialog with participants, the researcher defines and redefines the assumptions and research questions in light of the learning that emerges.

Multiple Interpretations

The multiple interpretations principle demands that researchers aggressively compare their historical and contextual interpretation of the phenomenon against all other available interpretations—and the reasons offered for them. Researcher preconceptions and biases are compared against competing interpretations, including those of the participants in the organization under study. Even if no conflicting interpretations are found during the study, the researcher should probe for them and document the process. In this way, the researcher strengthens the conclusions and interpretations derived from the analysis.

Suspicion

The final principle of interpretive research is suspicion, which requires the researcher to not accept an interpretation at face value. To avoid making false interpretations, the researcher must examine with a healthy dose of skepticism every personal preconception, conclusion, definition, and derived meaning.

An Interpretive Case Example

"What's So 'Special' about Airport Authorities?" is the title of a 2006 interpretive case study by Bacot and Christine. In this case the authors first established how airport authorities differ from the classical special district structure and then suggested a theory of the unique governance structures of airport administrative bodies. The subject of the case was the phenomenon of airport governance structures; the topic was picked to add to the body of knowledge and understanding of special governance structures and standings of airports in the United States. Benefits from increasing that understanding included determining whether governance structure had any impact on local airports' taxing and spending practices.

The administration of airports in the United States is complex in that while it is generally a local responsibility (city or county), the U.S. Federal Aviation Administration (FAA) has considerable influence over airport administration. The FAA offers considerable direction but does not dictate operations. In addition, both the Department of Homeland Security and Environmental Protection Administration provide operational advice.

Airports are generally owned by local governments. Ownership falls into one of four major categories: county ownership, city ownership, state agency control (as in Hawaii and Maryland), and authorities that are truly independent, distinct government units. Rather than being a part of the standard general-purpose administrative organization of the city or county, the latter ownership model is usually under the management of airport authorities or port authorities.

Although similar in many ways to the governance structure found in traditional special districts or special-purpose government organizations, governance of airports differs in several substantial ways. One of the biggest differences is that most airport authorities (80 percent) rely on user fees (or similar means) to pay for services they provide and for revenue bond capacity for capital construction. Special districts depend on their borrowing and taxing ability for revenue.

Other than their fiscal arrangements and governance differences, airport authorities differ from traditional special districts in at least four additional ways (Bacot and Christine 2006, 244–46):

1. Administration is not completely independent; it lacks autonomy from the local general-purpose governments.
2. Although theoretically possible, airport authorities can never be considered completely private because of federal, state, and local control.
3. Authority service areas are regional in scope, often crossing beyond city/county boundaries, whereas special purpose governments are usually limited to a county or part of a county.
4. Authorization for airports and, hence airport authorities, depends upon federal and state legislation, and local ordinance, while special-purpose districts are enabled by state legislative action.

In terms of lessons for other general-purpose government managers and academic researchers, Bacot and Christine (2006) concluded that airport authorities are "inappropriately included in most research on special-purpose governments . . . doing so, fails to note the significant distinctions between airport authorities and special-purpose governments."

Critical Case Research

Critical research, which evolved from approaches in Marxian critical sociology and Freudian psychotherapy traditions (Argyris, Putnam, and Smith 1985; Klein and Meyers 1999), is the third approach to qualitative case research in public administration. This approach is not used as often for case study research as the explanatory and interpretive approaches, although it can be a powerful tool for change.

A case study can be considered to be critical in nature if it exposes harmful or alienating social conditions. The purpose of the case study should be to emancipate members of the society or group from some harmful condition or undesired circumstances, thereby eliminating the causes of alienation. In critical case studies, members of the society are not told how to change their conditions, but are instead helped to identify on their own alternative ways of defining their society and for achieving human potential—men and women are seen as being free to, at least partially, determine their own existence; they are, in a word, emancipated (Kincheloe and McLaren, 1984).

According to White (1994), the primary objective of critical research is to help people change their beliefs and actions as part of a process of helping them become aware of the often unconscious bases for the way they act. By becoming aware of *why* they live and think the way they do, the "critique points out inconsistencies between what is true and false, good and bad; it compels (people) to act in accordance with truth and goodness" (White 1994, 46). The critical case study is the means for communicating these messages.

Critical public management case research begins with an assumption that a critical situation or crisis exists in some aspect of an organization, group, or society. The researcher approaches the study of this crisis from a deeply personal and involved commitment to help the people involved. Recognition of a crisis, then, is one of the key concepts of the approach:

> From [the crisis] perspective, society is seen as [torn] by social and political divisions which make the process of social reproduction . . . prone to actual or incipient breakdown. Society [is not] a harmonious, self-regulating system. Rather, it must be seen as a field of complex and contradictory possibilities for social actors who would . . . assume command of these possibilities and produce new social realities which would express their ability to act as empowered, autonomous agents. The task of critical research involves identifying these possibilities and suggesting what social actors might do to bring their lives under their conscious direction. (Hansen and Muszyaki 1990, 2)

Structural Themes in Critical Research

Schwandt (1997, 24–25) identified a number of structural themes that characterize critical research. The two that seem to appear most regularly in the literature of critical research methodology are distortion in the perceptions held by members of a group and rejection of the idea of the disinterested scientist. With the first theme, the goal of critical research is to integrate social theory and application or practice in such a way that the members of social groups become cognizant of distortions and other problems in their society or their value systems. Then, the group members are encouraged to propose ways to change their social and value systems in ways that improve their quality of life.

The second key theme in critical case research is the refusal to accept the traditional idea that calls for the social scientist to remain objective or disinterested. In its place, it substitutes an active, change-oriented researcher whose perspective is on motivating change processes in groups and individuals. Blyler addressed this issue of critical perspective:

> The critical perspective aims at empowerment and emancipation. It reinterprets the relationship between researcher and participants as one of collaboration,

where participants define research questions that matter to them and where social action is the desired goal. (Blyler 1998, 33)

Researchers employing case research in the critical tradition are typically concerned with three activities: research into the antecedents of the situation, education of the participants or population at risk, and action that the group takes upon itself to resolve the issue. The foundation of this research approach is critical theory, where a primary goal of the research is to effect a fundamental, emancipating change in a society.

A Critical Research Case Example

Participatory case research developed from social movements among oppressed societies in the third world, including Africa, Asia, and Latin America. It has also gained a strong foothold in North America, particularly in research involving minorities, the disenfranchised, and the discriminated against.

For example, a four-year study with residents of the town of North Bonneville, Washington, was the focus of critical case research conducted in the early 1970s (Comstock and Fox 1993). Groups of students and faculty from The Evergreen State College in Olympia, Washington, worked with some 450 residents of a Columbia River community that was scheduled for demolition to make room for a new dam spillway and power plant. The result of their combined efforts was written up as a case study.

During initial meetings with town residents, the U.S. Army Corps of Engineers refused to consider moving the town and instead offered payments for residents to move to other areas. Comstock and Fox described how residents overcame a critical hurtle in their path to achieving success in their dealings with the corps:

> Very early in the struggle, the residents discovered the contradiction between the corps's meaning of community and their own. To the corps the community was individuals and physical structures. This ignored the reality of community values, attachments to the land, and social networks. Through a careful description of their community, the residents gained a more articulate description of their community and vitality as a community. (Comstock and Fox 1993, 121)

Once residents learned how the corps perceived the community and its residents and how corps agents were using the agency's control of information as a wedge to divide citizen opinion, they moved to acquire technical information on their own. They then provided that technical information to everyone in a way that could be understood, thus breaking down the corps's monopoly of ideas. The town eventually won in its fight to survive. The Corps of Engineers constructed a new town in the location wanted by residents of the old town. The new city of North Bonneville was officially dedicated in July 1976.

Researchers using this model believe that if, through education, members of a society become aware of better ways to function, they will bring about the change themselves. Thus, a key part of the research process is helping community members become active participants in their study and its action aftermath. Participants are expected to take primary responsibility for the study, including its overall design, data gathering and analysis, and eventual distribution of the findings.

Comstock and Fox also noted the political nature of the participatory action approach in their case conclusions on how the experience changed the people of North Bonneville forever:

> Perhaps the most striking result of the North Bonneville experience has been the degree to which a self-sustaining political process was initiated. . . . The growth of self-direction continued as residents, no longer content with their original demand that a new town be planned and built for them, demanded (and got) control over the design of their own community. (Comstock and Fox 1993, 123)

Reliability and Validity Issues in Case Research

A question of case method researchers has long been how to improve the generalizability of the findings of research with one or a very few cases (Mertens 1998). In the positivist tradition of research, faith in the generalizability of study findings is achieved through designs that include provisions for achieving acceptable levels of reliability and validity. In large sample studies, these questions are dealt with through random selection of sample members and sufficient sample size. These preventive approaches are more difficult to apply in case research.

Validity and reliability are core concepts in all research, regardless of design, method, or analysis approach. Validity refers to the ability of a research design to do what it is supposed to do. That is, does the research produce the information it was designed to provide? Validity is concerned with only the results of the research activity, not the activity or the evaluation or test methods themselves. Reliability refers to the extent that the analysis or tools used in measuring or evaluating collected data work in the same way when applied is a similar study.

In research designs, validity is considered to have a number of different constructs. On the one hand, Salkind (2000) identified content, criterion, construct, and predictive validity. Yin (1994), on the other hand, referred to four types of validity tests as common to all social science research: construct, internal validity, external validity, and reliability. George and Bennett (2005) were more concerned with just one aspect of validity: conceptual, which refers to the extent to which a research study is able to focus on a point or points of particular interest to the researcher. They believed that the case method offered high levels of conceptual validity because it could focus on the indicators that best represented the concepts of interest to the researcher.

Construct validity refers to the ability of the study to meet its objective. Case research examples include establishment of a theory, testing of an earlier theory, comparing a phenomenon in two or more applications, and so forth. It is most often used in reference to a study measuring method—such as a survey instrument—to actually measure the phenomenon of interest. Examples include voting history, policy positions, and ethical standards.

Internal Validity

Internal validity is applied in experimental or quasi-experimental studies. It refers to the measurement of causality, and therefore it is seldom a major design issue in single-case research, where measurement of causality is more problematic. Predictability or criterion validity is similar, although that is found more often in descriptions of quantitative research methods. Predictability refers to the extent that the study design or measurement can predict some future event or behavior. An often seen example is the use of certain demographic characteristics as predictors of voting behavior.

External Validity

Measuring external validity is another difficult feature of case research. This is a determination of whether the case findings are generalizable to other, similar situations. In single-case designs, the only way to determine whether study results are generalizable is to conduct additional case studies. Researchers use multicase designs in an effort to address this issue.

Reliability in Case Research

Reliability refers to a core concept of all scientific research: replicability, that is, whether another research project following the same procedures with a similar case subject or subjects will produce similar results. According to Yin (1994), a good way of ensuring reliability is to carry out the study "as if someone were always looking over your shoulder." Keeping a documented history of every step taken in the study also helps.

Summary

The case method has become one of the most popular approaches followed in public administration research. The popularity of the case study approach is a result of its great flexibility. Case studies can be written to serve as examples of what a public administrator ought not to do, as well as what should be done. However, their primary purpose is to show public administrators what other administrators are doing. Different research objectives call for research designs to be explanatory, interpretive, or critical. The explanatory and interpretive approaches are used more often for research in public management and administration.

A typical purpose for explanatory case research is to explain to readers how public managers faced and solved a problem, implemented a program, or designed and put into practice an innovative approach to handle a new or recurring problem.

Interpretive case research is conducted when the researcher must not only describe or explain a phenomenon but also interpret the phenomenon. This requires researchers to provide their interpretation of what the phenomenon means as well as what it is.

The critical case study is often used to describe the results of an action research program. In this approach, the case researcher is often required to function as a participant in the empowering activity and often functions in an action-catalyst role. The chapter concluded with a brief discussion of validity and reliability issues in case research.

➤ 4 ◄

Single-Case
Research Designs

Effective single-case studies can be used to develop new generalizations and challenge existing ones, to develop and analyze scenarios, to illustrate exemplary solutions to recurring problems, and to analyze how practitioners frame their roles. Single-case studies can also display methodological approaches such as observation, thick description, normative reasoning, and program evaluation.
—Sandford Borins (2001)

The previous chapter introduced the three categories of case research strategies in terms of their underlying research objectives or mission: explanatory, interpretive, and critical. This chapter looks at case studies from two additional points of view. The first is based on the *scale* of the study; this approach focuses on the units of analysis included in the study. The second organizes case designs based on the *scope* and objectives of case research studies. Although the differences between the two approaches are not all that great, several classification schemes are discussed here so that the public manager will not be surprised when research reports are described in different ways. Single-case designs are introduced and defined in this chapter, and the process of carrying out single-case research is discussed in greater detail in the chapter 6.

The first broad categorization of all cases was suggested by Robert Stake in 1994 and is based on the scale of the case study. He concluded that cases can be grouped into three categories or types of studies based on the intent of their research design: *intrinsic, instrumental,* and *collective.* Intrinsic case studies are the most narrow in scale, whereas collective studies have the greatest scale.

The second categorization scheme identifies cases based on the scope of the study design rather than the intent or objectives of the study. Case research grouped by scope comprises three types, ranging from the most focused to the broadest focus: (1) single-case design, (2) multicase design, and (3) meta-analysis or case survey design (less seen than the first two).

Yin (1994) used a classification scheme that included components of scale and scope when he grouped case studies on the basis of two characteristics: the number of primary units examined in the study (scale) and the variations in numbers of subgroups studied in the research (scope). The first classification level divides cases into two groups based on whether they involve a single unit or multiple units, that is, the familiar single-case and multicase designs. The second level of categorization is based on the number of subgroups examined in the study, one or more than one, and is categorized by the terms *holistic* and *embedded.* This second level of classification can apply to either single-case or multicase designs, thus producing four design types.

Labels in Case Research

Sometimes confusion surfaces about the differences in the labels used for the case study and the case research method, as the different classification schemes suggest. Clearly there is a great deal of overlap in these classification schemes. This is nothing to worry about, given that the choices are really few. However, a brief discussion of some of the differences in labels is included here in an attempt to clear up any confusion.

First, there is an incorrect assumption of interchangeability between the terms *case study* and *single-case study.* The term *case study* is, of course, a collective phrase that refers to case research using any number of subject units, whereas a *single-case study* involves the study of only one representative unit or phenomenon. The opposite of case studies is any and all other research methods, whereas the opposite of single-case study is multicase study.

Second, various social and administrative sciences have shaped their own forms of the single-case model. Examples in education include Merriam's *Qualitative Research and Case Study Applications in Education* (1998) and Stake's *The Art of Case Study Research* (1995). Examples in clinical psychology include Franklin, Allison, and Gorman's *Design and Analysis of Single-Case Research* (1997) and Hersen and Barlow's *Single-Case Experimental Designs* (1976). The thing to remember is that there are only three basic designs, each with some variation: single-case, multicase, and meta-analysis.

Case Research in the Administrative Sciences

Case research has long been popular in the administrative sciences, including public management. An early example of the single-case study in organizational research is the analysis of the Glacier Metal Company in London by a team of researchers led by Jacques (1951). Jacques described the report as a case study of developments in the social life of one industrial community. He added that, as a case study, the report was not intended to serve as a statement of precise and definite conclusions. Rather, it was written to show how managers and employees in one company deal with change.

As its name implies, the single-case design focuses on a single individual, unit, organization, or phenomenon. Its purpose is to clearly analyze some topic of interest in that single unit. The single-case model is found in all the social and administrative sciences, making this model what Miles and Huberman (1998, 193) called the *traditional mode of qualitative analysis.* Also, the great majority of public management case studies are single-case designs.

Significance of Single-Case Research

Although it has been used for many years, as noted earlier, the case method has only recently been accepted as a legitimate research method for studies in the social and administrative sciences. In many disciplines during the 1970s and 1980s, qualitative research methods—including the case study approach—began to make serious inroads into the research traditions formed during the behavioralist movement of the 1940s and 1950s.

Case research was ignored by researchers who were convinced that research methods that followed the natural sciences model were the only scientific way of conducting research in the social sciences. However, once the ease of use and value of case method approach were recognized, it did not take long for a large body of journal articles supporting this approach to appear in the literature of the time. Typical of the published research was the *MIS Quarterly* article by Lee (1989) in which he sought to show how the case method was actually just as "scientific" as the natural science approach. In his article he pointed to a case study on implementation of management information systems by Markus (1983) as an exemplar of the scientific appropriateness of the single-case study approach for research in the field of management information systems.

Lee (1989) began with an overview of the key scientific research methodology problems associated with single-case research. He then showed how the case study produced by Markus (1983) successfully addressed those problems. In his conclusion, he suggested that the results of his study and that of Markus held important methodological ramifications for other social and administrative sciences as well. The Lee article proceeded on the assumption that a case study is an examination of a real-world phenomenon that actually exists in its natural setting.

Holding the single-case study to the criteria embedded in the general understanding of what is meant by *the scientific method,* Lee (1989) then identified four key problems that case researchers must address if their research is to be accepted as valid as a study that follows quantitative, natural science methods: controlled observations, controlled deductions, replicability, and generalizability. The problems and solutions are displayed in Table 4.1.

Four Problem Areas

The first of these problem areas is the need to make the controlled observations typical of natural science research. This involves observing the effects of one variable on another while controlling confounding-variable influences—using experimental methods with statistical probability measures. Recognizing that studying an organization in the real world is not the same as a laboratory situation, and that it

Table 4.1

Single-Case Methodological Problems and Possible Solutions

Scientific Method Principle	Scientific Method Solution	Qualitative Case Research Problem	Qualitative Case Research Solution
Making controlled observations	Design an experiment with test and control groups, control for influence of confounding variables; apply a treatment, measure for statistically significant change, and measure relationship and causality.	In case research and description, it is difficult if not impossible to control for confounding variables or establish control and treatment groups; increasing the number of variables rather than measurements is an appropriate solution.	Markus solved the controlled observations issue by using what Lee described as *natural controls*; the research focused on a single person in the organization, following the subject's attitude changes when moved to a new position. The treatment was the move to the new position.
Making controlled deductions	Employ mathematical measurements, subject data to statistical analysis, and base deductions on laws of probability for statistical significance.	Hypothesis testing with qualitative data requires predictions stated in narrative form, opening the door to researcher bias in analysis and interpretation.	Lee established that mathematics is just one subset of logic; thus, logical deductions do not require mathematics. Deductions based on verbal propositions are equally valid.
Allowing for replicability	Design experiments so that subsequent researchers are able to replicate the experiment using the same configuration of subjects, groups, treatments, measurements, and analyses.	Other researchers are unable to replicate the same configuration of subjects, events, or phenomena; even if it were possible, the passage of time makes additional learning necessary and further confounds the test situation.	While it is unlikely that the same circumstances can ever be evaluated, other researchers can apply the same theories tested in the original case to a different set of conditions in other, similar organizations. Even though the predictions would be different, the same theory would be tested.
Allowing for generalizability	Develop a generalizability theory; pay rigid attention to experimental design; random sampling; and statistical testing of null and alternate hypotheses	Because the case describes events in a single unit, organization, or phenomenon at a given point in time, the researchers' findings must be considered unique and not generalizable to other organizations or settings.	Lee sees generalizability as describing a theory that has been tested in a variety of situations, regardless of the research method. Thus, it is no more or less a problem for case research than for any research method for any study in any other discipline.

Sources: Lee (1989); Markus (1983).

44

is not appropriate or even possible to use statistical methods to analyze results of a single case, Lee (1989) suggested that because the in-depth study of a single case typically produces more variables than data points, the use of statistical controls is not relevant, thus rendering the argument moot. Moreover, studying the case in its individual setting resolves the laboratory control argument.

The second problem is that of making controlled deductions. In natural science research, these are typically based on mathematical propositions such as probability and confidence intervals, t-tests, analysis of variance results, and correlations. Pointing out that single-case research is rarely quantitative, numerical test results are not available to the case researcher. Instead, the researcher must rely on qualitative data. Not providing a suggestion for a way of resolving this problem, Lee (1989) concluded that, while not impossible, making deductions with qualitative case data alone is more problematic.

The third problem is the difficulty of achieving replicability. Because the case is unique—the study of a specific group or organization with specific actors, at a given time, under specific circumstances—it is next to impossible for another researcher to replicate exactly the same study.

The fourth problem—enabling the researcher to generalize the results or findings to other organizations—is similarly problematic; the findings of a single case are unlikely to be extended to other subject organizations or phenomena, regardless how similar in scope or mission.

Scientific Theory Requirements

Despite these difficulties, Lee (1989) concluded that Markus (1983) was remarkably successful in designing a case study that met each of these four scientific research characteristics. In addition, the Markus case study met the additional scientific theory requirements of falsifiability, logical consistency, greater predictive power than alternative theories, and survival of the empirical tests designed to falsify it.

Markus (1983) examined three alternative theories to explain the failure of many management information systems (MIS) implementations: the characteristics of the people, the characteristics of the system, and a combination of people and system. She then compared the predictions (deductions) for each theory's ability to explain people's resistance to the new technology. The validity of each theory was tested by using contrary predictions about what would happen in the same set of circumstances. The theory that remained unfalsified in this comparison was determined to be "scientific." Only the interaction-based theory satisfied the four requirements; a combination of people characteristics and the technology resulted in continual resistance to the system as implemented.

The Scale and Scope of Single-Case Research

Defining case studies by scale refers to the number of units, organizations, or phenomena studied for the case. As discussed earlier, the scope of case research

Figure 4.1 **Types of Case Research Designs**

	Scope		
Scale	Single-Case	Multicase	Meta-Analysis
Intrinsic	X	X	
Instrumental	X	X	
Collective		X	X

is represented by three designs: single-case, multicase, and meta-analysis design. In the single-case design, one unit of interest is examined in detail; the multicase design includes two or more similar units. In multicase design the researcher usually compares one case unit against the others in the study (although comparisons are not an absolute requirement for this approach). Meta-analysis design is an analysis of a group of already existing case studies.

The single-case design is the most common approach in case research. In this method, the underlying purpose of the case researcher is not to produce a representative picture of the world, but rather to explain what makes the chosen case or cases worth the effort of the study. Robert Stake (1994) placed case studies into three groups based on the scale of the study: intrinsic, instrumental, and collective. The intrinsic, single-case study is the most focused of the designs (Figure 4.1).

Regardless of their form, case studies should not be used to draw conclusions beyond the case or cases being investigated. However, good case studies do search out and highlight features and characteristics of the case or set of cases that are uniform and generalizable, as well as those elements in the case that have the appearance of being relatively unique to the case under study (Bailey 1994, 192).

Intrinsic Case Studies

An intrinsic case study design is chosen when the researcher wants to provide a better understanding of the subject case itself. It is not selected because it is representative of a larger genre or because it serves as an illustrative example of something. Nor is it selected because the researcher plans to build a theory upon what is found in the analysis of the case. Rather, the case is studied simply because the researcher is interested in it for some reason. It tends to be, therefore, the most focused scale of all the types of case studies.

Examples of Intrinsic Case Studies

The first example of an intrinsic public management single-case study discussed here is Soni's (2000) study of a regional office of the U.S. Environmental Protection Agency. The study focused on workplace diversity and the attitudes of agency personnel toward mandated awareness initiatives. Soni first determined how employees valued workplace diversity and then looked at whether the staff supported the agency management-development program. The program was designed to enhance worker acceptance of racial, age, and gender diversity in the organization. This included requirements for diversity-management initiatives in five-year strategic plans and diversity goals at the local or agency group level.

Analysis of this single case led Soni (2000) to conclude that workers accept and support diversity to a far less extent than the ideal published in the literature. In addition, diversity-management programs appeared to have only minimal effects in changing workers' sensitivity of differences or their acceptance and valuing of diversity, reducing stereotyping and prejudice, or any of the other goals established for the program.

Case studies such as that carried out by Soni should not be used by research-ers to imply similar behaviors or conditions in other or related organizations. The results of a case study are applicable only to the organization or group examined. No inferences can or should be made from the results. Soni (2000, 407) reflected on this possible limitation of the method by adding the following caveat at the conclusion of the article: "The racial and gender effects found in this case study may be a consequence of the many specific organizational characteristics and can-not be assumed to be representative of other organizations."

A Small-Scale Intrinsic Total Quality Management Case

In a public management example of a small-scale intrinsic single-case study, Poister and Harris (2000) examined a mature total quality management (TQM) program in the Pennsylvania Department of Transportation (PDT). The program began in 1982 with the introduction of quality circles and evolved into a major strategic force in the department, with quality concepts incorporated into all levels of the culture of the organization.

Poister and Harris (2000) pointed to the experience of the department as an example for other agencies to emulate—one of the key purposes of the case study. They concluded their study with the statement that the department had focused on the core values of quality and customer service to transform itself over a fifteen-year period. They added that they hoped the agency's experience would be helpful to other public agencies that have begun a transformation process after reading about the PDT experience.

A Single-State, Single-Program Intrinsic Case

Improving agency performance and service delivery in the government of the state of Washington was the topic of an intrinsic case study (Campbell 2004). A series of productivity improvement programs enacted during the administration of Governor Gary Locke resulted in what was described as a performance-driven approach to government in the state. Included were the Budgeting and Accounting Act of 1993; Personnel Systems Reform Act of 2002; Priorities of Government program, which aligned budgeting agency by agency and provided strategy-based budgeting processes; private-sector consultation on performance management; and several performance management, sustainability, and quality-related executive orders.

Although there was no attempt at developing or proving a theory of administrative management, the case did conclude with a set of lessons learned from the record of the Governor Locke administration that other governors might adapt for their own terms of office:

- Use the "bully pulpit" of the governor's office to engage citizens in the work of government.
- Use a strategy-based approach to budgeting; recruit other elected state offices in developing regular reports to state citizens.
- Have a clear agenda for the administration; engage cabinet officers to align agency strategies and resourcing decisions with the agenda.
- Support civil service reform; develop a performance-based culture among state government employees.
- Adopt common data architectures and integrate systems across the state to make government more seamless to citizens and reduce duplicate data entry.
- Support an entrepreneurial and strategic approach to delivering administrative or support functions.
- Use best management practices from other sectors as appropriate.

Instrumental Case Studies

Instrumental designs are used when the public administration researcher wants to gain greater insight into a specific issue that often involves more than a single unit or organization: it is, therefore, of wider scale than the intrinsic case study. In these situations, the subject case is expected to contribute to a greater understanding of a topic of interest. Examples include case studies on organizations' implementation of performance measurement procedures, e-government and other technology-enhanced service delivery programs, and outsourcing selected government services. In these and similar studies, the subject case itself is of secondary interest; examining the case helps improve understanding of the phenomenon, not the organization. The case study of the attitudes of employees in a regional office of General Services Administration (GSA) mentioned in chapter 1 falls into this category of case research.

An Example of an Instrumental Case Study

An analysis of natural disaster planning and the evacuation of some 7,000 residents of the island of Montserrat after eruption of the long-dormant Soufriere

Hills volcano was the subject of a 1999 large-scale instrumental single-case study. Kydd (1999) described and analyzed program-planning activities that occurred before and during the series of five significant eruptions that began in July 1995.

Montserrat, one of the Leeward Islands in the Caribbean, has been a British possession since 1632. The eruptions produced pyroclastic flows of super-hot dry rock mixed with hot gases. The series of flows covered the capitol city of Plymouth under forty feet of mud, destroyed the island's airport, claimed twenty lives, and forced evacuations of all residents of the southern half of the island. A similar eruption on the neighboring island of Martinique in 1902 resulted in the deaths of 28,000 islanders. Beginning in 1996, most of the population was moved to neighboring islands, the United States, or Great Britain.

The Montserrat case researchers began by identifying the affected population; they then conducted assessments of the needs of the population, identified when and where program-planning activities would be needed, and surveyed the population to identify the psychological and psychosocial needs of citizens evacuated to Great Britain, which were surfacing as a result of the large-scale relocations. From this situational analysis, the author developed sets of relocation guidelines for support agencies and personnel, and analyzed the application of the program-planning and evaluation approach. The final element was preparation of a set of program-planning and evaluation principles for possible use in other natural disaster and large-scale population evacuations.

Montserrat and the Five Key Elements of Case Research

The Montserrat case research report followed Robert Yin's (1994) five key elements of a case research design:

1. The questions upon which the study is framed
2. The study's propositions
3. Its units of analysis
4. The logic linking the data to the propositions
5. The criteria for interpreting the findings

The researchers addressed each of the five elements by answering the following five study questions:

1. Who were the groups and individuals involved in the project?
2. How was the program-planning and evaluation process implemented?
3. What outcomes occurred as a result of the program activities?
4. What were people's reactions to involvement in the project?
5. To what extent did the adapted version of the program-planning and evaluation process meet identified standards?

The purpose of specifying the propositions upon which the questions were framed is to help the researcher focus on what should be studied. In some studies the propositions may be listed as the researchers' assumptions. In the Montserrat case, the propositions included statements regarding (1) which subjects should be included in the study and which excluded, (2) why the subjects should be persons already relocated to Great Britain, (3) why the evaluation should occur when and where proposed, what outcomes were expected to occur and why, (4) what reactions and ramifications were expected as a result of relocation and its aftermath, and (5) which measures (objective and subjective) would be used in interpreting the collected survey data.

The Unit of Analysis in the Montserrat Case

The unit of analysis is what the case *is*; this process of defining of the unit of analysis is a "problem that has plagued many investigators at the outset of case studies" (Yin 1994, 21). Among the many possible forms, the case can be made up of a single individual or a group; it can be a program, a decision, an implementation of a program, or a change in an organization. In the Montserrat case, the individuals surveyed were *not* the unit of analysis. Rather, in this research the case studied was the program-planning and evaluation process used to develop relocation guidelines for this and future populations. According to Yin, as a general rule, defining the unit of analysis is related to the way that the researcher defines the original case questions.

The steps of linking the data to the study propositions and specifying the criteria for interpreting the findings are described by Yin (1994) as being the least developed elements of case research. Linking the data refers to the researcher's conceptions of which theory or theories are assumed to underlie the propositions. If, for example, the case is analysis of a decision, one or more of the theories of decision making might be tested in the analysis of the data. The author of the Montserrat case achieved this requirement by clearly specifying propositions that support each of the five study questions. Both objective and subjective measures were the criteria used for interpreting the collected data. The data were collected through answers to open- and closed-ended questions asked during personal interviews and completion of survey questionnaires.

Collective Case Studies

In this design, several individual cases are studied together as a group because it is believed that they can contribute to greater understanding of a phenomenon, a population, or some general organizational condition. Another name for this form of case is *multisite qualitative research* (Yeager 1989). Two variations of this design exist. The first is traditional multicase design, and the second is meta-analysis design. Multicase research designs will be examined in greater detail in chapter 5. The meta-analysis design, which is a study of case studies, has the broadest scale of case research. Meta-analysis will be discussed in greater detail in the chapter 7.

A Two-Level Case Classification System

The characteristics of the scale and the scope of the research also make it possible to identify a two-level classification system for case research. This classification system involves, first, the number of cases in the study (single- or multicase designs) and, second, the number of subunits contributing to the phenomenon under analysis (single or multiple unit of analysis). These characteristics result in four types of case study designs: single-case/single-unit design, single-case/multiple-unit design, multicase/single-unit design, and multicase/multiple-unit designs. Case studies in which a single unit of analysis is studied are *holistic* designs; designs in which multiple units contribute to the analysis are *embedded* designs (Yin 1994).

Holistic Single-Case Designs

In holistic single-case designs, researchers are concerned with the analysis of one complete unit of analysis, with no subunits analyzed independently. The key to understanding this design is the concept that only a single, complete unit is the focus of the case; the organization or unit is studied as a whole. A case study of the implementation of a new customer management software system in one city department is an example of a holistic design. Another example is a case study of the effects on the welfare client population in a single community or a single state that results from a shift from a government delivery system to a contract system, in which the services are delivered by one or more faith-based, nonprofit organizations.

Holistic Multicase Designs

The holistic multicase design is used when the case study includes more than one case. For example, the U.S. Department of Homeland Security (DHS) was established immediately after the terrorist attacks of September 11, 2001. More than two dozen organizations were removed from other departments and combined under the new cabinet-level department. A case study on the use of performance management processes and techniques in DHS could logically include evaluations of more than one of the agencies now under DHS management. The research would involve the study of this one concept, phenomenon, or program, but would analyze that concept, phenomenon, or program in more than one of the agencies now under DHS management. Yin described this as a study in which several holistic studies are analyzed.

Embedded Single-Case Designs

In this design the researcher includes more than one participant unit of analysis to contribute to understanding of a single case. Say, for example, the researcher is interested in developing a case study of the failures of government agencies during and after Hurricane Katrina. The effects of Hurricane Katrina is the single case. Each of any number or level of government agencies involved during and after the disaster is a subunit in the analysis of the whole. This case would fit the requirements of an embedded single-case design. If, however, it was not possible to identify any individual subunits, the holistic single-case design would have been the proper design.

Embedded Multicase Designs

This is the most complex of the case designs identified by Yin. It involves multiple cases, each with multiple subunits included in the analysis. Each of the cases or each of the subunits could conceivably be considered a case study in itself. An example could be a study of regional public transportation authorities. Say, for example, the public transit authorities in Boston, Chicago, Los Angeles, New York, and Seattle are the subject cases. Each receives funding from the federal government agencies and from sources that are particular to their region, such as cities, counties, or regions. The mission and networks of each transportation organization are varied in size, type, age, and governance structure. Thus, a number of subunits can be identified for each of the cases; to not analyze these and other subunits would severely limit understanding of the individual systems and problems faced collectively.

Factors Affecting the Design Decision

Three characteristics contribute to the decision of whether to use a single-case or a multicase design. First, the single-case approach is the most appropriate method to use when the case subject is deemed to be a critical case. This refers to a situation in which the researcher proceeds with a theory already well developed, with a clear hypotheses or propositions that are believed to be true. The purposes of the single-case study in these situations are to "confirm, challenge, or extend the theory" (Yin 1994, 38–40).

Second, the single-case design should be used when the subject under study can be considered an extreme or unique case. This situation occurs when the phenomenon in the case is so rare that it is intrinsically worth investigating. Yin pointed to examples in clinical psychology, but this design is certainly not limited to that discipline. In public management, for example, problems or failures with implementation of a new policy directive could easily fit this requirement.

Third, the single-case design should be used when the case reveals information that, until this case is identified, might have remained hidden or not fully understood; Yin calls this type a revelatory case because the analysis reveals information otherwise unknown. In some ways, this design is similar to investigative journalism.

The decision to choose a multicase design is similar to that of conducting multiple experiments in the natural sciences. However, in a multicase design, the additional or follow-on "experiments" are all conducted as part of the same multicase project. Accordingly,

> The logic underlying the use of multiple-case studies is the same. Each case must be carefully selected so that it either (a) predicts similar results (a *literal replication*) or (b) produces contrasting results but for predictable reasons (a *theoretical replication*). The ability to conduct six or ten case studies, arranged effectively within a multiple-case design, is analogous to the ability to conduct six to ten experiments on related topics. . . . (Yin 1994, 46; emphasis in the original)

Summary

Case studies are intensive studies of one or a few exemplary individuals, families, events, time periods, decisions, processes, programs, institutions, organizations, groups, or even entire communities.

Based on their overall scale, three types of case studies have been identified: intrinsic, instrumental, and collective. Intrinsic case studies, the narrowest in scale, are done when the researcher wants to provide a better understanding of the subject case itself. Instrumental case studies are used when the researcher wants to gain greater insight into a specific issue. The collective case study is a multicase design, with a group of individual cases studied together because it is believed that they can contribute to greater understanding of a phenomenon, a population, or some general organizational condition. Another term for this type of case is multisite qualitative research.

Case studies are also defined by their scope: single-case, multicase, and meta-analysis design. Most case studies conducted in the behavioral and administrative sciences—including public administration—are single-case studies; however, multicase studies are becoming nearly as common as single-case studies in public management research. A third model, the meta-analysis of many cases, is appropriate, for example, when investigators are interested in examining how research reports on a phenomenon have shifted in the literature over some period of time.

➤ 5 ◀

Multicase Research Designs

*The multicase study is a special effort to examine
something having lots of cases, parts, or members.
We study those parts, perhaps its students, its committees, its
projects, or manifestations in diverse settings.*
—Robert E. Stake (2006)

Although most case study research is constructed around an in-depth analysis of
a single case, multicase designs are also quite common. Multicase designs either
compare one case against another or involve analysis of more than one case collectively in an effort to attain even greater understanding of the phenomenon of
interest. Comparative public management cases are by intent all multicase studies
(Jun 1976 and 2000; Kaarbo and Beasley 1999). Multicase designs are introduced
in this chapter, and the process of carrying out multicase research is discussed in
greater detail in the following chapter.

Multicase research is a variation of single-case design and is done for more or
less the same reasons and with the same data collection methods. However, a multicase design is selected when the evidence gained from a single case is insufficient
to develop a theory, test an existing theory, or effectively illustrate the principles
existing in the case that the researcher wishes to bring to light.

While there is no ironclad rule for the number of cases to include in a multicase
study, Stake (2006) pointed out that researchers can do their best work if their
multicase studies include more than four but fewer than ten cases. Fewer than four
cases usually do not provide the researcher enough variability in the study question
for meaningful results. When the number climbs to fifteen or more, the cases may
become too distinct, varying from the study question enough to lack relevance; they
may provide too much variability for the researcher and readers to analyze.

Transforming Readers into Participants

Rosenwald (1988), in concluding his essay on the multicase method in the *Journal
of Personality*, justified his call for more multicase research in such administrative
and social sciences as public management with this statement:

> The multicase approach aims at an educational effect. It seeks to make readers into participants and thus to help them clarify their lives. Beyond this, it seeks to focus on the difficulties, including above all the silences and perplexities, which obstruct readers' and participants' endeavors to change their lives [and resolve the issues at hand]. It regards these obstacles as yet another kind of social object. . . . It should be clear that our ultimate interest is the lot of individuals. This must be socially comprehended and reconstructed. However, to understand what the social world is to individuals, we must consult them more than we ever have before. (Rosenwald 1988, 263)

The problems most public managers must deal with in carrying out their governance missions may also be considered to be social problems. They are social in that they typically have some effect upon one or more groups of people. The groups may be other members of the staff of the organization or other administrators in widely disbursed but similar organizations who find or will find themselves required to make decisions in similar circumstances. Or the group may be the constituency of the manager or administrator.

Rosenwald (1988) believed that social problems are often minimized, ignored, or denied by ordinary citizens. The passive consensus that this lack of interest engenders tends to perpetuate problems in administrative organizations. When this attitude prevails, administrators may be unable to resolve the impasse forged by the consensus.

Conducting multicase studies instead of focusing only on a single case often helps the administrator or researcher to draw out the underlying issues. This helps both the subjects of the case and the administrators to achieve resolution. In addition, even when a problem is acknowledged by individual members of a group, it appears in as many different forms as there are individuals within the group. By looking at more than one person's perception of the problem, multicase studies can identify the commonalities and core concepts that frame the issue.

Rosenwald (1988) emphasized that socially significant knowledge cannot be developed from single-case studies. Moreover, multicase studies are not and should never be considered to be merely a collection of single-case studies. The single-case study is important for what it is: an in-depth analysis of a single case. The information gained from single-case studies cannot serve an inferential role, nor should it be used for hypothesis testing. Rather, it helps to provide greater understanding. He concluded that "at best," multiple-case research "results in a clarification of personal and social experience." And in many cases, that may be results enough.

Some Advantages and Disadvantages of the Multicase Method

Multicase designs have both advantages and disadvantages in comparison to single-case designs. Advantages include the following:

- The findings of a multicase study may have greater force than that of a single case.
- From a scientific point of view, a multicase design may be more "robust," that is, have more convincing proof and, at the same time, be more flexible in design.

Disadvantages include the following:

- The researcher's rationale for selecting a case design may be less convincing for a multicase design than it might be for a single-case design.
- A multicase design may require far greater resources and probably take much more time to complete than a typical single-case design.

Three Categories of Multicase Research

Three multicase research designs are discussed in this chapter: comparative, interpretive, and longitudinal. The comparative research method focuses on the results of individual case applications of a concept, process, or other such phenomenon. The results are compared—often item by item—to identify best practices for others to emulate. Interpretive designs are an extension of the single-case approach. Here, the focus is on developing greater understanding of an issue or phenomenon, often for the purpose of generating or testing a theory. Therefore, choosing the cases to include in the study is particularly important. Longitudinal design is often used in studies of a few individual cases conducted over some period of time to identify and expose changes in conditions or events. The purpose of longitudinal multicase design is to direct the most attention possible to some aspect of an experience, circumstance, condition, phenomenon, or event so as to expand, dissect, and describe in detail the core dimensions of a phenomenon. The goal of this type of study is often to develop theory while at the same time illustrating some application of a process or program (Schneider 1999). Each of the designs is discussed in greater detail in the next sections.

Comparative Multicase Design

Multicase research design is often used to compare the findings of one or more case activities against the way the same activity is carried out in other cases. This comparative approach is one of the principal research designs in political science and its many subdisciplines, including public administration or public management. Pennings, Keman, and Kleinnijenhuis (1999) suggested that people use the "art of comparing" as they absorb communications from the environment in order to arrive at what most individuals believe is a sound interpretation of what is happening in public life. They offered the following conclusion about the comparative method:

The "art of comparing" is thus one of the most important cornerstones of the development of knowledge about society and politics and insights into what is going on, how things develop and, more often than not, the formulation of statements about why this is the case and what it may mean to all of us. In short, comparisons are part and parcel of the way we experience reality and, most importantly, how we assess its impact on our lives and that of others. (Pennings, Keman, and Kleinnijenhuis 1999, 3)

The Comparative Method Defined

In their article on comparative case research in political science, political psychology, and, by inference, public administration, Kaarbo and Beasley (1999, 372) defined the comparative method as "the systematic comparison of two or more [cases] obtained through the case study method." Their analysis of the literature revealed that most of the published comparative research in political science was focused on comparisons of cross-national politics, with little research on such subfields as public administration or public management. They recommended that researchers planning comparative case studies follow this six-step procedure:

1. Identify a specific research question or questions for focused comparison.
2. Identify variables from existing theory.
3. Select the cases for analysis and comparison based on determined
   a. comparability of cases;
   b. cases with measurable variation in the focused question(s); and
   c. cases with representation across "population" subgroups.
4. Construct a case codebook and define ("operationalize") selected variables.
5. Record code-data from collected evidence and analysis of case data.
6. Make comparisons and implications for theory development or testing.

A Comparative Case Example

In an economic development study, Yager (1992) used a comparative case design to evaluate the transfer of technology from firms in four industries to affiliates in Hong Kong, Singapore, and the Guangdong Province of China. The objective of his study was to identify patterns in international technology transfers and the contexts in which transfers take place. The industries selected included athletic footwear, food processing, electronics, and building materials. Contextual variables included the home country of the technology supplier, the host country of the recipient, relationships between the two governments, and characteristics of the global industry in which the supplier and recipient firms operate. Yager's comparative case analysis identified sets of conditional factors and relationships that facilitated or hindered technology transfer.

Yager (1992) noted that research in such complex and changing spheres of interest requires flexibility in researching economic, social, and political environments, as well as the ability to synthesize the complex relationships existing in international commerce. He concluded that the case method of research is particularly well suited in such circumstances.

Comparing Benchmarking Projects

Ammons, Coe, and Lombardo (2001) used a multicase approach to compare the success of three public sector benchmarking projects. Two of the projects were national in scope, and the third was a single state program. The first project was a 1991 program sponsored by the Innovation Groups to collect performance measurement information from cities and counties across the country.

This information was eventually incorporated into a national performance-benchmarking information network, eventually named the *PBCenter*. Participants were charged a $750 fee to join the project. Although the effort started aggressively by measuring forty-three programs, ultimately both participation and enthusiasm among potential users of the information were disappointing.

The Ammons, Coe, and Lombardo (2001) study concluded that all three programs had failed to deliver results that even closely approached the expectations of their participants, and many felt that program costs exceeded any benefits. On the basis of their comparative analysis of the three cases, the authors recommended that administrators of similar projects in the future should make sure that participants have realistic expectations for benchmarking before they buy into their programs.

Interpretive Multicase Designs

Multicase design is also used to study a collection of cases in order to develop greater understanding of a phenomenon of interest—what Robert Stake (2006) labeled the "quintain." Because the multicase design involves the study of a selected group of parts or units functioning in diverse settings, with different resources and operational environments, each part contributes to the enlargement of this understanding. Naturally, each case selected for the study has its own set of problems, networks, and other characteristics. Only by studying each component part of the whole does the researcher develop an understanding of the whole. Accordingly,

> We seek an accurate understanding of the quintain [the greater whole]. We seek to portray its cases comprehensively, using ample but nontechnical description and narrative. Our observations cannot help being interpretive, and our descriptions are laced with and followed by interpretation. We offer readers the opportunity to generate their own interpretations of the quintain, but we offer ours too. (Stake 2006, vii)

An Interpretive Case Example

Falleti's 2005 multicase study of decentralization in Latin America is an example of a case study in which the author proposes a theory that supplants or enhances

Table 5.1

Applying Case Elements in a Multicase Design

Process Step	Government Decentralization Case Examples
Frame the research question.	Has decentralization led to the expected shift in the balance of power among executive, gubernatorial, and mayoral levels of government? The study proposed a definition of decentralization as a multidimensional process involving political bargaining over the content and implementation of policies resulting in power sharing at the national, provincial, and municipal levels.
Define key constructs.	Key constructs defined include decentralization and its three forms: administrative, fiscal, and political decentralization; decentralization as a process; sequences of decentralization; and intergovernmental balance of power in Latin America.
Define units of analysis.	The units of analysis in this case were the large Latin American countries (Argentina, Bolivia, Brazil, Chile, Colombia, Mexico, Paraguay, and Peru). The study first compared decentralization activities in Argentina, Brazil, Colombia, and Mexico, and then focused on comparing decentralization progress in Argentina and Colombia. The specific unit measured consisted of historical reports of decentralization successes and failures within the two focus nations.
Collect the data.	The data were collected by a study of government documents, published academic and popular literature, academic journal articles and books, and personal interviews carried out by the research in the focus nations. Both English and Spanish language sources were investigated.
Analyze the data.	Data analysis methods and procedures were not described in the published document.
Prepare and present a report.	The report was produced as a comparative multicase research report in Falleti (2005).

Source: Falleti (2005).

existing theories. The purpose was to increase understanding of the decentralization phenomenon, not to compare how well different agencies or jurisdictions accomplished the task. The research question addressed in the case was this: Has decentralization in Latin America led to expected shifts in the balance of power among the executive, gubernatorial, and mayoral levels of government?

After describing liberal and economic theories of benefits accruing from decentralization, the author proposed a "sequential theory of decentralization" as an alternative. Liberal theory argues that decentralization helps to expand and strengthen democracy by bringing power to local governments. Those following a market theory of local expenditures contend that decentralization of government improves resource allocation because of greater knowledge of local needs and preferences.

Three types of decentralization were identified in this case study: administrative decentralization (polices that transfer the management and delivery of social services), fiscal decentralization (policies designed to increase revenues or fiscal autonomy of governments below the national level), and political decentralization (constitutional amendments and electoral reforms to increase representation for government below the national level). Each type would have its own forum and level of success in decentralization. Sequential theory suggests that decentralization processes go through two or more of these steps sequentially.

The author then described levels of government decentralization that occurred between 1978 and 1999 in Argentina, Brazil, Colombia, and Mexico. This was followed by an in-depth comparative analysis of the widely different, extreme approaches to decentralization taken in Colombia and in Argentina. The design of the study is shown in Table 5.1.

Decentralization began in Colombia in 1986 with passage of a constitutional amendment supported by President Belisario Betancur. The legislation would, for the first time in more than 100 years, require popular election of mayors. Prior to the amendment, the president appointed regional governors who then appointed local mayors.

This administrative decentralization was followed by fiscal decentralization. This was then followed with a series of reforms that gave local administrators greater control over local resources. By all measurements applied at the time, Colombia's decentralization was a success.

Government decentralization activity in Argentina was a different story, however. There, decentralization followed a national path, in which the military junta in power in 1978 began with decrees that administrative control of all national preschools and primary schools be transferred to the provinces. Retroactive to the first of the year, some 6,500 schools (with 65,000 employees and 900,000 students) were transferred from national to local administration—although neither revenues nor fiscal powers were transferred with the schools. The federal budget was immediately cut by something in excess of 200 million pesos.

Fiscal decentralization finally followed ten years later. When the ruling party lost its majority in the House of Representatives after the 1987 midterm elections, the president agreed to the governors' demands for changes in the distribution of revenue-share taxes. Political decentralization followed, beginning in 1994, when the city of Buenos Aires was granted political autonomy. However, other legislation that would have increased political decentralization failed to pass. As a result,

> The sequence of administrative, fiscal and political reforms followed by Argentina resulted in a small change in the relative power of the governors and mayors. The share of expenditures increased, but by a lower amount than the changes experienced by Colombia, Mexico, or Brazil. . . . Despite the introduction of decentralization policies that transferred responsibilities, resources, and authority to subnational governments, the sequence in which the reforms took place meant that the intergovernmental balance of power remained unchanged in Argentina. Compared to their situation prior to 1976, governors had acquired more responsibilities and fewer fiscal resources, with no change in their political authority. (Falleti 2005, 343)

A City/County Multicase Interpretive Study

Another multicase interpretive study example is the *Center for Performance Measurement* case. This case involved a study of a national program sponsored by the International City/County Management Association (ICMA). This program was established in 1994 by a consortium of thirty-four cities and counties with populations over 200,000. Performance measurements were collected and shared in these four core service areas: police services, fire services, neighborhood services, and support services. Neighborhood services included code enforcement, housing, libraries, parks and recreation, road maintenance, garbage collection, and street lighting services.

Longitudinal Multicase Designs

Longitudinal studies are often conducted to evaluate such outcomes and the long-term effects of a new federal policy or program, local implementation of a mandated change in an existing policy or program by a state and/or local government, and other actions that cannot be evaluated until after the passage of some period of time. In these studies, the underlying design is usually that of an interpretive study; the researchers want to understand the impact of the change or whether the objectives of the policy or program have remained in place through the period of implementation, as Rist warned:

> One message has come back to policy makers time and time again: Do not take for granted that what was intended to be established or put in place through a policy initiative will be what one finds after the implementation process is complete. Programs and policies make countless midcourse corrections, tacking constantly, making changes in funding levels, staff stability, target population movements, political support, community acceptance, and the like. (Rist 1998, 414)

Longitudinal Multicase Research Examples

Wineburg (1994) conducted a longitudinal multicase study of faith-based organizations' growing involvement in the delivery of human services at the local level. The longitudinal study focused on congregations as open systems in order to interpret their public mission orientation. The six cases included in the study were traditional mainstream congregations in Greensboro, North Carolina; all were members of the Greensboro Church and Community Forum. Wineburg found that the more a congregation became involved as a contract service provider, the more they appeared to demonstrate moral influence on local welfare reform issues, and the greater they emerged as local power brokers in policy decisions.

Kelly and Rivenbark (2003) highlighted another longitudinal multicase comparative study in their book on performance budgeting for state and local governments. They examined a local government improvement initiative that began in 1994 in

North Carolina; its purpose was to provide performance reports to the state's city managers. By 1995, it had evolved into the *North Carolina Local Government Performance Management Project* and was run by the Institute of Government at the University of North Carolina–Chapel Hill. By 1997, thirty-five cities and counties were participating.

Summary

Multicase designs are used to compare two or more cases for gathering extended evidence across a group of like cases. Multicase research is a variation of the single-case design and is done for the same reasons and with the same data collection methods. A multicase design is selected when the evidence gained from a single case is insufficient to develop a theory, test an existing theory, or effectively illustrate the principles existing in the case that the researcher wishes to bring to light.

This chapter reviewed three different multicase designs: comparative, interpretive, and longitudinal. Comparative research is often conducted to identify best practices of a phenomenon. Interpretive research is traditionally the design adopted when the objective is to develop greater understanding of a phenomenon for the purpose of developing or testing a theory. In the longitudinal approach, multicase research is often used in studies conducted over relatively long periods of time to identify and expose changes in conditions or events.

➤ 6 ◄

Getting Started in Single-Case and Multicase Research

*To study a case, we carefully examine its functioning and activities,
but the first objective of a case study is to understand the case. In
time, we may move on to studying its functioning and relating it to
other cases. Early on, we need to find out how the case gets things
done. By definition, the prime referent in case study is the case, not
the methods by which the case operates.*
—Robert E. Stake (2006)

The case research method is a way of examining one or a small number of cases of
a phenomenon in considerable detail. It can involve a number of different data collection methods, but will more than likely involve personal interviews, participant
observation, and/or the analysis of documents or other archival materials. Like other
methods, case research may be used for exploratory, descriptive, or explanatory
purposes (Johnson, Joslyn, and Reynolds 2001). This chapter describes processes
that researchers follow when carrying out case research in both single-case and
multicase research designs.

The Single-Case Research Process

Gordon and Shontz (1990) have offered a set of guidelines to follow when conducting what they called *representative case* research—what we now call the single-case
method. Representative case research focuses on individual units, such as persons,
governmental units, problem situations, or leadership styles.

These types of case studies involve studying the unit in depth to learn how the
individual administrator or governing unit manages circumstances, experiences,
processes, and events in situations or under certain conditions. As such, it is an ap-

Figure 6.1 **Steps in the Representative or Single-Case Research Process**

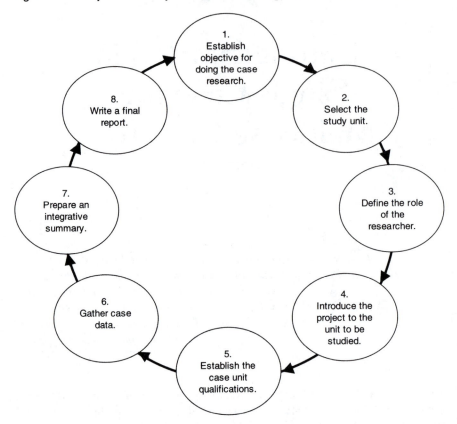

propriate approach to follow when researching how public administrators perform assigned tasks, deal with uncertainty, and cope in crisis situations. The procedure follows the eight steps displayed in Figure 6.1.

The discussion that follows each of the eight steps in the representative case research process includes examples from two case studies. One is Thompson's (2000) review of the performance management experiences of the U.S. Social Security Administration (SSA) during the first four years following the National Performance Review (NPR) Act of 1993 (The NPR was renamed the National Partnership for Reinventing Government in 1997. However, the NPR acronym was still in general use at the time this case study was written.)

When launched in 1993 by President Bill Clinton and Vice President Al Gore, NPR had four guiding principles: (1) cut government red tape, including stream-lining the federal budget process and decentralizing personnel decisions; (2) put customers (citizens) first; (3) empower employees for results by giving frontline employees more freedom of action, but with greater accountability; and (4) go back to basics by consolidating field offices and cutting duplication in and among agencies and increasing productivity through greater use of technology (Nesterczuk 1996).

Define the Reason for Doing the Case Study

All research should begin with a thorough description of the problem or concept for which the study is being conducted. This means you must specify the reason or reasons why this case study is an important one. Otherwise, why do it? The case study is almost always designed to provide information about an event, problem, or situation for which the case and the experiences of the subjects involved will offer guidance and serve as an example. Thus, the study problem must be one that contributes to the level of knowledge in the discipline.

Thompson (2000) selected the SSA for a case assessment on how well the agency was accomplishing the reinvention mandates of the NPR. Key elements of his assessment included measuring whether NPR had (1) reduced the number of employees, (2) made the agency more efficient, (3) reduced costs, (4) reformed administrative systems and decentralized authority, (5) improved customer service, (6) shifted the organizational culture from complacency and entitlement, (7) empowered frontline agency employees, and (8) reengineered work processes to improve productivity.

Thompson (2000) noted that an advantage of the case study method for the research was that it "is conducive to an understanding of causal relationships and thereby facilitates the generation of answers to 'why' questions." His key *why* question was: "Despite . . . five or six years of effort, why hasn't NPR achieved the critical reinvention objectives that it was designed to accomplish?"

Select the Unit to Be Studied

The unit may be a person, an office, a department, a jurisdiction, a group, a state, or any group or individual of interest. When deciding which unit to study, it is best to use a set of characteristics that qualify the unit as one that will produce expert knowledge about the research question or situation of interest..

This research method is only effective when the researcher and coinvestigator have established a close, mutually respectful relationship. Individuals in the chosen research unit must be "articulate, motivated, cooperative, and self-reflective" enough to provide the researcher information that is useful. Thus, in case research with individuals, Gordon and Shontz (1990) called the subject the *coinvestigator*; this term is equally apt if the case is a group.

The Chicago Social Security Office was selected because it was identified as being well suited for reinvention action and therefore represented a useful test case of whether reinvention of government really works. The researchers were convinced that the evidence they would turn up in the study would provide the expert knowledge that would help other administrators understand how to cope in similar situations.

Define the Role of the Researcher

If there is a research team, roles should be defined for all members of the team. Because the data are subject to individual interpretation, the relevant characteristics (both personal and professional) of the individual collecting the data must be described. In addition, the motives for conducting the study and what the researcher's beliefs about the results might reveal should also be aired.

Thompson, then an assistant professor of public administration at the University of Illinois at Chicago, was an outside observer and interviewer. He conducted thirty-one personal interviews of SSA staff at levels ranging from frontline supervisors and field office managers to deputy commissioners at the national office. He also conducted interviews with officials at the Government Accountability Office and at the NPR offices. The data were collected between December 1997 and January 1999. Secondary data were also collected in the form of a 1996 merit principle survey of all federal government respondents, including SSA personnel.

Introduce the Project to the Study Unit

The subjects or individuals within the unit function in the role of expert on the events, circumstances, activities, and experiences of the life of the study unit. The researcher is the trained investigator, seeking answers to questions that focus on the research question. In addition to providing formal, written consent, the subjects must also be assured of anonymity and have the right to withdraw from the study at any time. They must also know that if permission for the study is withdrawn for any reason, all records to that time will be destroyed.

Thompson gained the support of the National Partnership for Reinventing Government office and the national SSA office before contacting local SSA personnel for the interviews and conducting his telephone and in-person interviews.

Establish the Case Unit Qualifications

Pre–case study interviews and written tests may be used to certify that the case unit selected will provide the knowledge and experience that the study is designed to gather. Public administration cases typically provide a record of one agency's successes or failures—or both—so that other administrators in the same situation do not repeat unsuccessful activities while learning to use the best of what others have done. Therefore, the subjects of the case should be central players in the drama taking place in the case. The case unit should also qualify as a (good or bad) example of the study question or theme.

The SSA was selected by Thompson because it met the requirements spelled out by Osborne and Gaebler (1992) for an agency ripe for a reinvention initiative: the agency's technology made it a good candidate for reinvention; it was a "production" organization with an "assembly-line" approach to processing claims; it had multiple management layers with a strict, vertical chain of command; and work was guided by strict rules and regulations. Thus, the agency seemed to be a classic example of an industrial-era bureaucracy, in which employees paid strict attention to standard operating procedures and standardized services.

Gather the Case Data

Gathering information about the case takes place in a series of cycles of data collection. At the close of one interview session, for example, the researcher should prepare a series of new questions suggested by information brought out during the preceding session. In this way the researcher achieves deeper levels of understanding that build on earlier records. These deepening levels of knowledge about the case unit and experiences of the subjects in the unit may also be used to clarify ambiguities. In addition, they can provide greater detail about some points or serve to confirm the accuracy of earlier observations.

Gillham (2000) showed that data for case research may be gathered in a number of different ways, including but not limited to individual in-depth and group interviews, participant or nonparticipant observation, or analysis of official documents and other published or archival documents or artifacts. Other approaches to data gathering for case research include questionnaires, analysis of physical artifacts, and role-playing, among others.

This multisource aspect of case data was reflected in the use of telephone and in-person interviews and use of secondary data sources for comparing the results of the SSA with all other federal government agencies.

Prepare an Integrative Summary

An *integrative summary* is a preliminary overview of the information gained during the case study. It also serves to signal the end of data gathering. It should include the researcher's initial reactions to the information. As case reports that follow a set of phases or milestones illustrate, this step should also include preparation of a timeline that notes the sequence of actions that occurred during the investigation. Each milestone in this timeline should include the key accomplishment achieved at that level.

Often, this phase in the study centers on one or a series of conferences, with all members of the research team contributing to the discussion. This summary is a record of the complete study and is characterized by the thick description possible by case study research. As such, it is far too detailed for the final case report; it must be condensed and synthesized—made into a readable, interesting report. This step was not discussed in the case report. Therefore, it was not possible to determine whether the findings were shared with agency administrators.

Write a Final Report

The final report of the case study should be an informative record of the actions taken and the findings reached by the researcher. It begins with an executive summary, starting with reasons for conducting the study and a brief background of the subject and closing with a discussion on the implications or lessons learned from the study. It describes the methods and physical circumstances of the data gathering and includes a timeline of the steps and milestones. It should not be an overly detailed record of everything done, seen, heard, or learned. Rather, the final case report should be an informative, condensed narrative of the key themes and topics uncovered during the period of the study. Most published reports also include suggestions for further study.

The findings of the SSA case study were published in *Public Administration Review* (Thompson 2000). Thompson included an excellent discussion of the possible explanations for the failure of NPR to be as effective at changing organizations as its supporters envisioned. Two areas of alternative explanations were provided: (1) errors of implementation, including political pressures and diversion of funds to other projects; and (2) design flaws, including errors in downsizing and contradictory elements with the NPR program.

The final case report must clearly show that the researcher has accurately explained what are perceived to be the facts in the case or cases. It must also contain some discussion of relevant alternative interpretations, as well as an explanation of why the researcher chose not to accept those alternatives. Finally, the case research report should end with a conclusion that is soundly based on the interpretation and theory adopted by the researcher (Yeager 1989).

The Multicase Research Process

Just as for a single-case research project, designing and preparing a multicase study takes place through a series of interlocking phases. These are illustrated in Figure 6.2, beginning with the need for framing the research question.

Frame the Research Question

In the first phase, the research question must be *framed*, meaning that the researcher must determine what should be studied in what cases, and why. *Framing* is a term for placing the case in a frame of reference, that is, deciding what specifically about the set of cases is to be studied, analyzed, and communicated.

For example, the researcher might focus on some managerial or service delivery aspect of a program. Studying the phenomenon across the group of cases will bring

Figure 6.2 **Steps in a Multicase Research Process**

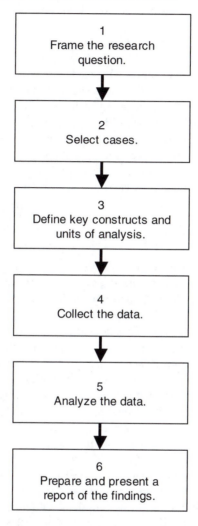

to light concepts that have increased understanding of the implementation process, the problems associated with its delivery, unexpected repercussions resulting from its implementation, or its applicability to other organizations. The frame of reference in this situation is program implementation in selected organizations.

Select Cases to Include in the Study

Researchers face at least two challenges when deciding which cases to include and which to exclude (Mahoney and Goertz 2004). The first is selecting an appropriate group of cases from the larger population of cases dealing with the issue under study. The second is establishing the boundaries that distinguish relevant cases from irrelevant cases.

In other than comparative case research designs, the key characteristic influencing the selection is that the cases should clearly add to the understanding of the phenomenon of interest. For example, if the case is about administration of Medicaid programs in local governments, the cases should (1) focus on comparable local governments rather than state or federal agencies and (2) be about issues pertaining to local administration of elements of Medicaid programs.

The boundaries separating cases are of more importance in comparative studies than descriptive designs. Furthermore, the decision on which cases to include should never be based only on their availability; some legitimate criteria upon which the selection to include the case should be established and spelled out early in the study report.

Define Key Constructs and Units of Analysis

In the second phase, key constructs, variables, terms, and the like, are defined and discussed so that no confusion occurs when they come up again later in the analysis process. Defining or operationalizing relevant themes, issues, research questions, and variables is the third step in this process.

Once defined, these become the key constructs that form and shape the research. This step also requires identifying all limitations and assumptions made for the research. Strauss and Corbin (1998) defined this step as a process of applying order to collected data by placing them in discrete categories.

Operationalizing activities can take place before, during, or after the data are collected. In case research, however, this process usually happens before data collection. When operationalizing is done after the data are collected, the study is more appropriately a *grounded theory* study. In grounded theory, the structure and order emerge from the collected data.

Regardless of when it takes place, the objectives for operationalizing the study constructs are the same: first, to impose *order and structure* to the data and, second, to bring to light any limitations or assumptions. Order and structure established beforehand will help to ensure that the needed data will be collected during case interviews and observations. Finally, when a researcher operationalizes the salient themes or constructs before collecting data for a case study, it is much easier to organize the data later on, as it is being collected.

Include Categories and Codes

Defining the categories also involves providing some amount of descriptive information for each of the categories. Overlaying a detailed structure on data also includes adding some amount of descriptive material along with the code descriptions and category definitions; this preformed description becomes valuable when writing the final report. Gathered information is coded as it is assigned to its proper category. Coding is based on a researcher-selected set of general properties, characteristics, or dimensions.

In their discussion on coding of qualitative data, Strauss and Corbin (1998) stated that conceptualizing is also the first step in theory building. A concept is the researcher's description of a significant event, object, or action-interaction. Naming the researched phenomena and organizing them into logical categories is necessary so that the researcher can group similar events, things, and so forth, into common groupings, classifications, or categories that share some common characteristic or meaning. Thus, "a labeled thing" is something that can be located, placed with a group of similar objects, or classified in some way.

Define the Units of Analysis

The next activity in this step is defining the *units of analysis*. This critical step hinges upon how the researcher has defined the problem in the first phase of the case study. *Defining the units of analysis* refers to the act of establishing if the "actors" in the case will be individuals, groups, neighborhoods, political units, jurisdictions, or any other unit of interest.

Much case research in public management focuses on the actions of individual units or persons, on pairs (dyads), small or large groups, that people follow, or the organizations in which people perform the action of interest (Marshall and Rossman 1999). However, the unit of interest can also be a decision or a set of decisions made by administrators, supervisors, or work teams. The research can focus on programs, agencies, small subunits of agencies, or groups of agencies that address a similar problem or service. Cases can even be about entire communities, groups of communities, and entire nations.

Deciding on the unit of analysis is what Yin (1994) called *a narrowing of the relevant data.* Narrowing the data allows the researcher to focus the study on topics identified in the research objectives. Taking the unit-of-analysis decision to the data-gathering level depends always on the way the researcher has defined the study question.

For example, a case study designed to bring to light the effects of a reduction in the number of beds available at a state mental health hospital could be addressed from several points of view. First, the study could chronicle the effects that inability to access treatment might have on one or a group of patients.

Another approach might focus on the impact the closures will have on community-based treatment centers. An even more focused case could limit the investigation to locally funded charitable organizations that treat the client base. A broader view might look at the economic impact that funding the services locally will have on other community-based programs competing for shares of the same funding pool. Clearly, defining the unit of analysis is a critical first step that must take place before moving to the next step, collecting information.

Finally, operationalization requires that researchers identify each of the procedures that will be followed in conducting the case research, both in data collection and analysis. It also requires identifying the data coding plans and methods that will be used. This process includes preparing a preliminary list of categories for the subsequent analysis as well.

Collect the Data

Data are collected in this phase of the research. This can take place in a variety of ways. The techniques used most often in public administration and political science research include in-depth interviews with key informants, simple (unobtrusive) or participant observation, and analysis of internal and external documents and other physical evidence. One of the hallmarks of a good case study is the selection of two or more of these methods for the same study (Arneson 1993)—a process known as *triangulation*. Triangulation refers to studying a phenomenon in two or more ways to substantiate the validity of the study findings. Each of these data collection methods will be discussed in greater detail in the next chapter.

Gathering data by interview may take one of several different forms. The form used most often in public administration research is the in-depth personal interview. Individual interviews occur as conversations between a researcher and a subject or respondent. To keep the conversation focused, the researcher uses a conversation guide in which are listed the key points to be covered in the interview. The respondent is free to provide any answer that comes to mind. Another type of interview is the more structured type, in which respondents must reply to specific open-ended questions.

Gathering Data by Observation

Observation takes several forms. *Naturalistic* or *simple observation* is used most often in public management case research. Marshall and Rossman (1999, 107) described this method as "the systematic noting and recording of events, behaviors, and artifacts in the social setting chosen for study." The researcher records events and behaviors as they happen. In this type of observation, the researcher does not seek to be accepted as a member of the group, staying instead as an outsider. When the researcher joins the group in all its activities, the method is called *participant observation.*

It is a toss-up as to which is used more often in the case study approach to research: personal interviewing or simple observation. Each has its own advantages and disadvantages. Interviews, for example, allow researchers to delve deeply into a subject, encouraging respondents to provide the reasons for their behavior or opinions. They are time-consuming, however, and require interviewers with special questioning and listening skills.

Observation has long been an important data-gathering technique used in social science research. While it may indeed be called *simple observation*, it is not an easy process to put into action. According to Marshall and Rossman,

> Observation is a fundamental and highly important method in all qualitative inquiry: It is used to discover complex interactions in natural social settings . . . It is, however, a method that requires a great deal of the researcher. Discomfort, uncomfortable ethical dilemmas and even danger, the challenge of managing a relatively unobtrusive role, and the challenge of identifying the "big picture" while finely observing huge amounts of fast-moving and complex behavior are just a few of the challenges. (Marshall and Rossman 1999, 107)

Gathering Data by Document or Evidence Analysis

The study of documents and archival data is usually undertaken to supplement the information the case study researcher acquires by interview or observation. The documents may be official government records, internal organization reports or memos, or external reports or articles about a case subject.

An analysis technique that is often used in document analysis is called *content analysis*. This process may be qualitative, quantitative, or both. One of the key advantages of document analysis is that it does not interfere with or disturb the case setting in any way. According to Marshall and Rossman (1999), the fact that document and archival analysis is unobtrusive and nonreactive is probably its greatest strength.

Analyze and Interpret the Data

The analysis of qualitative data takes place in a progression of phases. An important tenet inherent in all data analysis is that the data be reduced in volume at each stage of the analysis. Unless this occurs, the researcher can be inundated with reams of unrelated information. This flood of data can make logical interpretation impossible.

Organizing the data into sets of mutually exclusive categories is one way that data reduction occurs. The primary responsibility of the analyst is to remain focused on interpreting information that sheds light on the study question. This may mean ignoring or leaving to a later review highly interesting but extraneous data.

The Data Analysis Process

Analysis of case data involves looking at and weighing the collected data from a number of different viewpoints before writing the final case narrative. This is done during a progression of steps:

1. Defining and reorganizing key constructs.
2. Grouping the data according to key constructs.
3. Identifying bases for interpretation.
4. Developing generalizations from the data.
5. Testing alternative interpretations.
6. Forming or refining theory from the case study.

Data analysis does not always take place in a logical, ordered sequence, however. Rather, two or more of the activities may be occurring at the same time. In addition, data analysis does not simply end with the first set of conclusions; it should be looked at as part of a circular process.

Parts of any analysis step may be moved forward to the next step or steps, while other parts, even whole sections, may butt up against conclusions with dead ends. When this happens, the researcher must search for alternative explanations, test these against the themes that evolved in the operationalization phase, and then either reach new and different conclusions, or adjust the themes and categories to reflect the reality of the data.

The Process of Interpreting Case Data

Case researchers must subjectively interpret what they see and hear in the case group or groups. They must interact closely with individuals in the groups they are studying, often becoming active participants in the phenomenon under study (Lee 1999). In this way, they not only record what they see, but are also able to place their interpretations of the interactions in the group or organization within the context of the social situation.

The objective of the interpretation of data collected during case research is to improve people's understanding of the phenomena of interest. Case studies are also conducted for performance analysis and identification of best practices and exemplars in public organizations.

The Issue of Objectivity

A foundation of the quantitative research approach that is not as relevant in case research is researcher objectivity. The case researcher is not expected to function as an unbiased, unobtrusive observer, reporting only what happens or what is heard. Survey researchers on the other hand maintain a deliberate distance and objectivity from the group they are studying; they avoid making value judgments about what they see in the group; and their goal is to measure behavior. Case researchers seek to understand behavior and the context in which it occurs.

Prepare and Present a Report of the Findings

The final step in the process is producing a comprehensive narrative of the case. The narrative is a descriptive account of the program, person, organization, office, or agency under study. It requires that all the information necessary to understand the case be addressed. It typically revolves around the researcher's interpretation of the behaviors and events observed in the case during the study period, along with the connections between key concepts and study objectives.

Summary

This chapter reviewed the differences and similarities in single-case and multicase research processes. Like all research activities, case research is best carried out in a series of logical steps. The key benefit of using a checklist of steps is to make sure that you don't skip any important process. Two such lists of steps were discussed in this chapter: one for single-case studies and one for multicase designs. The lists are not mutually exclusive, however; in a pinch, one can always be substituted for the other.

Readers will also find different lists of steps in other texts; don't be alarmed over these differences. All such lists are simply the brainchildren of other researchers; they are best considered as suggestions, not hard-and-fast rules. They all serve the same purpose, however: helping to ensure that you cover all bases in your research study.

The nature and scope of data collected can also influence selection of the case study approach. Ethnographic methodology that enables the thick description of the antecedents, events, and circumstances is a common data collection method in these instances.

➤ 7 ◄

Meta-Analysis Research Designs and Processes

Meta-analysis refers to the analysis of analyses. I use it to refer to the statistical analysis of a large collection of analysis results from individual studies for the purpose of integrating the findings. It connotes a rigorous alternative to the casual, narrative discussions of research studies which typify our attempts to make sense of the rapidly expanding research literature.
—Gene V. Glass (1976)

The third form of case study research discussed in this text is the meta-analysis or survey of cases model. This approach involves analyzing many cases and looking for commonalities and discrepancies in findings. In this design a group of previously researched cases is selected and subjected to comparative analysis.

In meta-analysis, instead of studying individuals, groups, organizations, or other such phenomena as subjects, previously prepared research reports are compared or evaluated. Meta-analysis is used to summarize and compare the results of studies produced by other researchers. A meta-analysis is often done to establish the state of research findings on a subject; in this way it provides the researcher with an overview of what others are saying about the subject rather than another discussion of one or a few parts of the question, problem, or issue.

The Focus of Meta-Analysis

Meta-analysis should only be applied to empirical research reports—that is, studies that have analyzed primary data (data collected by the researcher who prepared the findings report). It should not be used for qualitative studies that summarize a set of other research studies; this would mean preparing a summary of summaries— clearly meaningless.

An excellent example of this design is the Dubé and Paré (2003) meta-analysis of ten years of case research on information systems. These authors examined 210 case articles published from 1990 to 1999 in seven major information systems (IS) journals. The objective of the analysis was to determine the level of rigor appearing in a sample of published IS case research reports. Selection of case reports for the analysis was based on whether they met the following key characteristics (Dubé and Paré 2003, 600):

- Did the case researcher examine a current phenomenon in a real-life context or setting?
- Were only one or a few subject units examined (e.g., individuals, groups, organizations, technology, or processes)?
- Did the researchers analyze the unit or units intensively?
- Were the unit or units not studied in isolation from their context or environment, particularly during the data analysis stage (a hermeneutic concept of analyzing a phenomenon only in light of its context and time period)?
- Did the researchers remain objective during their data collection and analysis, avoiding any variable manipulation or treatment?

The case reports were evaluated on three broad characteristics: research design issues, data collection methods, and data analysis. A major finding of their analysis was that a large proportion of the case researchers ignored the case research methods that had been developed by a number of case research methodologists. For example, only 42 percent of the articles in their database included clear research questions; only 58 percent described their data collection methods; and only 23 percent described their data analysis processes.

The meta-analysis resulted in recommendations on each of the three characteristics included in the design. For example, among the chief recommendations in the area of design issues were to always identify clear research questions, specify rules for study unit (sample) selection, do more longitudinal studies, and consider alternative theories.

In the area of data collection, suggestions included providing detailed information on data collection methods, sampling strategies, the use and number of interviewers; using tables to summarize information; and triangulating findings by using more than one data collection method. Data analysis recommendations included describing the analysis methods and procedures; making greater use of preliminary analysis techniques such as field notes, memos, and similar techniques; and comparing the findings with current literature on the topic.

Advantages and Disadvantages of Meta-Analysis

Measurement and statistics researchers at the University of Maryland have identified what may be the single most important advantage of meta-analyses of large numbers of studies (MetaStat 2008): The human mind may be unable to effectively process and evaluate a large number of alternatives. Individuals have a difficult time when asked to evaluate the results of, say, 20 similar studies. When the number of studies is increased to 200—a not untypical number in many meta-analyses—the mind reels. Fortunately, statistical methods and software are readily available for coping with the complexity inherent in large numbers of cases.

In addition to the advantage of synthesizing large volumes of case research data, the three key important advantages of meta-analyses of cases are: First, the process of coding and establishing criteria for selecting studies (what is referred to as a *survey protocol*), reading the study reports, coding the material, and subjecting it to a rigid statistical analysis, imposes a discipline on the researcher that is sometimes missing in qualitative summarizations and comparative analyses.

Second, the summaries of research on similar topics may produce finer gradations of themes that might otherwise have been missed with only one or two case analyses. The application of common statistical tests across all the studies can correct for wide differences in sample size, for example (Bengtsson, Larsson, Griffiths and Hine 2007).

Third, because the meta-analysis examines many case studies, it may make it possible to find effects or associations that one or a smaller number of other comparative processes may have missed. And finally, the meta-analysis process provides a way to organize and structure diverse information from a wide variety of study findings.

Finally, Lipsey and Wilson (2001) identified four additional advantages of a meta-analysis: (1) the method can improve research discipline, (2) supply improvements in data quality, (3) make it possible to locate and compare missed points, and (4) produce improvements in study and report structure.

Some Disadvantages of Meta-Analysis

Meta-analysis is not without its disadvantages, however. A few of the criticisms that have been identified for the method include the following:

1. The large amount of effort and expertise it requires is an often-cited disadvantage of the method. Properly done, a meta-analysis takes considerably more time than a conventional research review. Also, it may require specialized knowledge of case information that the researcher may not have.
2. The case analysis may miss some important issues, including but not limited to the social context of the study, theoretical influences and implications, methodological quality, design issues, and procedures.
3. The mix of studies (an apples and oranges issue) combined into larger groups may hide subtle differences seen in individual studies.
4. Finally, inclusion of studies that are methodologically weak can detract from the findings in strong studies.

Getting Started with a Meta-Analysis

A meta-analysis follows the same system of procedures as primary case research. Researchers first identify a research question (the purpose for the review) and establish their objectives for the review. They then select an organizational framework for the analysis; that is, they determine what variables they will measure across the entire sample of cases.

The next step is to select a sample and specify why individual sample elements will be chosen. Cases selected for a meta-analysis are most often studies that have included the entire population of interest. Researchers then collect, code, and tabulate the data. This involves investigating and reporting on the relationships found between the studies included in the review. Reporting the findings involves connecting the findings back to the study question, purpose, and objectives of the analysis (Bangert-Drowns and Rudner 1991).

Fink (1998) recommended a series of steps for conducting a meta-analysis. His recommendations have been synthesized and coordinated with other research process lists and are presented in Figure 7.1. Each of the steps is discussed in greater detail in the next sections.

Identify the Problem

The first step in all research involves identifying the reason for doing the research. This is what is meant by defining the research problem. In a meta-analysis study, the core problem is deciding what questions or hypotheses should be examined, and what evidence should be included in the review of the selected cases. In meta-analysis, this means deciding what body of research results should be examined. Most often, the research results are seldom concerned with theoretical or methods studies.

Say, for example, that a researcher is interested in knowing more about the role of government collaboration with faith-based organizations in the delivery of emergency services after a natural disaster. The research problem might be perceived variation in services delivery.

Set Criteria for Selecting Cases

Criteria for selecting cases to be included in the analysis might include characteristics of the client population, geographic location, history, experience level of the delivering organization or its sponsoring government agency, or research method used by the case writer. The point is that each selected case should add to the research question knowledge base.

Cases that function as outliers and do not address the issues included in the study are a waste of the researcher's time and resources. A good meta-analysis is not concerned with drawing a representative sample of the literature on the topic. The meta-analysis does seek to include the entire population of studies on the topic; the objective is to include a broad spectrum of representative case studies in the analysis. Deciding which cases to exclude should not be a casual activity; specific criteria should be determined in advance.

Figure 7.1 **Steps in the Meta-Analysis Procedure**

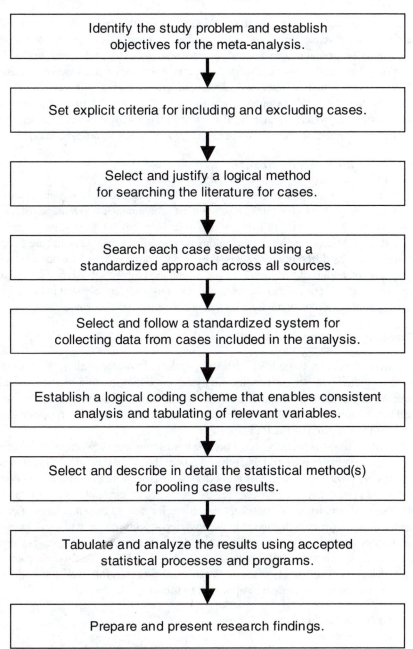

> Identify the study problem and establish objectives for the meta-analysis.

> Set explicit criteria for including and excluding cases.

> Select and justify a logical method for searching the literature for cases.

> Search each case selected using a standardized approach across all sources.

> Select and follow a standardized system for collecting data from cases included in the analysis.

> Establish a logical coding scheme that enables consistent analysis and tabulating of relevant variables.

> Select and describe in detail the statistical method(s) for pooling case results.

> Tabulate and analyze the results using accepted statistical processes and programs.

> Prepare and present research findings.

Sources: Bangert-Drowns and Rudner (1991), Fink (1998).

The Literature Search for Cases

There are two kinds of literature from which to choose the cases for inclusion in the meta-analysis: (1) cases published in the professional literature or government documents, and (2) internal reports, records of analyses conducted and maintained within an organization, and other unpublished materials archived within the organization (Gillham 2000). Whichever source is adopted, the criteria for accepting the case should always be the same. For example, a case may be accepted because of a common theory-testing approach, the nature of the participants within the case under study (such as government workers or citizens), or any other relevant decision criteria.

Standardize the Points for Analysis

The meta-analysis design involves an analysis of analyses, and all analyses are different in some way; this represents one of the most problematic disadvantages of meta-analysis. This has been referred to as an "apples and oranges" problem. Since the cases are studies of different aspects of a phenomenon or different subjects and are done at different times by different researchers, the cases are different; they are not all studies of "apples" or studies of "oranges." To get around the problems that these desired differences entail, it is critical that the researcher examine the same element in every case, ignoring information or characteristics that are peculiar to the one case alone.

Standardize the Analysis Procedure

This step is closely associated with the previous two steps, although this step concerns method rather than focus. Analysis procedure in meta-analysis usually implements standard statistical techniques. However, the techniques and procedures used in the individual cases are often specific to that researcher, the research question, or the discipline of the topic.

The meta-analysis reviewer must be able to differentiate between what the original report writer supposes and what the results of the study indicate. McMillan and Schumacher (1997, 151) offered this good advice: "Be careful to distinguish between study- and review-generated evidence." At this stage of the analysis the researcher must establish and follow a consistent procedure for pulling relevant data out of the cases. Coding—which is discussed in the next step—is one element of the data selection process. Another approach might involve developing précis of key paragraphs and matching these across the full sample. Still another might be to identify and compare the descriptions of key points or terms. Whatever approach is followed, it is important to know that there is not one best approach to follow in all situations.

Select a Coding Scheme

Most researchers tend to follow a coding approach that is similar to data analysis methods used in ethnographic studies. The coding of variables for comparison or tabulation must be consistent across the body of literature reviewed in the meta-analysis. Again, there are no rules for coding, other than to retain consistency. Numeric coding is the preferred approach since most researchers use computers and statistical software for their analyses.

Describe the Statistical Processes Used

In addition to the statistical processes used by the researcher conducting the meta-analysis, the researcher must describe the statistical processes used in each of the cases included in the study. Selecting what process to use in the final analysis has been simplified by the development of statistical software for use with qualitative research studies. Much of this software is available for free. *MetaStat* from the University of Maryland is an example of free meta-analysis software; the online user's manual for MetaStat may also be downloaded free of charge.

Tabulate and Analyze the Data

The last two steps in the meta-analysis procedure are combined here. Data analysis is a product of the statistical software used by the researcher and, as such, is rather straightforward. Standard statistical analyses used in meta-analyses range from simple descriptive statistics and correlation analysis to regression analysis and analysis of variance, to name just a few of the popular tests included in such studies.

Prepare and Present Research Findings

Writing the report introduces a subjective element to the study. The researcher must decide how much information to include and how much to leave out of the report. Care must be taken to control for issues of validity, although statistical inferences are generally not made with meta-analysis findings. Because most meta-analysis case studies involve some degree of comparative analysis, care must be taken to ensure that like concepts, ideas, or themes are compared and an explanation provided for elements left out of any comparisons.

Document Analysis in Meta-Designs: Hermeneutic Analysis

Because meta-analysis involves the interpretation of written materials, a discussion on the underlying method of document analysis is included here. Meta-analysis of many cases has been found to be significantly facilitated by following principles of hermeneutic analysis. Hermeneutics is a method of analyzing all types of data, but is particularly relevant for analysis of written material as in published cases.

Hermeneutics follows a set of principles that requires the analyst to (1) decipher the meaning in the texts through the eyes and intent of the writer or creator,

(2) frame the meaning in the time period of the case research and writing (often referred to as the *context* within which the document was prepared), and (3) determine the meaning considering the political and social environments at the time of the creation of the text or artifact.

Analysis and the Act of Explaining

Hermeneutics owes its long history of interpretive applications to the analysis of religious and legal documents and written administrative rulings such as government pronouncements (Gadamer 1990; Bauman 1992; Alejandro 1993). The term *hermeneutics* originates from the Greek word *hermeneutikós,* which refers to the act of explaining. *Explaining* means making clear or clarifying the obscure (Bauman 1992).

Hermeneutic analysis requires that the researcher take a holistic, or *contextualist,* approach to analysis of the written case studies. The meaning of a text or social phenomenon that is analyzed hermeneutically depends on the whole—that is, the words, the authors, and the context. Meaning cannot be deciphered without understanding the context as well as the text or phenomenon (Wachterhauser 1986).

Hermeneutic analysis is particularly relevant when studying historical documents in public administration, such as past legislation, the records of discourse that occurred during legislative or administrative meetings and hearings, and similar applications. In this way, public administration hermeneutics can help establish meaning and historical trends in previously studied cases dealing with government texts or documents as its material object. And it can do so within the scope of the intent of the participants at the time of the passage or implementation of legislation. Thus, laws enacted years ago that might seem irrelevant today may be interpreted as logical and meaningful when considered in the light of events and circumstances at the time of their enactment or failure to be enacted.

Analysis Using the Meta-Analytic Schedule

An analytical tool useful in carrying out a meta-analysis is the *meta-analytic schedule.* This is a summary table in which the rows are case studies analyzed and the columns are research findings and related study information. The individual cells are used to record specific information, which can be as direct as a simple checkmark noting whether the study includes a relevant characteristic (Garson 2008). Excerpts of an analytic schedule are displayed in Table 7.1.

A Meta-Analysis of Transformational Change Cases

Bushe and Kassam (2005) used a meta-analysis technique to evaluate twenty published case studies using the appreciative inquiry (AI) method of bringing about transformational change in organizations. Details of three of the AI cases—DTE

Table 7.1

Meta-analytic Schedule Showing Results of an Appreciative Inquiry Analysis

	Case		
	DTE Energy Services	NASA	United Religions
Appreciative Inquiry (AI) Outcome	Building the use of AI into the culture of the company	Development of a broadly accepted OHR strategic plan	Establishment of a representative United Religions organization
Is It Transformational?	Unknown	No	Yes
New Knowledge or New Processes	New processes	New process	New knowledge
Generative Metaphor	Unknown	No	Yes
Figure or Ground	Figure	Figure	Ground
Improvisation or Implementation	Improvisation	Improvisation	Improvisation

Source: Bushe and Kassam (2005).

Energy Services, NASA, and United Religions—are displayed in Table 7.1. Six of the case studies were nonprofit organizations (three educational institutions with religious affiliations, two social service organizations, and one nonprofit health maintenance organization [HMO]), and one case was a U.S. government organization (NASA).

The remaining cases dealt with AI change initiatives in private organizations, most of which were Canadian organizations in the service industries (such as public accounting, real estate, energy, and medical services). The analysis showed that only seven, or 35 percent, of the case studies indicated that a transformational change had occurred in the subject organization of the case study. One of the success stories was the NASA case.

The authors used a variety of measures in their independent analysis of the cases, including seven principles and practices taken from the theoretical literature on AI. Of these measures, the two AI features seemed to have the greatest influence on the change process: (1) a focus on changing how people think instead of what people do and (2) a focus on supporting a self-organizing change process that emerged from new ideas rather than implementing centrally determined changes.

The advantage of this meta-analysis in terms of the AI organizational development process is twofold. First, the study authors, Bushe and Kassam, evaluated a large number of recommended factors that theorists suggest are necessary for a transformational change to occur, and second, the number of cases across which the determining factors were evaluated was likely to be considered large enough for subsequent researchers to accept the results and use only those metrics that seem to have universal application.

Meta-Analysis in the Twenty-First Century

Arizona State University professor Gene Glass's small article in 1976 has become one of the most influential references for discussions on this increasingly popular research design. It is only fitting, then, that he was asked to write a summary of the method after twenty-five years of use. He described the growth in popularity of the process in a 2000 conference paper:

> In 25 years, meta-analysis has grown from an unheard of preoccupation of a very small group of statisticians working on problems of research integration in education and psychotherapy to a minor academic industry, as well as a commercial endeavor. (Glass 2000, 1)

Glass (2000) pointed out a number of weaknesses in the approach as he concluded that meta-analysis needs to be replaced with some more useful and accurate ways of summarizing research findings. According to Glass, the method is limited because of old but persistent use of abbreviated reporting styles and substitution of simple statements instead of fully describing complex relationships. He averred that social science researchers need to stop thinking of themselves as "scientists testing grand theories" and instead recognize that they are technicians collecting and collating information. Finally, continuing to refer to their research as "studies"—with the idea that a study concludes with a test of a hypothesis and that a theory underlies the hypothesis—has been the greatest barrier to progress.

To surmount these difficulties, researchers should stop thinking they are testing "grand theories" and begin recognizing that what they are really doing is collecting and sharing collected data. "We aren't publishing 'studies,'" said Glass, "rather, we are contributing to data archives."

Summary

A lesser-seen form of case study research is the meta-analysis or case survey model. It involves analyzing many cases, looking for commonalities and discrepancies in findings. In this design a group of previously researched cases is selected and subjected to comparative analysis. A meta-analysis is a type of survey research in which, instead of people being surveyed as subjects, previously prepared research reports are compared. Meta-analysis of many cases is usually carried out according to the principles of hermeneutic analysis.

Meta-analysis is facilitated using a meta-analytic schedule or cross-case table. Rows are cases; columns are the results of the analysis on the items or attributes of interest. Cell entries may be brief summaries of the findings or as simple as a checkmark. The schedule makes it easy to record and communicate analysis results.

The meta-analysis technique has grown dramatically since its adoption in 1976. However, Glass, its originator, suggested that despite its increasing popularity, it might be time to replace it with some approach that more closely reflects the nature of modern research in the social science.

➤ 8 ◀

Collecting and
Analyzing Case Data

All evidence is of some use to the case study researcher: nothing
is turned away. It will vary in relevance or trustworthiness or
completeness (but you won't know to begin with). You accumulate.
Because this can easily get untidy—and difficult to access—you need
to be organized in this respect, mainly by sorting out types of evidence.
—Bill Gillham (2000)

A core objective for case research is to develop an understanding of the roles and actions people display in their social groups (Whiting and Whiting 1973). Thus, public management case researchers focus on the actions and interactions of people in their economic, political, and administrative environments. This chapter looks at the most common ways researchers collect data about how people function in organizations, and how they react to and, in turn, influence organizational culture. To collect and analyze these data for their case analyses, many social scientists follow a data collection framework developed for ethnographic fieldwork. Ethnographic research methods are common in such social science research as sociology, anthropology, political science, and the administrative and organizational sciences. They include participation, interviewing, and analysis of cultural artifacts such as documents and physical possessions. Participation and interviewing are discussed in this chapter; document and artifact analysis are the topic of chapter 9.

Ethnographic Research Approaches

Most, if not all, of the data collection methods used in ethnographic research have been used at one time or another in single-case and multicase research projects. Ethnographic research is almost always case research. Therefore, case research employs the three primary methods in ethnographic research: conducting in-person or group interviews, observing behavior either as a participant in the group or as a nonparticipating, silent observer, and analyzing internal and external documents and other products (artifacts) of the subject group or groups. Usually, a case study research project will employ two or more of these methods—either for collecting additional data that can only be acquired in that way or as triangulation in an application of validity testing (Kawulich 2005).

Observation, interviewing, and document analysis may be best known for providing a rich description of the research subject or case. On the one hand, the use of detailed description means that ethnographic methods are an excellent design choice when the study objective is to provide deep background information for long-term, strategic public policy formation and implementation. On the other hand, ethnographic methods are generally not appropriate when a public management decision must be made immediately on the basis of the findings of the research.

Ethnographic Data Collection Methods

Case research is often the method of choice when researchers need to collect and present large amounts of explanatory data. Case research is generally considered to be of qualitative design, and one that is closely related to ethnographic research, historical studies, biographies, grounded theory, and phenomenological studies (Westgren and Zering 1998). Case research is mostly concerned with the study of contemporary phenomena rather than historical concerns (Yin 1994). The following section examines more closely ethnographic approaches as used in case research.

Data collection in these types of research designs follows in the tradition of thick description that grew out of ethnographic research. The process of developing thick description for a case study has been described as a two-part process: First, the researchers write down everything that they see in the subject of the case. This recording is done as a detailed description of events, settings, and behaviors, thereby capturing the sense of the social actors, groups, and institutions being described. Second, the researchers' own interpretations are recorded, and these interpretations are typically what shapes the final description in the case report. Together, the two-part process of observation and interpretation moves from one activity to the other, then back again, repeating the process over and over (Duveen 2000).

Types of Ethnographic Research

There are several different types of ethnographic case research methods, including ethnomethodology, community-based ethnography, and ethology. Each of these research approaches has its own advocates and detractors, but all are considered to fall under the larger category of field research in the family of case research designs.

Ethnomethodology has been defined as "the study of commonsense knowledge" (Neuman 2000, 348). It combines themes from sociology and philosophy, and is usually seen as an application of *phenomenology,* which is the study of human experiences (Adler and Adler 1998). Researchers who follow this approach focus their concern on how people in organizations and groups, as well as individually, go about living their everyday lives. Ethnomethodologists study these everyday behaviors in exceptionally close detail. They often use audio- and videotapes, films, and other methods to record the behavior of people they study. The data they collect are then analyzed in minute detail, using what Adler and Adler (99) described as "an intricate notational system that allows [them] to view the conversational overlaps, pauses, and intonations to within one-tenth of a second . . . they have directed a particular emphasis toward conversation analysis."

Community-based ethnography (CBR) is closely associated with the critical approach in action research (Stringer 1997), but CBR focuses on the study of groups rather than individuals. CBR is often the method of choice for conducting critical research case analyses such as empowerment studies.

Ethnology case research methods address many of the same issues as traditional ethnography, but focus on comparisons between cultures or groups. This approach is often used in organizational research using the case study approach. In this mode, the method focuses on identifying and describing the behavior of people in their social settings. *Ethology* case research focuses on the study of animal behavior as it occurs in the environment. The behaviors of humans as animals are often studied in this way. Importantly, all of these approaches use research methods developed by ethnographers.

Advantages and Disadvantages of Ethnographic Methods

The approaches followed during collection of data in ethnographic case study designs typically involve simple observation that can be either visible or hidden (unobtrusive). Organ and Bateman (1991), examining ethologic observation in the context of organizational behavior research, referred to this method as "naturalistic observation." They identified a number of desirable characteristics of this approach, as well as some of its shortcomings. Possibly the most important advantage is what Organ and Bateman call the "contextual richness" that is possible with observation. This includes more than the thick description that characterizes ethnographic field notes—it also refers to the fact that this type of research has enjoyed wide acceptance over the years, with results published in many articles, books, autobiographies, newspaper stories, conversations, and speeches.

Among the disadvantages of observation in case research is that it often results in a report bias that is traceable to the natural tendency of people to exercise selective perception and selective retention. *Selective perception* means that from all the myriad stimuli people encounter, everyone sees what they want to see, what they are interested in, and what they think is important. Whether they do so consciously or unconsciously, people ignore much of what else goes on. This idea has been suggested by a number of different investigators. John Dewey, for example, noted that human perception is never neutral. Rather, human knowledge and intelligence, what we think of as past experience, always influence perception. Furthermore, judgment is involved in all perception. Otherwise, the perception is nothing more than a form of sensory excitation (Phillips 1987; Hanson 1958).

Because observation is recorded as the field notes of one or more researchers, it will always contain what the researcher feels is important, or what action or actions the researcher thinks caused or influenced a reaction. Researchers will often omit from their field notes what they believe to be trivial or unimportant; this is what is meant by *selective retention*. We are all drawn to the dramatic or exciting in situations—it makes for interesting reading, even when it has little or no bearing on the central issue or issues. Both field notes and the material that is eventually included in a report must pass through a filter formed from the perceptions and memory of events held by the researchers.

Therefore, researchers must always struggle with this question: Would another observer have drawn the same conclusion from these events? Researchers use thick description in an attempt to provide an answer.

Case Research as Fieldwork

Fieldwork is the key activity in narrative or qualitative research designs. Thus, it is also a popular method for data collection in case research. The basic methods and techniques of collecting data and data analysis are the core elements of "doing ethnography" (Fetterman 1989; Bernard 1995). Deciding on what equipment to select and use—tape recorders, videotaping, and actual interviewing, among others—is a major decision in fieldwork. This process produces case information through the analysis of collected data during the entire process of ethnography—in field notes, memos, interim reports, published studies, articles, or books. It is a valuable tool for gathering information about behaviors embedded in, and specifically for the study of, organizational culture and subculture. In its public administration application during the early decades of the twentieth century, it was often used to identify administrative options for making decisions on matters of public policy.

Yeager (1989, 726) described participant observation as an "old and widely used research method both in public administration and in other fields of study." In public administration case research it incorporates many different techniques, including simple, group, and unobtrusive observations; in-depth interviewing of key informants; ethnography; and controlled observation techniques.

> Participant observation includes material that the observer gains directly from personally seeing or hearing an event occur. Often the participant observer establishes personal relationships with subjects and maintains those relationships over a period of time. . . . Rapport and trust are established with subjects to a far greater extent than in other methods. Typically, more exhaustive data are gathered on fewer subjects using participant observation that with other methods. (Yeager 1989, 726)

The most important part of fieldwork is not the length of time spent with a group, but rather, simply being there to observe, ask questions, and write down what is heard and seen (Fetterman 1989). Participant observation, like ethnography, has changed from its original concept of total immersion in a society under study to include new and different topics and locations of study, in addition to a wide variety of data-gathering tools and techniques.

Ethnographic field research requires the most intense connection between the researcher and the subjects of the study (Kornblum 1996; Flick 1999); it is not unusual to see ethnographers who have lived and worked within a group for many years to begin to take on a self-identity that places a greater loyalty and connection to the study group than that of the researcher's prior connection to his or her own society.

An example of participant observation case research is the report of a study to document the impact of a clinical information system on an AIDS treatment organization in Uganda (Pina 2006). The researcher participated with the staff management in the clinic's seven departments as they implemented the new system and delivered clinical services. The case highlighted complications in implementation of the system that resulted in poor record quality and low system utility. Insufficient staffing within the clinic's data-entry department resulted in producing either duplicate records or multiple entries on individual patient records; patient records were not updated between visits; and backups in patient service were common. The case revealed that implementing the system without sufficient training or staffing voided the expected benefits of the new system.

Collecting Case Data by Observation

Observation methods have a long and important history in social and human science research (Neuman 2000). Among many different situations, observation case research is carried out in studies of individuals, small and large groups, and government and nonprofit organizations; in the inner cities of modern societies; suburban and rural government jurisdictions; cross-cultural comparative cases; and investigations into the interactions of people in societies, cultures, and subcultures, as well as of the interface between people and their government organizations.

Collecting data by observing takes place through a process of watching and recording the actions of individuals or groups during the exercise of their daily activities. This way of collecting data is one of several data collection methods developed by early anthropologists—researchers who originally studied the behaviors of individuals and groups in distant or isolated societies. Those early observers of cultural phenomena often lived with the group they were studying and participated in the group's daily rites and social behaviors (Becker et al. 2004; Manicom and Campbell 2005).

These early anthropologists recorded everything they saw in detailed, written notes—their field notes—or on film and other recording devices. They then returned to their own societies to study and interpret what they had seen. They sought to identify patterns of behavior, cultural norms, and beliefs that took place in the groups they studied. Because of the voluminous notes they kept, the phrase *thick description* came to be used to describe the written records of their observations. Thick description is used today to refer to rich, detailed stories and descriptions of individuals, groups, or societies studied by ethnographic methods. Eventually, sociologists, educators, psychologists, political scientists, and other behavioral and administrative researchers adopted the techniques of data gathering by observation that were developed by the early ethnographers.

Case researchers are no longer satisfied with simply describing social phenomena. Rather, they seek to interpret social behavior. The observation method alone is not always capable of achieving this goal.

Forms of Observation Research

Modern observation techniques can take either of two chief forms: observing alone or observing and participating. Because the data-gathering, note-taking, and recording and analyzing processes are the same in both forms, only participant observation is discussed here. Participant observation always occurs in the participants' own environment, in a setting believed to have relevance to the study question. By simply observing, the researcher remains an outsider. People do not always share their thoughts with outsiders. By participating alongside the people being observed, the researcher is more readily accepted and taken into the subjects' confidence. A list of steps to guide observation researches is presented in Box 8.1.

Advantages and Disadvantages of Observation

Several advantages and disadvantages of observation are described in the following two sections.

Disadvantages of Observation

Observation methods provide researchers with a number of advantages (Kawulich 2005). First, they make it possible to observe and record nonverbal expressions of feelings, discover with whom individuals in an organization interact, see how members of the group communicate with one another, and see how much time people spend on various activities.

Also, researchers are able to observe actions or events that people may not be willing or able to share with an interviewer; by participating alongside the individuals included in the study, information that might otherwise be missed may come to light. Case research by observation makes it possible for researchers to unearth

Box 8.1

Observation Research in Family Health

In their qualitative research methods guidebook for family health researchers, Manicom and Campbell (2005) included a two-part list of steps. The first section has steps to follow when preparing to engage in participant observation; the second part has steps to follow after the observation. The steps are listed in the following two sections.

Preparing for Observation

1. Establish the goal for the observation activity in terms of the research project.
2. Determine what subjects, organization, and type of site will be needed to do the case research.
3. Get permission to do the study and to participate in the group's activities.
4. Investigate possible sites for the study; select the best alternative.
5. Establish a timeline for completing all tasks.
6. Assign tasks to other members of the research team, if any; include completion schedules.
7. Establish what your role (i.e., stance) should be during the participation in order to result in relationships that produce the most information. That is, should you participate or just observe without participating?
8. Plan how and when to take notes (during or after participating?).
9. Keep a field notebook and writing materials ready for use at all times.

After the Participation

10. Schedule time after participation to transfer and expand on your notes.
11. Type the notes into computer files; make at least one additional copy of the notes and follow-up interpretation. Adopt the attitude that if something can be lost, it will.

Source: Manicom and Campbell (2005).

valuable insights into the context of a social situation, as well as the relationships and behaviors exhibited by the people in the setting.

Disadvantages of Observation

Observation methods also have a number of disadvantages. They typically produce great quantities of information, take long periods of time to complete, and may not unearth the root cause of a problem or situation. Not all of the large amounts of data collected will be equally important or even relevant.

The length of time often needed to collect the data is the chief disadvantage of the observation method. Observation studies can continue over many months or even years; public administrators are usually neither able nor willing to devote that length of time to a case research project. For example, an observation study may take six months to a year or more just to collect the raw data. It then takes at least as long or longer to analyze, synthesize, and interpret the collected information. As a result, an observation study can take several years to complete.

When observation techniques are used, however, they can produce powerful narratives that provide deep insight into the functioning of a group or administrative unit. Because of the long time they may require, observation methods alone are not commonly used in public management case research; rather, observation is generally used with one or more other data-gathering techniques.

The practice of producing voluminous notes as thick description—a hallmark of all participation research—is another potential drawback of the technique. As noted, thick description refers to the great depth, detail, and complexity that characterize most ethnographic reports. An example cited by Neuman (2000) is the description of a social event that might last three minutes or less, but which takes up many pages of descriptive narrative.

Another disadvantage of observation is associated with the recording of everything that is said or done during the long study period. This makes interpretation of the data highly problematic. Another disadvantage is that what is recorded in researchers' field notebooks cannot help but be subjective rather than the objectivity science desires. A researcher's notes include what the researcher chooses to see and to write down.

One way to carry out an observation research project is to use the series of steps in ethnographic fieldwork shown in Figure 8.1. This process begins with defining the research problem and culminates with preparation of a written case study (Jones 1996; Kawulich 2005). Much of the first four steps in the process are involved in preobservation planning. Research has shown that careful planning before embarking on a research journey eliminates or greatly reduces many of the potential problems that can and will come up once the research is under way. Only in steps five and six does the actual data gathering take place. The next four steps are involved with taking, translating, and interpreting field notes—the actual data upon which the researcher will draw conclusions. The next step is to formulate a theory from the data analysis. The final step is to prepare and present a report of the research findings. There are many formats and targets for the final report, among which are a report to senior administrators, a report made available to voters, or an article published in a professional journal.

Collecting Data by Interviews

Interviews are conversations between a researcher and a person or persons with the purpose of collecting information about a subject or subjects of interest. In these conversations, one person—the interviewer—takes the lead in the discussion by

Figure 8.1 **Ethnographic Fieldwork, Analysis and Presentation Process**

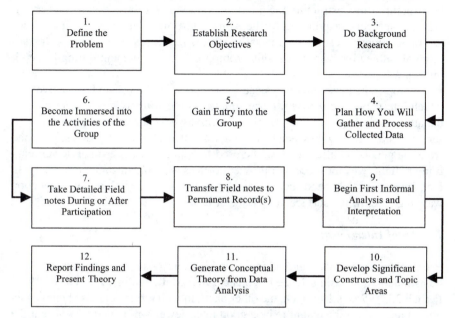

Source: Russell A. Jones (1996).

asking questions and probing for more or deeper responses. The person (or persons) being interviewed—called the respondent or, less commonly, the interviewee—is asked to answer questions in as much detail as is appropriate; the respondent is also often asked to elaborate on the answers. Beyond these questions and answers, the respondent is also often asked to simply talk about a subject with little or no guidance by the interviewer.

There are two major forms of interviews: single-subject and multisubject. If they occur between a single interviewer and one subject, they are personal or single-subject interviews. These one-on-one, in-depth interviews are often used in journalism, psychology, and education, as well as in researching individuals or organizations for the preparation of case studies. Although these interviews usually take place in a face-to-face situation, they may also occur by telephone (voice-to-voice). Single interviews by Internet or e-mail occur far less often.

When several subjects are interviewed at the same time, the sessions are known as group or multisubject interviews. The focus group is a popular type of multisubject interview that involves from ten to twelve participants in the interview session. For many reasons, the focus group has become one of the most commonly used interview forms in such subjects as anthropology, sociology, public management, and business administration; the focus group has become a major data-gathering approach used in marketing and communications research.

In all applications, both the single- and multisubject forms of interviews may be structured or unstructured. Structured interviews follow a prepared script, with all subjects responding to the same questions. Unstructured interviews use open-ended questions and usually call for the interviewer to probe for additional, subjective responses. This probing is a major element during in-depth interviews.

The topics of these interviews can be as varied as the research objectives for which interviews are planned. For example, they can be used to collect data on the attitudes and opinions of organization employees, purchasers or recipients of services, individuals with special knowledge about a place or thing, or just someone from the general public. They can be used to help a researcher-interviewer team bring to light relevant success or problem factors in an organization or activity. In fact, anytime a study needs deep understanding of an issue, interviews are a good way to get below the surface of an issue or problem.

The Art of Interviewing

People who use this data-gathering method in their jobs consider interviewing to be as much an art as a science (Goodale 1982; McLaughlin 1992; Pascal 1983; Perlich 2007; Weiss 1994). On the other hand, most interviewers also believe that almost anyone can be taught to be a good interviewer—provided they accept the premise that the key to becoming good at interviewing is learning how to listen to what people are saying. This includes not making value judgments or using biased prompts.

In *The Art of the Interview,* professional media interviewer Martin Perlich (2007) distilled what people need to know about the art of interviewing down to just two activities: prepare and listen. Perlich, of course, went into the subject in much greater detail than this; if he hadn't, there would be no need for his book. He said that interviewing requires such skills as attentive listening, nonthreatening probing for often unspoken attitudes and beliefs, and an ability to accept things as they are without being judgmental.

Good interviewers do not interpose their beliefs or biases into the interview session; they become what might be called "empathetic sponges." They ask intelligent questions, and then they listen in such a way that people want to tell them what they know. With practice, good interviewers are often able to get valid data from subjects with minimal cooperation; they read as much from what is not said as what is said. This is what is knows as being "sensitive to nonverbal cues" (Pascal 1983, 7).

Purposes for Interviewing

No interview should ever occur without the interviewer first establishing the objectives for the action. Although every interview has a purpose and a specific information target in sight, achieving the desired results during the actual interviewing activity is often lost in the flood of information offered. To keep focused on the topic and goal, interviewers must understand the purpose and process of interviewing.

For example, in their qualitative research methods manual for practitioners working in drug use interventions, the Boston University Social Scientists Working Group (SSWG) described the purpose of in-depth interviewing:

> An in-depth interview is a qualitative technique that allows person-to-person discussion. It can lead to increased insight into people's thoughts, feelings, and behavior on important issues. This type of interview is often unstructured and therefore permits the interviewer to encourage an informant (respondent) to talk at length about the topic of interest. . . . The in-depth interview uses a flexible interview approach. It aims to ask questions to explain reasons underlying a problem or process [activity] in a target group. You use the technique to gather ideas, to gather information, and to develop [concepts for later application]. (SSWG 2000, 3)

Becoming a good interviewer takes time and practice. Throughout the skill-building process, interviewers are urged to refer to the five stages of interviewing identified by human resources interviewer James Goodale (1982) in *The Fine Art of Interviewing* and paraphrased here in Table 8.1. Goodale emphasized the importance of the opening sequence to the success of an interview.

Advantages and Disadvantages of Interviews

Interviewing requires the interviewer to be more than just a good listener; the interviewer must also know how to creatively pick out key points from the mass of collected data that in-depth interviews produce. Keeping interview subjects focused on the topic you're interested in goes a long way toward making interpretation easier. Despite researchers' best intentions, however, what gets recorded is subject to the forces of selective perception and selective retention. People will remember having seen a phenomenon in terms of what point or points attracted their interest—not necessarily what really happened. And they will remember what they think was important.

This means that the data that are collected in an interview are subjective, no matter how hard the interviewer works to keep it purely objective. There is much evidence that suggests that if two people interview the same subject at different times, the story each receives as the outcome of the interview will be different (Goodale 1982). One reason for this is called the *learning effect*; the second interview will cause the respondents to think of things that they think they should have brought up during the first interview, or it will cause them to weigh "the facts" internally and decide that what they initially thought was important was not important after all, or was less important than something else.

Table 8.1

Stages and Question Examples in Interviewing

Sequence	Stage	Discussion	Example Questioning
1.	Initiate	Explain the purpose of the interview and begin with questions to get the interviewee talking.	Use open-ended questions.
2.	Listen	Actively listen and record key topics for later expansion.	Listen for key terms and phrases that reflect the objectives of the research.
3.	Focus	Direct the subject's attention to the key topics raised earlier and generate discussion on topics that meet the study objectives.	Use open-ended phrases like "you mentioned . . . " and "I'd like to hear more about . . . "
4.	Probe	Probe for additional information on topics raised by the interview subject and introduce additional topics that had been planned to be covered in the interview.	Use such nondirective techniques as pauses, head nodding, and simply waiting for the subject to continue; ask such questions as "How did . . . ," "Why . . . "
5.	Use	Use the information gathered during the interview to generate a theory and develop possible explanatory conclusions.	End the interview with positive reinforcement for the subject's contribution.

Source: Goodale (1982).

Getting Beneath the Surface in Interviewing

The greatest advantage of an interview is its ability to let the researcher get beneath the surface of a stated opinion, attitude, or action and, in the process, come closer to determining a cause or causes of the phenomenon. Open-ended questions are particularly useful in this way. However, the interviewer must take care to keep the respondent focused on the study question. Asking questions and getting answers is not as easy a task as it might seem (Fontana and Frey 1998).

Interviewing has some important limitations, however. Interviews are incredibly time-consuming; a single interview can take two hours or longer. This generally results in cutting down the size of a sample. In addition, interviewers need to be trained. Even after training, a large element of subjectivity remains. Everyone looks different, acts and talks differently, and responds differently to subjects' answers.

One way that researchers try to get around the time and skills limitations of in-depth interviewing is with the use of group or focus group interviewing. Focus groups consist of six to a dozen individuals with similar interests or characteristics who are interviewed together in the same room. The researcher functions as a moderator, ensuring that any one or a few participants do not monopolize the conversation or intimidate other subjects. Rather, each participant is called upon to contribute and others to comment on the contribution. In this way, group interaction often appears, thus providing for a richer, more meaningful discussion of the topic or topics.

Taking Notes or Recording the Interview

One important decision that an interviewer must make is whether to take notes during the interview or tape-record the interview. Taking notes can be time-consuming and may slow down the flow of the interview. Also, it often leads to accidentally missing one or more important points made by the respondent. While using a tape recorder makes it possible to collect and retain a complete and accurate record of the session, the respondent must be asked for permission beforehand. In a few situations, the device may be intimidating or the respondent may simply not want a recording to be made. Therefore, always get the respondent's permission to use a tape recorder (Blau, Elbow, and Killgallon 1992).

The Interviewing Process

When planning to conduct an interview for any research project, it is usually best to follow some systematic procedure that ensures that you achieve your data-gathering objectives. One such system is the simple six-phase procedure, with several simple steps in each phase, as shown in Figure 8.2. The phases of interviewing help to establish a foundation or background for understanding the underlying structure of the interviewing process.

While it is not always necessary and depends largely on the purpose for the interview, it is generally a good practice to give the interview respondent or respondents an opportunity to review your written report before publishing it. Often, their review results in gaining additional or crucial data that might have been missed or glossed over in the earlier draft.

Summary

This chapter reviewed ethnographic research methods for collecting data in single-case and multicase research. The two most commonly used methods are participant observation and in-depth interviews. Ethnographic research methods were developed over many years by anthropologists and sociologists to identify and describe patterns of human behavior in group situations. This makes these methods ideally suited for use in case research in public management. The chapter reviewed the steps researchers follow in ethnographic data collection.

103

Figure 8.2 **A Six-Phase Interviewing Process**

Phase 1: Plan the Interview
1. Choose a person to interview.
2. Make an appointment.
3. Prepare for the interview.
4. Have a focus in mind.
5. Make up a list of questions.

Phase 2: Conduct the Interview
1. Set the tone for the interview; arrive on time prepared to work; begin with a friendly, open-ended question.
2. Relax and listen; try active listening.
3. Probe when appropriate.
4. Thank the respondent when finished.

Phase 3: Transcribe and Organize Notes
1. Transcribe the tape or notes.
2. Organize the material.
3. Select a format (narrative or series of questions and answers).

Phase 4: Write First Draft
1. Write an enticing introduction.
2. Select the major points and write topic sentences for each.
3. Fill out the rest of the story.
4. Write a conclusion with a logical conclusion.

Phase 5: Review the Draft and Rewrite
1. Be sure that like things are together.
2. Check for flow and sentence construction.
3. Make a final check of spelling and syntax.

Phase 6: Publish and/or Present the Story
1. For legal reasons, make sure you have your respondent's permission to publish the story.
2. Send a copy of the published story (if published) to the respondent with your thanks.

Two types of observation are used in public administration case research: participant observation and silent or nonobtrusive participation. In participant observation, the researcher essentially joins the team or organization under study. Notes are then taken away from the research situation. In nonparticipant observation, the researcher takers notes or films the situation while watching actions and behaviors without participating in the situation or organization.

Personal interviews are possibly used more often in public management research than either of the participation approaches. Developing the ability to conduct meaningful and informative interviews is as much an art as it is a science. It takes a great deal of practice and a sympathetic and open attitude to do it well.

➤ 9 ◄

Document Analysis Methods

Researchers supplement participant observation, interviewing, and observation with gathering and analyzing documents produced in the course of everyday events or constructed specifically for the research at hand. As such, the review of documents is an unobtrusive method, rich in portraying the values and beliefs of participants in the setting. Minutes of meetings, logs, announcements, formal policy statements, letters, and so on, are all useful in developing an understanding of the setting or group studied. Similarly, research journals and samples of free writing about the topic can be quite informative.
—Catherine Marshall and Gretchen B. Rossman (1999)

This chapter examines the use of the written record as a data source in the case research method. This record includes documents, reports, statistics, manuscripts and other written and visual materials, as well as a variety of elements that can be measured using unobtrusive methods (Webb et al. 2000). Hodder (1998) referred to this group of resources as a society's *material culture,* and included physical artifacts as well as the written word and graphic symbols. This chapter is concerned with the written word and, particularly, document analysis—the third major way that case researchers gather data. It will also include a review of document analysis methods. The chapter begins with a description of textual material as a source of case research data.

Textual material can be grouped into four broad categories. The first consists of *published texts.* These include sources such as books, periodicals, narratives, reports, pamphlets, and other published materials. This group of sources also includes reports published in the mass media. To differentiate this approach to data collection from field-work, research using these sources is often referred to as *desk* or *library research.*

The second category of textual material consists of *formal* and *informal documents*; it includes personal messages and assorted types of archival information, such as personal notes and memos, government records and vital statistics, and other informal written materials, including e-mail.

The third category of sources is made up of the wide variety of *nonwritten*

Table 9.1

Sources, Examples, and Analysis Methods in the Study of Texts

Source	Examples	Typical Analysis Methods
Published texts	Professional literature	Hermeneutic analysis
	Mass media	Content analysis
	Narratives	Narrative analysis
	Books and stories	Meta-analysis
		Literature review
Informal documents and other written records	Archival information	Hermeneutic analysis
	Government reports	Content analysis
	Vital statistics	Archival analysis
	Records, documents, notes and memos	Semiotics E-mail
Nonwritten communications and material culture	Photos and drawings	Semiotics
	Films and videos	Discourse analysis
	Tools and artifacts	Hermeneutic Analysis
	Graphs and tables	Site surveys
Nonverbal signs, symbols and other communications	Body language	Semiotics
	Gestures	Proxemics
	Music and dance	Kinesics
	Nonverbal sounds	
	Signs	
	Noise	

communications. This group includes such graphic displays as graphs, tables, and charts; photographs and illustrations; tools and other artifacts; and recorded films and audio- and videotapes.

The final category includes all *nonverbal signs and symbols.* Among these are the silent messages in body language, facial expressions, gestures, nonverbal symbols and signs, music and dance, animal sounds and behavior, and even noise. Symbols used as directions or for identification—as in road signs and logotypes—are also included in this category.

Case researchers employ a variety of analysis tools and methods in their study of texts, symbols, and artifacts. Among these are hermeneutics, content analysis, meta-analysis, semiotic analysis, proxemics, kinesics, discourse analysis, site surveys, and more. Table 9.1 displays the relationship between various sources of data and methods used in their analysis. The analysis approaches seen most often in public management research are the analysis of texts in a formal literature review, archival analysis, and meta-analysis of existing cases.

Categories of Written Record Data Analysis

From the case researcher's point of view, textual or documentary research can be grouped into a number of categories. One classification scheme gathers research of the written record into three groups: traditional literature review, study of archival records, and analysis of analyses—the meta-analytic research design.

The traditional *literature review* is a fundamental element in all scientific research. A major purpose of the literature review is to provide background information that can then be used to design a complete research project. In addition, case researchers use the literature review to discover what other researchers have said about the topic or organization they are studying.

The second strategy, *archival studies,* refers to the study of recorded public and private formal documents, records, and other material of a historical nature. These records are often not in general circulation, although they may be stored in a library. When noncirculating records are needed, special permission is often required to access them for the research project.

The third approach is the *meta-analysis* research design, in which researchers use other case studies as subjects for analysis. Meta-analysis is a quantitative technique for summarizing other investigators' research on a topic. As such, it considers existing literature a source of data in its own right. This method was discussed in chapter 7.

The Episodic or the Running Record

The second way of classifying the written record is by the framework within which the record falls. It includes both an episodic record and a running record (Johnson, Joslyn, and Reynolds 2001). Episodic records are not elements in an official record-keeping program of an organization but rather are preserved in a more casual manner, often by individuals rather than organizations. Examples include personal diaries, e-mail and other correspondence, manuscripts, brochures, stories and memoirs, biographies and autobiographies, and temporary records of associated organizations and individuals. The papers of past presidents and other elected officials fall into this category.

The running record, on the other hand, consists largely of the official records of organizations. They are collected and maintained in official archives and are often retained for many years. The statistical and other records of federal, state, and local governments are examples. Some of the running record databases of interest to public managers and political scientists include election returns, voting records of legislative bodies, court decisions, official government policy records, demographic and other statistical indexes, speeches and official position papers, mass media stories, biographical data, and others.

A 2002 study of congressional voting is a good example of a case study using the running record—in this case, the voting records of the U.S. House of Representatives (Bovitz 2002). The study question was to identify under what conditions members of Congress might vote in opposition to their colleagues on perceived pork barrel legislation and whether there are any positive benefits resulting from the record of such negative votes. The phenomenon in question was voting behavior on proposed termination of pork barrel legislation by members of the House of Representatives. Votes were compared across seven units in the case:

1. Clinch River Breeder Reactor (Tennessee), July 1981 (whether to fund a proposed atomic research project)
2. Bonneville Unit of the Central Utah Project, July 1986 (terminate $83.7 million water supply system construction)
3. Appalachian Regional Commission, June 1987 (terminate regional economic development by construction on a variety of public works)
4. Magnetohydrodynamics Program, University of Oklahoma, June 1987 (terminate $9 million scientific research project)
5. Superconducting Super Collider, Waxahachie, Texas, May 1991 (terminate $8 billion atomic particle accelerator)
6. National Endowment for the Arts (proposed elimination of NEA funding)
7. National Biological survey, June 1994 (terminate the program and $167.2 million allocated in fiscal 1995 to track population levels of selected species on the verge of being threatened or endangered)

Bovitz (2002) found that in some instances, legislators were rewarded for voting against pork barrel programs that were proposed for their own districts, despite knowledge of receiving rewards for favorable votes (rewards were defined as reelection at the next election or endorsements that translated into votes). To the researchers' surprise, the representatives were not penalized politically for voting against their party-supported projects in other members' districts.

The Literature Review in Case Research

A crucial early step in the design and conduct of all case research is an investigation of the literature on the study topic, the research question, and the methodology followed by others who have studied the same or similar problems. Sometimes called a *review of the relevant literature* or simply a *literature review,* the process has been defined as "a systematic, explicit, and reproducible method for identifying, evaluating, and interpreting the existing body of recorded work produced by researchers, scholars, and practitioners" (Fink 1998, 3).

A literature review can help case research in three ways: First, it shows the readers of the final research findings your awareness of the work already done on the topic. Second, it clearly identifies what other researchers believe are the key issues, crucial questions, and obvious gaps in the field. Third, it establishes a set of guiding signs that help you evaluate theories and principles others used to shape their research design and analysis as you prepare your own (Denscombe 1998). In sum, a well-conducted literature review can do all of the following:

- Help to set specific limits for subsequent research.
- Introduce new and different ways of looking at the problem.
- Help avoid errors and omissions in planning the study.
- Suggest new ideas.
- Acquaint you with new sources of data and, often, totally different ways of looking at an issue.

Avoiding Pitfalls in Literature Analysis

Despite the critical importance of the literature review, some case researchers skip this step in the mistaken belief that theirs is a "unique" study problem, or that by studying their case, they are examining all the relevant documentation. Or, if they do look into the literature of the study topic, field, or discipline, they treat the review as just a summary of the articles and books that they read to prepare themselves to do their research—something like the book reports they had to write in school. Or, they include the review only as a list of the authors with whom they agree (or disagree). A little preinterview planning can help researchers avoid these pitfalls.

Among the most meaningful strategic purposes to which the literature review can be put are those listed by Piantanida and Garman (1999). The important thing to remember about this list is that none of the purposes are mutually exclusive; a good literature review can achieve many goals at the same time.

1. The review can *trace* the historical evolution of the study problem or key issues, themes, or constructs pertaining to the problem.
2. The review can provide a schematic of the different schools of thought that have developed or are developing with regard to the study problem.
3. The review can look at the study problem from several different disciplines, such as looking at welfare reform from the point of view of social work and from an economic viewpoint.
4. The review can examine the positions of different stakeholder groups, such as public administrators, citizen groups, nonprofit organizations, and so forth.
5. The review can trace different conceptual schools of thought that have emerged over time and may currently be taking opposing or conflicting views in the literature.

Lang and Heiss (1994) summarized a similar list of points into two fundamental purposes. First, that the review can help the researcher hone his or her attack on a specific study problem. Second, it can provide a point of reference to use when discussing and interpreting the findings of the research.

CHAPTER 9

The Literature Review Analysis Process

A good document analysis typically follows a series of steps. One suggested set is displayed in Figure 9.1. This model begins with an encouragement to researchers to study all their options before embarking on their journey through the literature. This means that all potential sources should be considered. Limiting a literature search to a quick perusal of the Internet or a run through a single database is not the way to conduct a thorough review of the literature.

The second step in the literature review process is made up of several equally important activities: First, establish some basis for selecting the cases to study. This process is called establishing content criteria. Second, decide on some method to follow in selecting the cases, such as should they all be quantitative or qualitative studies? Should they all be single-case or multicase studies? If they are to be multicase studies, should they all be of a certain minimum or maximum number of cases? Were the case members or site randomly selected or predetermined? The decision will be based on the study question and may change somewhat when collecting the relevant literature is under way.

Once the literature is collected, the analysis process can begin. As the material is studied, relevant categories of information will begin to stand out. These categories can then be classified and coded to provide some structure for further analysis. Repeated key themes in the literature should be considered for organizing the final review; these themes can serve as discussion points during the writing of the final research report. You can begin summarizing the material by writing interpretive notes in the form of comments on the material in the literature. These memos can then be carried into the final report with little or no revision.

During the early stages of the analysis of the material, researchers must be sure to record all the important bibliographic information pertaining to the source documents. This includes information about the author(s), the discipline in which they did their research, all information about the source, and any connections to other sources that have been or might be also investigated.

Relevant categories of information should begin to become apparent as the review stage continues. Categories must be coded, with the pertinent information copied onto cards or in computer files, worksheets, or portable memory devices. Repeated key themes found in the literature often serve as discussion points during the writing of the final case research report. During the process of coding and organizing, researchers may summarize the material, add comments, and begin the final report.

Researchers record all the important bibliographic information on the source documents during the next-to-last stage in the process. This includes information about the author(s), information about the source case studied, and any connections to other sources that have been or might be investigated later.

Fink (1998) encouraged researchers to first study all their options—internal and external sources; published and unpublished material, and the like—before

112

Figure 9.1   **Steps in a Literature Review Process**

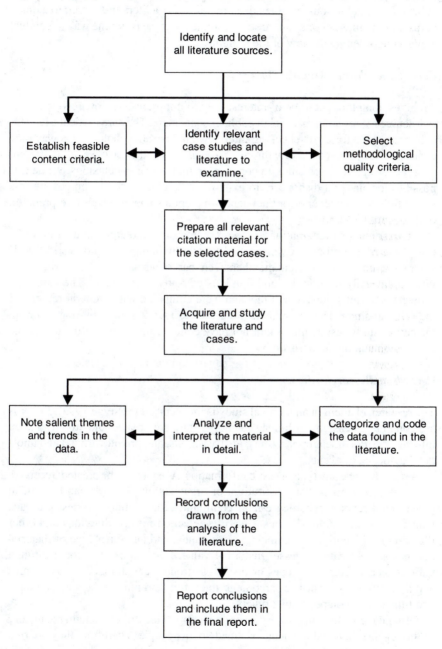

embarking on their examination of the literature. Only then should they begin to collect all available sources. She added that limiting a literature search to a quick perusal of the Internet or a run through a single database is *not* the way to conduct a thorough, scientific review of the literature.

Case Research with Archival Data

Archives, long thought to be of interest only to librarians, are now recognized as rich sources of research material in public management. They are particularly valuable as a source for cross-checking interview and narrative data. In this way they contribute to improved validity through *triangulation*—the use of several different approaches in a research study to corroborate findings or conclusions. While it is possible for bias and dishonesty to exist in archival data, these sources are less susceptible to researcher error than depending upon someone else's interpretation of the primary sources.

An example of triangulation in case research in which archival data played a role is the Monopoli and Alworth (2000) study involving Navaho World War II veterans. Four surviving tribal members were part of a panel who had participated in a 1950s study of attitudes and opinions of Native Americans. The surviving subjects were interviewed, and the data were compared with archival records of the original study. The researchers were able to identify some biasing errors in the earlier study results that might not have come to light without the use of the archival data in the modern study.

Records as Research Elements

The research element in an archival study is the record (Dearstyne 1993). Records are concrete extensions of human memory. They are created and stored to keep information, document transactions, justify actions, and provide official and unofficial evidence of events.

A record can be any type of saved information. A record can be created, received, or maintained by a person, institution, or organization. Records can be official government reports, recorded e-mail communications, letters, diaries, journals, ledgers, meeting minutes, deeds, case files, election results, drawings and other illustrations, blueprints, agreements, memoranda, and any other type of material that has some greater or lesser historical value. Records can be stored through various means: computer tapes or disks, electronic data storage, words, figures and illustrations on paper or parchment, microfilm and microfiche, cassette tape, and film and videotape, among others.

Official records maintained by an organization or institution contain the history of the organization and the decisions made by its people. Therefore, they are rich information sources for public management case researchers.

The National Historical Publications and Records Commission recently estimated that there are more than 4,500 historical record repositories in the United States alone. In addition, almost every state has its own historical society; personnel at these agencies can often direct the researcher to sources not kept in official government archives. A few examples include voter registration lists, the *Congressional Record,* actuarial records (i.e., vital statistics), records of quasi-governmental agencies (e.g., weather reports), the mass media, professional and academic journals, company and organization records, personal histories, and published and unpublished documents.

Content Analysis in Case Research

Content analysis is the name of a method for statistically interpreting nonnumerical, written records. Content analysis is, therefore, the quantitative component of document analysis (McNabb 2008). It is used to describe attributes contained in documents and other forms of records, but it is not intended to determine the intentions of the sender. The process involves breaking down the written material into researcher-selected categories or units. The researcher then prepares an *item dictionary* in order to clearly define identified constructs. Measurements of the occurrence of these items in the text make statistical analysis of the data possible.

Holsti (1969, 14) defined the content analysis process as "any technique for making inferences by objectively and systematically identifying specified characteristics of messages." The point he was making is that content analysis does not illuminate "truth." It can only measure usage. Holsti did not limit analysis of data gathered by the process only to quantitative analysis, instead stating that he believed that a "rigid qualitative-quantitative distinction seems unwarranted." He concluded that researchers using content analysis should use both qualitative and quantitative methods to supplement each other. In this way, Holsti combined aspects of hermeneutics with the traditional quantitative interpretation of content analysis.

Bernard (1995) referred to content analysis as a "catch-all term" that is used to describe a variety of techniques for making inferences from textual material. Bernard saw the purpose of these techniques as a way to reduce the information in a text to a series of quantitative variables that can then be studied for correlations.

Advantages and Disadvantages of Content Analysis

Content analysis can be used for analyzing the content of written documents; transcripts of films, videos, and speeches; and other types of written communication. The main advantage of content analysis is that it provides the researcher with a structured method for quantifying the contents of a qualitative or interpretive text in a simple, clear, and easily repeatable format.

The main disadvantage of content analysis is that it contains a built-in bias of isolating bits of information from their context. Thus, the contextual meaning is often lost or, at the least, made problematic. Furthermore, content analysis has great difficulty in dealing with implied meanings in a text. In these situations, interpretive analysis may be more appropriate, with content analysis used to supplement the primary analysis method. A major difficulty with the process is the subjectivity of the researcher in identifying the original codes and categories that are to be counted. It is nearly impossible to avoid interjecting some researcher bias into this step of the analysis.

When to Use Content Analysis

Content analysis is best used when dealing with communications in which the messages tend to be clear, straightforward, obvious, and simple. The more that a text relies on subtle or intricate meanings, the less likely the content analysis can reveal the full meaning of the communication. Thus, content analysis is used most often to describe attributes of messages without reference to the intentions of the message sender or effect of the message on the receiver (Denscombe 1998; Holsti 1969). Counting how many times in a speech a candidate denigrates the character of a political opponent is an example application of content analysis.

The major purpose of all content analysis is to be able to make inferences about one or more variables uncovered in a text. It accomplishes this by systematically and objectively analyzing the content of the text, the process of communication itself, or both (Sproull 1988). Content analysis takes place in the nine-step process displayed in Figure 9.2.

The content analysis process begins with establishing objectives for the content analysis research. The first step in the process should be a familiar one by now: Establish objectives for the research process. This means determining in advance of the research what you want to accomplish by its conduct. Next, assuming that the researcher has some familiarity with the larger issues or themes at stake in the phenomenon, a list should be made of what variables are to be counted in the text. Variables are not the same as words; rather, they tend to be constructs that describe or refer to broader complex issues of behavior or attitude. This list is clearly embedded in the study objectives.

Once the researcher has decided what to look for and where to look for it, the next step is to establish a system for coding the content items while also determining how the items are going to be counted and recorded. The texts themselves are then collected. Holsti (1969) recommended that at this time researchers should draw a random sample of the materials for a pilot test of the study. The pilot test will provide important clues about the relative effectiveness of the research design. For example, since the variables of interest are established before measurement takes place, there is a possibility that the variables are not treated significantly in the sample of sources chosen. In that case, the researcher would have to go back and identify new variables for the study.

The final steps in the study involves conducting statistical analysis on the mea-

Figure 9.2 **Steps in Content Analysis Research Design**

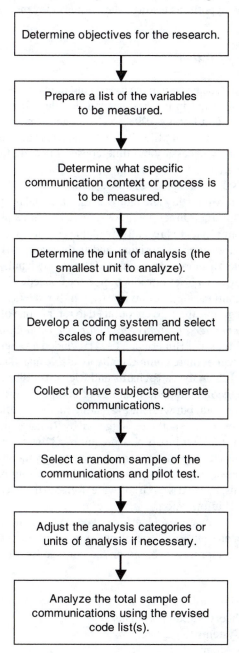

Determine objectives for the research.

Prepare a list of the variables
to be measured.

Determine what specific
communication context or process is
to be measured.

Determine the unit of analysis (the
smallest unit to analyze).

Develop a coding system and select
scales of measurement.

Collect or have subjects generate
communications.

Select a random sample of the
communications and pilot test.

Adjust the analysis categories or
units of analysis if necessary.

Analyze the total sample of
communications using the revised
code list(s).

Source: Adapted from Holsti (1969), Sproull (1988), Denscombe (1998).

surements. When possible, these should include descriptive statistics, correlation analysis, and simple hypothesis testing. The findings may then presented in tables or graphs.

Computer Analysis of Textual Data

There has been a dramatic growth in the use of computers in research and the availability of analysis software in the past several decades (Tak, Nield, and Becker 1999; Este, Sieppert, and Barsky 1998; Richards and Richards 1998; Miles and Huberman 1994; Weitzman and Miles 1995). In some research settings, technology has simplified the many necessary but time-consuming and often-boring tasks of the data analysis process.

Although today's computer programs are capable of processing large volumes of text material and records, sorting and indexing the data, and retrieving information from a variety of different directions, few researchers have used the qualitative data analysis programs that are presently available (Richards and Richards 1998). Instead, data coding, sorting, categorizing, and analysis are still often done the way they have been done for more than a hundred years—by hand.

This section provides a brief introduction to the concept of computer analysis, using a single program package for an illustration. If readers seek more information about these programs, they are encouraged to refer to one of several published reviews, such as *Computer Programs for Qualitative Data Analysis* by Weitzman and Miles (1995). Miles and Huberman (1994) included a valuable point-by-point comparison of a dozen or more commercially available analysis programs in their text on qualitative data analysis. Richards and Richards (1998) provided a useful introduction to the theoretical underpinnings of computer software programs for analyzing qualitative data, but without evaluating many specific programs.

In the taxonomy of analysis software suggested by Richards and Richards (1998), software is divided into two broad classifications: (1) general-purpose software packages and (2) special-purpose software developed specifically for data analysis. General-purpose packages include standard word-processing programs, database management systems, and text-search software. Refer to the Richards and Richards review for additional information.

Special-purpose software packages are what their name implies: programs developed for a special purpose. These can be grouped into at least five categories of special-purpose programs based on the purpose for which they have been designed:

- Code-and-retrieve software
- Rule-based, theory-building systems
- Logic-based systems
- Index-based systems
- Conceptual, or semantic, network systems

Of these, the two approaches that seem to offer the most promise at this time for case research are logic-based systems and conceptual network systems. Richards and Richards (1998) provided an extensive review of the logic-based system they created, NUD*IST (Non-Numerical Unstructured Data Indexing, Searching, and Theorizing). With NUD*IST, a user is able to code themes and categories by just attaching labels to segments of the text (Tak, Nield, and Becker 1999).

Like a majority of the systems discussed by Richards and Richards, NUD*IST is built around a code-and-retrieve facility. It has been expanded to include a number of different optional processes—a feature that may have turned out to be one of the program's greatest faults. Potential users of the system should consider their caveat about the early versions of the program:

> NUD*IST appears, compared with the other systems described here, as a rather awkward hybrid, containing features of code-and-retrieve, ways of handling production-rule and other types of conceptual-level reasoning, conceptual representations alternative to conceptual network systems, and database storage facilities, all interacting through interlocking tools. . . . And, perhaps most important, the software offers many ways for a researcher never to finish a study. (Richards and Richards 1998, 237)

Despite the potentially confusing complexity of NUD*IST, it has become one of the, if not the most, popular computer software program for analysis of qualitative data. It is particularly popular in education, nursing, and other medical studies, and some sociological applications. It seems to be used less often in ethnographic studies and is hardly ever seen in political science research. Despite its slow adoption, a few innovators in political science and nongovernment organization research have started to test its capabilities.

The second software program to receive special mention by Richards and Richards was the conceptual network system ATLAS/ti. Mühr (1991) developed ATLAS in Germany during the 1980s, when most of the work on analysis software was under way. ATLAS is built on a code-and-retrieve foundation, to which has been added an excellent memoing capability; codes can be assigned to memos as well as the original text. Its distinguishing feature, however, is an ability to create conceptual graphic displays that show relationships and linkages that relate the text to the systems or theories in the case being studied (Richards and Richards 1998, 240). ATLAS and NUD*IST are just two of the many programs available for analyzing qualitative case research data. Among the others are HyperRESEARCH (Hesse-Biber, Dupuis, and Kinder 1991) and AQUAD (Huber and Garcia 1991).

In conclusion, the application of special-purpose software packages for qualitative data analysis is probably here to stay. As more and more professional researchers discover the capabilities of the packages and more students are exposed to them in their research methods classes, this growth should accelerate. As of today, however, because of their complexity—due in large part to their extensive capabilities—many researchers still analyze their data using traditional, minimal techniques and processes.

Summary

The chief data collection methods used in public management case research are conducting in-person or group interviews; observing behavior either as a participant in the group or as a nonparticipating, silent observer; and analyzing internal and external documents and other artifacts. Often, two or more of these methods are used, either for collecting additional data or in triangulation for a test of validity.

This chapter reviewed two procedures for analyzing textual material: the traditional approach to a literature review and the statistically based process known as content analysis. The chapter concluded with a short discussion on computer programs for analysis of textual data. A number of special-purpose computer programs have been developed for analyzing qualitative case research data. Two of these were discussed: NUD*IST and ATLAS/ti.

➤ 10 ◀

The Case Research Report

As a general rule, the compositional phase puts the greatest demands on a case study investigator. The case study report does not follow any stereotypical form. . . . Moreover, the report need not be in written form only. Probably because of this uncertain nature, researchers who do not like to compose [write] probably should not do case studies.
—Robert K. Yin (1994)

Although there does not appear to be any one right way to prepare a case report, a number of guidelines are available to help researchers prepare case study reports (Hamel, Dufour, and Fortin 1993; Marshall and Rossman 1999; Gillham 2000). For example, Yin (1994) identified five key principles that have been applied in the best and most informative case study reports.

The first of these guiding principles is that the case study must be significant. Cases that are significant are those that stand out as superior examples of the best in their class. They illustrate a particular point in a better or more succinct way than others that could have been chosen. In this way, the researcher indicates that selection of the case or cases was not only appropriate, but also that the study adds to the body of knowledge about the topic or issue; the study makes a significant contribution.

Research problems that are trivial do not make good case studies. Yin (1994) concluded that the best case studies are those in which one or more of the following are true:

- The single case or sets of cases are unusual and not "mundane."
- The case or cases are what the public would be interested in reading about.
- The fundamental issues brought to light in the case have wide appeal—they are "nationally important," either as theory, as policy, or in practical application.

The second guiding principle is that the case study must be complete. Cases that are complete leave the reader with the feeling that all relevant evidence has been collected, evaluated, interpreted, and either accepted or rejected. The operative word here, of course, is *relevant*. Thus, a case is not absolutely complete unless it is complete on three distinct dimensions:

- Dimension 1: A complete case is one in which the phenomenon of interest in the case is explicitly addressed.
- Dimension 2: All the relevant information is collected; no information that fits this dimension should be left ungathered or, if collected, left uninterpreted and discussed in the final narrative.
- Dimension 3: The researcher or case author must not impose any artificial conditions during the analysis or evaluation of the collected data. This means, for example, that the researcher must not stop collecting relevant information because he or she ran out of money or time, or for any other nonresearch constraint.

The third principle is that the case study should also consider alternative perspectives. It is important that the researcher not limit the analysis of case data to a single point of view. Alternative explanations for a social phenomenon always exist (Marshall and Rossman 1999). Throughout the analysis of the case data, the researcher is obligated to identify alternative explanations or interpretations of the raw data, and to show why they are rejected in favor of the adopted explanation. Evidence that supports the selected interpretation must also be presented.

The fourth principle is that the case study must display sufficient evidence. Data reduction solely for the sake of brevity in a case analysis is not desirable. All the relevant evidence must appear in the final narrative. Certainly, condensing, distilling, and combining data take place at each step of the analysis; otherwise, the final report would end up little more than a hodgepodge of unrelated raw data. The researcher must analyze the data to fully interpret and evaluate what was collected. In this process, some data reduction naturally occurs. However, the researcher should probably err on the side of including too much material rather than omitting what could be important evidence from the final case report.

The fifth principle is that the case study should be composed in an engaging manner. This advice is particularly relevant because it influences whether the case will be read, understood, and, where appropriate, published or used in policy development or similar public management situations.

Writing in an engaging manner is a question of style, which can mean many things. Length, word selection, paragraph construction, headlines and subheads, the flow of ideas, summaries and conclusions, punctuation, citations, and references: These and other concepts are all a part of writing style.

Complaints that are often heard about case study reports are that they are too long, they are cumbersome to read and interpret, or they are simply boring. In a word, they lack style. By style, Yin (1994) meant that writers of case reports should always strive to engage readers' intelligence, entice their interest by early hinting at exciting information to come, and seduce readers into accepting the underlying premise.

Universal Recommendations for Case Reports

Writing a report of a case study does not differ much from writing other types of research reports. The biggest differences are the greater importance of explaining in detail the circumstances surrounding the choice of the case subject and in the description of the case subject itself.

Once the case data have been collected and analyzed, the researcher must then organize the information and choose a structure for presenting the findings and conclusions. There are many different ways to organize the final case report, although only several stand out. An often seen way is the *chronological* organization, in which events and circumstances are detailed as they occurred, capped at the end with a section of conclusions and implications.

A better approach is one that organizes the case information from the *general to the specific;* an alternative of this approach is to organize the report from the specific to the general. In another approach, the researcher could use the points established in the *definition of the study question* or *the research hypotheses* as a structure for the final case report. This means inserting a starting paragraph with a point or a hypothesis early in the report, then using material from the literature to show how the point or points were applied in practice. Many cases follow this design.

Three Steps of Report Writing

Patton (1980, 304) referred to the case narrative as "the descriptive, analytic, interpretive, and evaluative treatment of the more comprehensive descriptive data" (collected by the researcher). He consolidated the report-writing phase into three distinct steps:

1. Collect and categorize the raw case data. This is all the information that can be gathered by interviews, in observing, and by reviewing any relevant documents and/or literature.
2. Write a preliminary record of the case. This case record includes the researchers' coded and subsequent distillation of the mass of raw data. It involves establishing categories and assigning the data to those categories in a logical order. A draft of the report eventually emerges from completion of this and the first step.
3. Produce a case narrative. This is the final written narrative that presents the case information in a readable, informative, and evaluative form. This document communicates how the case meets the original objectives for the research. It includes all the information that readers need to fully understand the subject. It can be presented in three forms: (1) a chronological record of events, (2) according to a set of themes, or (3) as a combination of both approaches.

Because there are no ironclad rules to follow when deciding how to organize research findings and present ideas, most case writers use different designs at different times (Gillham 2000). However, if you are going to write many cases, it is probably best to avoid jumping around from one point to another or to write a report with no underlying plan whatsoever.

Remember: A fundamental goal of your case writing is that it be read. For that to happen, it must be interesting and readable. This requires adopting a structure and then sticking to the plan and format you chose.

Five Key Elements of Case Research Reports

For many years, the structure of case reports in the social sciences has tended to follow the design with five key elements for case studies proposed by Robert Yin (1994). The first key element is to begin with a statement of the research question or questions that sparked the case study in the first place. Many of these are stated in terms of *how* or *why* questions.

The second key element includes what Yin (1994) called "study propositions." The propositions outline what the researcher believes will emerge from analysis of the case. In positivist research, the researcher's hypotheses serve this purpose. In narrative case reports, however, the study proposition is typically stated as a short paragraph stating what the researchers hoped to accomplish by the case study. An example is this statement of purpose from a 2003 multicase study on the provision of emergency contraception in Brazil and Colombia:

> This paper highlights the particular programmatic and political contexts for introducing emergency contraception (EC) of two of the five study countries [targeted by the International Planned Parenthood Federation, Western Hemisphere Region; other countries included Chile, the Dominican Republic and Venezuela]: Brazil and Colombia. In each case we explore the role of health sector reform and the strategies adopted in these two countries to expand EC use. (Heimburger, Gras, and Guedes 2003, 151)

The third element is a description of the units of analysis; that is, establishing the "case" as an individual, a group of individuals, a unit in an organization, an organization, agency, or department, or, in the broadest sense, a nation. The case can also be an event, such as the transformation of an organization for greater operational efficiency or effectiveness or of national policy as described in the emergency conception case.

The fourth element should be the researcher's analysis—the *logic*—involved in the interpretation and conclusions reached about what happened or is happening in the case and, therefore, what is the connection to the study question. The fifth element is a description of what criteria the researcher used to make the conclusion. For example, if the case was a study of how an organization developed an effective performance-oriented pay and recognition system, upon what measurement and other criteria was the system judged to be effective?

Establishing a Point of View for the Case Research

A key step in organizing and presenting research findings is to select a point of view that matches the objectives of your research. This involves deciding how to structure the report so that the ideas flow smoothly from section to section. The chances of the report being read can often be improved by following a simple, standard structure and using a writing style consistent with the writing in that field of study. Different points of view are described in the next section.

Sample Points of View

Different disciplines in the social and administrative sciences and the humanities often recommend a variety of ways to structure or organize their written reports. A valuable overview of some of the different directions or points of view that researchers can take when planning and writing reports of their findings has been suggested by Sorrels (1984), who lists these seven points of view or patterns:

1. The *indirect pattern* point of view. This pattern moves from factual parts of a case to a general conclusion.
2. The *direct form,* which reverses this order. This form moves the reader from a general conclusion to the facts that support the conclusion.
3. A *chronological pattern.* In this form the reader is taken through an order of events, such as a sequence of dates as in a typical historical account of some phenomenon.
4. A *spatial pattern.* An example of this method is a case report that moves the reader from one department or location to other related or equally impacted units in some researcher-selected logical sequence.
5. An *analytical organization,* in which the whole is separated into its parts. Each part is addressed completely before moving on to the next part. Typically from three to five parts is probably the most appropriate number of parts to include in such a study.
6. A *comparative pattern.* As the name implies, elements of a whole are compared point by point. Multicase designs, cross-national, or cross-state cases often follow this pattern.
7. A *ranked method,* where portions of the report are presented in the order of their importance or impact; the importance may be in ascending or descending order. This method is often used in cases describing events leading up to some important climax, such as winning an election or achieving the meaningful transformation of an organization's culture.

Box 10.1

Components of a Case Research Report

1. Title
2. Abstract
3. Introduction or rationale for the case
4. Review of the literature examined for the case
5. Discussion of the methodology and/or research design used for the study
6. Complete discussion of the findings
7. Conclusions, implications, and/or recommendations
8. Detailed list of the references and sources cited
9. Appendices if any

Components in a Case Report

Written research reports contain, at most, nine or ten parts or sections. These are often organized in the manner presented in Box 10.1. However, it is also important to remember that not all papers and reports follow this format, and not all include every one of these major components.

Notice that this list does not include any mention of charts, tables, graphs, drawings or other illustrations, models, or other graphic communication tools. That is because these tools are not limited to any one section. Naturally, graphic items are not found in the title, abstract, or references sections of the report. However, they can certainly be used in any or all of the other sections. They should be used where they achieve the desired impact or communication objective. When used correctly, graphic tools greatly improve the ability of a report to communicate. They allow the researcher to present detailed information clearly, succinctly, and at a glance, regardless of where they are used in the report.

The Title

The title is often one of the most important components of the report. It should leap off the page, grabbing the reader's attention. This does not mean that it should be cute. It is usually best to avoid the use of slang in your writing unless there is a specific and pertinent reason to do so. If for some reason slang must be used for special effect, for example, it should be set off in quotation marks or in italics.

Most students and beginning researchers tend to use titles that are too general or that do not say anything about what the research or assignment involves. For example, "A Report in Compliance with the Research Assignment of February 2" is not an appropriate title, even if it is true. A different approach to take with that title might be "Environmentally Harmful Logging Practices Approved by the State Bureau of Water Resources: A Case Study."

Although this rewritten title contains fifteen words, researchers are cautioned not to make the title too long; eight to twelve words is the preferred length. A rule of thumb to remember is this: Fewer is best. However, it is not good to be terse. Research papers are not newspaper stories. Therefore, short, tricky, or cute headlines as titles are not appropriate—even if they are explained in the first section of the case report.

Elements of a Good Title

Good titles should contain four key components: (1) They identify the *topic*; (2) they spell out the *specific dimension* of the study; (3) they name *who* the study is about; (4) they explain what *methodology* was followed—in this situation, the methodology is a case study. The purpose of the title is to tell the reader what the paper is about—and to capture the reader's interest so that the finished product is examined in full.

Finally, the title page should include the title of the paper, the name of the author or authors (usually in alphabetical order based on the first letter of the last name), and any other relevant information.

Examples of Qualitative Study Titles

1. "How Glide, Oregon, Used Community Meetings to Overcome Negative Public Attitudes toward Public Safety Planning: A Case Study."
2. "Implementing Federal Port Security Requirements in Stockton, California."

Examples of Quantitative Study Titles

3. "A Case Study of Consumer Attitudes about Smoking in Olympia, Washington."
4. "An Analysis of Minority Hiring Procedures: The Case of Two Oregon State Government Agencies."

The Abstract (or Executive Summary)

The abstract is a concise summary of the research study and report. It is placed at the top of the first page of the paper, immediately below the title and before the introduction section. While most reports are typed double-spaced, the abstract is usually single-spaced and indented five spaces on both sides of the paper (Box 10.2).

Typically, the abstract ranges from 100 to 200 words. In some journals, editorial

Box 10.2

An Example of a Case Research Title and Abstract

Comprehensive Management and Budgeting Reform in Local Government:

The Case of Milwaukee

Since its new mayor was elected in 1988, Milwaukee, Wisconsin, has been undergoing comprehensive budget and management reforms similar to those currently occurring at all levels of government. This article presents a case analysis of the events and conditions surrounding the initiation and implementation stages of reform in the city from their inception to the mid-1990s. The analysis focuses on variables relating to structure and process, leadership characteristics, managerial capacity, and culture that have been identified in other cases and comparative studies as either facilitating or hindering the two stages. Milwaukee's experience also shows that political factors seem to be more important to these stages than what often is related by other studies of reform.

Source: Hendrick (2000, 261 and 312–37).

instructions for authors call for the abstract to be less than 100 words. Whatever length, in this short space, the abstract must inform readers what was done, how it was done, the most significant results or findings, and what readers will find when they read the entire paper. Abstracts contain enough information to accurately inform the readers about the key ideas in a paper while also encouraging them to read the full paper. Abstracts are found in all professional journal articles and in the long-form listing of papers included in CD-ROM databases and similar electronic sources. It is a good idea to examine these abstracts to get a feel for how other researchers write theirs.

In a report prepared for internal distribution, such as a study done for management of a nonprofit organization, a slightly longer form called an executive summary takes the place of an abstract. The executive summary is often used to guide an audience through an oral presentation of the paper. While abstracts follow normal sentence and paragraph construction, the executive summary may be presented in outline or bulleted form.

The Introduction

In some professional journal formats, the introduction may be called the background section. In others it is referred to as the "rationale for the study." In some journals, the section may have no label or headline; the writer just begins with the writing. Many but not all public administration and administrative science journals continue to use an "Introduction" label at the beginning of the case report text.

The purpose of the introduction section is to explain for the reader in some detail what the study and paper are all about. Beyond this, there are few specific rules about what goes in the introduction, only suggestions. The following ideas are some of the things you might wish to think about as you write the introduction for the case report:

The introduction section is where readers are introduced to the full scope of the subject of the case study. It includes background information on the topic or situation, the organization or administrative unit, and any other relevant preliminary information. It is the place to state why the case subject or subjects were selected. It is also where the steps taken in developing the study are listed. The introduction also explains how or why the study was first considered and what the researcher hoped to learn by studying this particular case subject or topic.

The introduction sometimes includes a brief discussion of some key items of the literature so that readers can see how the research relates to other work done on this topic. This is done so that the researcher can interpret other case reports and/or articles about the issue topic and ultimately indicate how they relate to the new study.

The introduction is the first place where the writing should begin to sparkle. This section must be carefully written and rewritten. It is the first chance to hook the people who are in a position to judge your research and writing. The following statement regarding instructions for contributors that appears in all issues of the *American Management Review* emphasizes the importance of careful attention to style:

> In addition to their substantive content, writing style, structure, and length also will be considered. Poor writing and visual presentation are also reasons for reviewers to reject a manuscript. Editors of the journal look for clarity and logical presentation, as well as a "provocative, challenging orientation that stimulates debate." Of course, the requirement for "professionalism" is important, if not paramount.

To summarize, the introduction section should include the following:

1. A brief (no more than two or three paragraphs) review of the background of the study
2. A statement explaining why the topic was selected
3. If appropriate, a brief introduction to other research on the subject
4. An indication of what will be presented in the pages to follow
5. Any additional information that logically could be considered as an introduction to the research project, study, topic, or paper

Review of the Literature

The section that follows the introduction is the review of the literature. It should contain the majority of your analysis of what other researchers and authors have said about the topic. This is where results of the library and/or Internet investigation are presented. Since everything included in this section comes from the work of others, the researcher must be careful to always cite sources; if someone else did the work first, that person *must* be given appropriate credit.

For case research studies that follow a document analysis strategy, this section might more appropriately be called the discussion section. For example, for a case about how managers in public organizations exercise one or more aspects of good leadership, all data might come from already published sources, such as one or more broadly focused public management journals, or sources on CD-ROM or the Internet. Once this is complete, the researcher might then carry out a more extensive search of the public administration literature for specific articles on the managers in the public sector specifically. This is not as difficult as it sounds because good examples tend to get lots of attention in the media.

The researcher may include introductory paragraphs defining the topic and variables in question; in this example it means describing specific leadership traits. Then, the literature that addressed each of the traits might be examined. In this way, the researcher might do all his or her research examining already published sources.

Or, the researcher might be asked to prepare a more structured case study that involves observing leadership traits as exhibited by managers in the researcher's own organization. The method of gathering this data may be qualitative, quantitative, or a combination of the two. In this situation, the literature search can provide suggestions about what traits might be more important than others, how leadership traits are or might be measured, and other relevant foundation material.

To summarize this discussion, the review of the literature (or discussion section in a shorter paper) should do the following:

- Review earlier work done in the field.
- Explain how earlier work relates to this investigation.
- Give examples of directions being taken by other investigators.
- Give a sense of continuity or closure to your work.
- For a shorter paper, it may provide the body of the ideas to be expanded upon in the rest of the study.

Methodology

Sometimes called research methods, or methods and materials, or simply the methods section, this is the part of the report where how the research work was done is finally and fully explained. In case research studies, this section should describe in some detail where the data came from, how it was collected, and how it was processed. Some of the questions answered in this section might include the following:

- Were the data gathered for the case taken from published literature—in a library study—or was the research limited to a study of Internet sources? Why was the method chosen?
- Did the data gathering involve more than one method? Why or why not?
- Were the data gathered by observation? If so, was the researcher functioning as a full participant or as unobtrusive bystander?
- If a personal, in-depth interview data-gathering approach was used, did the research involve conducting a single interview or a series of personal interviews?
- If interviews were used, was a custom-designed discussion guide (or questionnaire) developed, or was the study guide or questionnaire one that was used in an earlier study? Why was the approach taken chosen?
- Was an experiment designed and carried out?

These are only a few of the many different factors that shape research methods and that should be identified in the case study report. The methodology employed will depend in the final analysis on the nature of the study problem, the relevant study variables, access to the chosen case subject, and the resources available to the researcher.

Review: Methods and Data Differences

It might be worthwhile here to briefly review one of the key differences in data as they relate to all research methods. This is the primary–secondary data dichotomy. *Primary* data are data that the researcher generates; they are specific to the research project at hand. An example consists of the collective responses to the questions asked by the researcher during an in-depth interview.

Secondary data are data that were collected by someone else for a different purpose. Examples include published economic and demographic statistics. The case data examined during a meta-analysis of cases are also secondary. Typically, secondary data are cheaper and quicker to gather, although primary data tend to be the more reliable of the two data types. There is a place and purpose for each.

If the study is a library or Internet research design for a short paper, it will usually involve gathering secondary data exclusively. If the research study means conducting an experiment to evaluate citizens' responses to various public service announcements, it means gathering primary data.

When gathering secondary data, remember that every source of information used must be identified in the paper. This means including a complete bibliographic citation, as well as page numbers for actual quotes you use in your paper (page numbers should *not* be used with source citations when they are paraphrased).

A research study can entail studying published books and articles in the library or checking sources over the Internet. It can require examining artifacts or observing behavior in the field. It can involve developing a set of questions and asking people to respond to a questionnaire. Or, it can require carefully designing and conducting an experiment with human subjects. In every case, the researcher must describe exactly what was done and how it was done. That information goes here, in the methods section of the research paper.

The Findings Section

Once readers have been told what was researched and how it was done, it is time to tell them what the research revealed—what it accomplished. Sometimes this section is called discussion, results, or findings. Whichever, this is where readers are presented the final results of the research effort; in the process, it explains the reasons for conducting the research in the first place.

This information must be present clearly, factually, simply, and without editorial comment. It is not the place for the researcher to introduce opinions or reactions. This means that conclusions, judgments, or evaluations of the information should not be interjected into this section of the report. The job of the author is simply to explain what the data reveal, nothing more.

It is not a good idea to editorialize about the data in this section. Rather, try to remain cool and objective; simply "tell it like it is." Avoid strongly negative opinions such as "the manager really made a stupid mistake." However, it is possible to describe the behavior in ways so that others might think the mistake was what you think it was. It is always best to let your readers make their own evaluations and conclusions; never tell them how to think.

Typically, quantitative research reports are written in the third person, and qualitative study reports may be written in the first person or third person. It is a good idea to get in the habit of using the form used most often in your field of interest or study. For example, researchers are often encouraged to avoid using the first-person approach in reports on management or economics research, whereas many public administration journals include papers written in both forms. The topic and research methodology followed should dictate the form used in the presentation. As a rule of thumb, it is difficult to get into trouble when always using clear, objective writing and writing in the third-person format.

Conclusions and/or Recommendations Section

Writing a case research report can be much like writing a speech. In both cases, the writer selects a topic, finds something out about the topic, and then writes about it. The writer closes with a summary and shares conclusions about the process with an audience. People who teach speech making have reduced this to a three-part structure: (1) Tell your audience what you are going to tell them, (2) tell them, (3) and then tell them what you told them.

In a sense, we have been following these directions as we moved from section to section in this chapter. In the introduction, readers were told what the research and report were going to be about. The methodology section described the way the data were gathered and processed. The results section presented the main body of your research findings. Now is the time to wrap things up by telling the audience what was learned from the research.

A good conclusions section can be one of the most valuable components of a paper (Markman, Markman, and Waddell 1989). The well-written conclusion is part summary, part conclusion, and part recommendations. This section can be used for several different purposes. First, it provides an opportunity to summarize the main ideas gleaned from the literature. It also permits repeating any critical findings from any experimental research that might have been conducted.

Second, a good conclusions section allows the researcher to interpret the findings and to write a subjective interpretation in his or her own words. In a good public administration paper, this may be the only place where the researcher can be original. To this point, the writing must have remained completely objective. Only the facts are reported. Finally, the conclusions section gives the researcher a chance to prove to the readers that the research idea, design, and project were valid and worthwhile. Now, however, the researcher must explain what it all means. To do this well requires the researcher to finally be creative, analytical, and persuasive. At the same time, this is where the author tries to influence the audience or to convince them that the presented interpretation is the right one.

Preparing the Conclusions Section

Begin the conclusions section with a brief summary of the research, add your interpretation, and close the report with what you see as either implications of the findings, or close with your recommendations. The conclusions section should do the following:

- Summarize the main ideas.
- Say what these ideas mean.
- Include a personal interpretation of the findings (your opinions).
- Convince readers that the research was worth the effort.
- Make recommendations, if any, to the reader.
- If a report is to be included in a professional journal, this section may also include mention of implications or recommendations for further research.

References (Bibliography)

The references section is where the writer identifies all sources of information. Typically, there are two parts to this section: (1) the location of the information used in your study and (2) an alphabetical list of all sources cited, studied, or examined during the study. The first part of this section is known as the notes or sources cited section and can be presented in the report as endnotes, footnotes, or in-text citations. Notes are presented in chronological order as they appear in the paper, from the first to the last. In-text citations are included in the body of the paper; they appear as the source information is used. The in-text citation method was used throughout this book.

Writers may use footnotes, endnotes, or in-text citations to inform readers of the location of their information sources. Location information is needed for others to either replicate the study or test for flaws. For papers of approximately ten to twelve pages, authors are no longer required to follow the requirement for endnotes or footnotes. This does not mean that authors can use the work of others as their own. Doing so is plagiarism, and plagiarism is theft. The practice is unethical, immoral, and, in most cases, illegal. At some universities and colleges, students can be expelled for plagiarism.

What it does mean is that the citations issue can be dealt with by placing the author's name and date of publication in parenthesis at the beginning or end of the section dealing with that work. This is called the in-text citations form. The in-text citation method is growing in popularity; most publications and organizations prefer that this method be used exclusively. It is the method used throughout this book.

The references or bibliography section contains complete bibliographic information about all sources used in the study. Many different styles for presenting bibliographic information are used in research writing. It is usually best to follow the style used by the most influential writers in your field, or to follow the style employed by the best journal in the discipline. Public administration and public management papers and journals most often follow standard American Psychology Association (APA) style, although other styles are also found in the industry literature. In addition to APA, two often-used styles include the Modern Language Association (MLA) and the University of Chicago (Chicago style). The references section of the research paper must include a complete bibliographic citation only for the sources used in the research. If a source has been examined for the study but not used, it is not necessary to include it in the references.

In summary, the information used as background for a research project can come from published books; periodicals (magazines, newspapers, journals); interviews or surveys; films; electronic sources such as the Internet; government or company brochures, reports, or pamphlets; television programs; or any other source you find. There are a variety of rules for how to list these sources, both as notes and references.

In the past, some stylebooks called for both notes and references to be included. Today, however, in-text citations are usually substituted for endnotes or footnotes. Most periodicals require that in-text citations be used instead of endnotes or footnotes, together with a formal bibliography at the end of the paper.

Appendix or Appendices

The appendix is usually the last component of a research paper. This word has two plural forms: *appendixes* or *appendices*; you may use the one you prefer. The appendix is the place for any attachments that might relate to the paper but which cannot or should not be placed in the body of the paper itself. A brochure or advertisement is an example. Other examples include a copy of the questionnaire used in a research study, a complicated mathematical table, or a copy of an article from a magazine, journal, or newspaper. There are no limits to what can or what should be included in the appendices.

The wide variety of materials that could qualify as appendices suggests that there is no one rule or special format to follow for appendices. Style manuals with recommendations pertaining to the appendix tend to agree with the following conclusions, however:

- Research papers for public administration, business, or economics seldom require an appendix.
- When appendices are used, they should be attached after the bibliography.
- Although it is not completely necessary, a single title page (with the label "Appendix") should be placed before all the attached material.
- Only the number of the appendix title page is noted in the table of contents.
- When more than one appendix is used, the word "Appendices" is placed in the table of contents and on the section title page.
- More than one appendix may be labeled chronologically as follows: *Appendix A, Appendix B, Appendix C,* and so forth.

Style and Format in Case Research Writing

The words *style* and *format* are often used interchangeably to refer to the way a paper is put together. They shouldn't be, however, because they mean different things. *Format* refers to the way the research paper is structured or organized. It includes headlines, subheads, and the order of the components of the paper. *Style,* on the other hand, refers to the choice of words and sentences used in the report. It includes punctuation and grammar.

Format often varies from discipline to discipline, journal to journal, and the purpose of the paper. Sometimes, when people talk about style they are referring to the writing rules endorsed by an organization like the American Society for Public Administration, the American Political Science Association, the Academy of Political Science, or the University of Chicago. At other times, they mean the subjective, creative, artistic part of writing: selecting words that sparkle, using the active rather than the passive voice, using a variety of sentence lengths.

What kinds of textbooks and articles do you hate to read: a volume with sentences that ramble on forever? Those books with huge seas of black or gray that put you to sleep because the author refused to paragraph, did not use headlines or subheads, or did not include illustrations or graphics to perk up the text? Do some books offend you because they either talk down to you or, on the other hand, assume that you have twenty years' experience in the field and that you understand the complicated or esoteric jargon the author insists on using?

135

Most people prefer textbooks and articles that can be easily read and understood. These are the examples to use as models for your own writing. Good writing *can* be learned, just as poor writing can be avoided.

When editors talk about style, they usually mean these writing features: (1) an author's choice of words and sentences, (2) how the author employs the basic rules of grammar and punctuation, or (3) the mechanics of footnotes, endnotes, in-text citations, and various ways of recording bibliographic (reference) notation.

Case Reporting Guidelines at *Public Performance and Management Review*

The public administration journal *Public Performance and Management Review* recommends that writers of public management cases studies follow guidelines such as those listed in the following sections. These should not be considered a checklist to follow religiously, but rather to guide the case report through to its logical conclusion.

Introduce the Case

Introducing the case is easier when the writer provides answers to the following questions:

- What are the issues, problems, and interests relevant to the case?
- What is the purpose of the case?
- Who are the key actors; can—and should—they be identified?
- What constraints or problems in the organization are faced by the decision makers or main actors?
- What is the case study setting: where, when, and why?
- Is the location of the case clearly stated? Should it be hidden?

Establish the Background of the Problem or Situation

The reader must know what and why the problem occurred, and why and how the problem was addressed. Answers to questions such as these can help make these points clear for the readers of the case report: (1) What is the history of events that led up to the situation examined in the case? What recent developments have contributed to the issue, problem, or situation?

Report Your Findings

- What is the story and case content?
- What characters are involved in some type of action that engenders a decision or a solution to a problem?

- What is the chronological sequence of the case? (Use time markers such as next, subsequently, etc.)
- Was a solution implemented, and if so, by whom?
- What were the decision-making processes?
- Did the solution produce the intended results? What evidence, if any, supports this conclusion?
- What alternative solutions were considered?
- What events were critical to success or failure?

Describe Your Analysis and Conclusions

The following questions are typical of the points that a case researcher may use to ensure that the conclusions section of the case provides readers and fellow researchers with the confidence that the case study followed accepted scientific principles.

- Does the case support or conflict with existing public administration theory or assumptions?
- Under the case study circumstances and the problem, what should be done?
- Is the resolution appropriate to the circumstances and useful in dealing with the problem?
- What other options are available?
- What lessons can other public managers learn from reading the case?

Summary

This chapter included discussion on two related topics: (1) the elements to be included in a case research study report and (2) the format and style of the report.

This chapter provided a discussion of the sections that are included in most research project reports. Case research reports are often organized to include nine major components: (1) title and title page, (2) abstract, (3) introduction or rationale for the study, (4) review of the literature, (5) discussion of the methodology used for the study, (6) complete discussion of the results produced by the study (often called the findings section), (7) conclusions and/or recommendations, (8) references, and (9) appendices, if any.

Both format and style were discussed in this chapter. *Format* refers to the logical way papers and reports are structured or organized. *Style* refers to the choice of words, the way words are used in sentences, and how sentences are formed into paragraphs. It includes punctuation and grammar. A related aspect of style is the form used to present references and works cited in the paper.

Part II

Case Research in Public Management

This section briefly introduces an issue concerning public management and then goes on to provide a wide variety of examples of case research in selected areas of interest in public administration and management. The areas were selected because they were either relevant topics of interest in the public administration and public management literature, or because of the quality of the cases.

The section begins with a chapter on cases in public policy and citizen engagement. This chapter is included because policy formulation is the core of all subsequent government actions and programs. Other chapters cover cases in performance management, sustainable government, technology management, security and emergency management, social and health services, public infrastructure, and public transportation. It concludes with a chapter on changes occurring in the work and governance models of government, including shifts from individual bureaucracies to a system of networks, collaboration, and cooperation. If your favorite topic was not included, keep in mind that the case research method is the same, regardless of the subject studied. A review of the public management literature will surely reveal cases on most topics of interest to public administrators and managers.

The chapters begin with several pages in which the topic is reviewed for researchers in that particular field of inquiry. This is followed by reviews of various cases that have been selected to illustrate research in the topic area. Additional thematic discussion may also be found scattered throughout the chapters.

Any errors that may have occurred in my interpretation or emphases in my reviews of the cases are due to my biases in the reviewing and paraphrasing processes. I apologize to the original authors in advance for these. My goal was to give readers an opportunity to gain from the case research method; for more information, readers are encouraged to consult the original case report to learn directly from the researchers' contributions.

➤ 11 ◄

Case Research in Public Policy and Management

> *Policy making is always a complex interplay of values, ideologies, and power, but how a policy idea becomes a piece of legislation is more like creating a work of art or solving a puzzle than producing a mechanical and predictable event.*
> —Anna Ya Ni and Alfred Tat-Kei Ho (2008)

This chapter and the next focus on two closely related aspects of public management: (1) how public policy shapes the strategies and tasks of public managers and (2) innovations in the ways that these public services are delivered and public feedback is received. Forces driving the changes that are occurring in these two core components of government are economics, market-driven structural trends, and a shift in the social framework within which public managers must function.

Traditional public administration theory holds that public managers implement policies formed by elected leaders—elected officials, members of Congress, the president, and the judiciary—who base their policy decisions on their analyses of the needs and wants of citizens and such interest groups as business and nonprofit organizations. However, this concept no longer describes the true picture of how policy is formed and implemented (Kull 1978; Gerston 1983). The more appropriate view is that public managers and citizens themselves also influence and shape public policy. Public managers do so through their role as implementers of policy; the public—at least in those states that allow them—shapes policy directly using such tools as the initiative, referendum, and recall; and indirectly through public opinion.

The policy initiatives that are eventually implemented by public agencies are shaped by the skills and experiences of the workers at the levels of government charged with their implementation. The way that a policy is implemented is also shaped by the assets and resources made available to government agencies through the appropriations process. During the actual implementation of a policy, the manner in which the relevant agencies follow through on its provisions is also influenced by the organizational culture of the agency and the values and mores of the people

Figure 11.1 **Some Factors with an Influence on Public Policy Decision Makers**

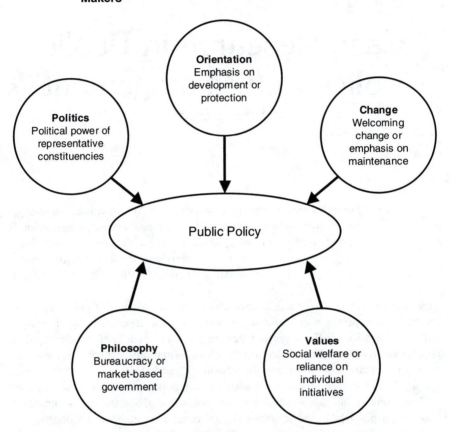

charged with carrying out the work of the unit. Thus, it is clear that policy and delivery are closely related. Figure 11.1 displays some of the factors with the power to influence the direction and implementation of public policy.

Public managers exercise great influence over public policy in many ways, as this statement explains: Government organizations "influence public policy through rule making, adjudication, law enforcement, program implementation, policy initiation, comments on proposed policy changes, and bureaucratic routines" (Meier 1979, 102–3).

Case research on public policy and public management focuses on these issues as well as those that reflect the influence of politics on professional public managers. Case research can describe the pros and cons, successes or failures, and key issues that are shaped during the process of policy implementation. Although public administration case research tends to focus on the management processes of policy implementation far more than it does on the processes involved in policy formula-tion, some case research in policy formulation is found in the public management literature (Kim 2000).

Themes in Policy Case Research

Kettl (2005) identified two main themes in research on policy formulation and public administration: focus and change. The first of these themes is research on *policy orientation*. This theme refers to the broad policy questions: What should government do? How much should it do? How should government performance on policy-based programs be measured? The second theme focuses on what poli-cies, if any, should be changed, when, and how. It addresses such questions as: Should the policy be retained or allowed to fade away? Should it be revised? If so, what changes should be made, and how and in what way should the changes be implemented? Who should be involved in establishing and implementing the changes, if any?

Policy orientation refers to the political and philosophical leanings of the policy-making bodies. For example, is it the prevailing orientation of legislators to invest more funds in social programs, or is more funding for defense, security, or economic stimulus programs of greater concern? Legislators focus on deciding what exactly it is that government should do, how deeply government should be involved in the social and economic affairs of the country, and what values underlie policy decisions. Public managers must then wrestle with decisions on how best to allocate limited resources to carry out the policy directions they receive.

Policy influences are ultimately decided by the political orientations of the decid-ers and the willingness of the electorate to accede to the decisions taken. Deciding whether government should compete or contract with private industry for the delivery of services and utilities such as cable television, waste management, and the like is an example of a policy orientation question shaped by political orienta-tions. Another is establishing how much of the federal highway budget should go toward building and repairing roads and bridges, compared with how much should go toward improvements and expansions to local mass rapid transit systems.

How Policy Shapes Government Services

Public policy is shaped by such institutions as legislative bodies, the media, interest groups, and the bureaucracy (Gerston 1983). National policy is usually a product of presidential or congressional action. However, when Congress fails to act, the courts often step in with decisions that result in policy based on precedent (Lee and Greenlaw 2000). At the state and local levels, policy is shaped by initiative and/ or referendum as well as by the actions of elected and appointed officials. Case research is possible in all of these approaches.

Congress and other legislative bodies are able to shape public policy through a variety of methods established at the same time a program is authorized (Hall 2008). The most common are the ex ante and ex post approaches. Ex ante[1] controls available to Congress include, among others, the following:

1. Limiting agency activities to a specified set of activities
2. Specifying which groups are to be covered by regulatory actions, or limiting the state or local government activities the federal agency can fund
3. Placing a limit on the actions or tools the agency can use to carry out the policy
4. Requiring an agency to perform the service itself, or demanding that it contract with other government agencies, nonprofit organizations or private firms
5. Specifying the scope of the agency's regulatory actions
6. Including auditing and performance measurement requirements in the authorizing legislation
7. Limiting the program authorization to a set time period and making its reauthorization possible only after congressional examination and adjustments

Short- and Long-Term Implications

Policy decisions can have short- or long-term implications. Short-term authorizations can range from one-year funding authorizations to programs that remain in effect for four to six years, as with some federal transportation programs. This use of short-term authorizations provides two types of control. First, it allows Congress to maintain the stability of a program by limiting pressures for legislative consideration of policy changes, thereby opening the door to program changes that can occur in set time frames: when hearings on reauthorization occur in the period just before the program is expected to expire. Second, scheduling reauthorizations force Congress to take another look at the program to ensure it is doing what it was intended to do, and that agency staff are implementing the policy as Congress intended. Case research focusing on changes that occur in programs often follows these periodic adjustments.

A Global Policy Single-Case Example

The World Commission on Dams (WCD), a global cooperative commission, was formed on February 16, 1998, to help ease growing tension between opponents and supporters of large dams. The strictly advisory role of the twelve-member commission endorsed by the World Bank was to inform political and economic decision makers about the positive and negative impact of large dams. The commission was not to be involved in establishing sites for dam construction or financing decisions.

Jennifer Brinkerhoff of Georgetown University studied the first five years of the WCD for a case research project published in 2002 in *Public Administration*

Review. Her study took the point of view that the global partnership that emerged after formation of the commission illustrated the potential for partnerships to achieve resolution on two major challenges in public service: (1) what she described as an "evolving sociopolitical context of public service, that is, the increasing incidence and intensity of conflict among diverse stakeholders," and (2) the processes involved in the development of an acceptable and feasible global public policy. The case focused on the global partnership that evolved from efforts to form the organization.

Two fundamental characteristics distinguished the WCD partnership model from other forms of intersector collaborative organizations. The first was the concept of *mutuality*, which refers to the mutual coordination and accountability of all actors instead of the domination by one or more partners. The second was the concept of *organization* identity, which is built on the partnership retaining its commitment to the mission, values, and interests, and the partnership continuing to hold the characteristics of the sector from which it originated. On a foundation of these principles, the partnership model exemplified by the WCD was then defined as a

> . . . dynamic relationship among diverse actors, based on mutually agreed objectives, pursued through a shared understanding of the most rational division of labor based on the respective comparative advantages of each partner. This results in a mutual influence, with a careful balance between synergy and respective autonomy, which incorporates mutual respect, equal participation in decision making, mutual accountability and transparency. (Brinkerhoff 2002, 325)

Brinkerhoff's study of the WCD included analysis of organizational and external published reports and a number of personal interviews with key personnel at the organization. She concluded that the organization included all of the forces shaping public service in the early years of the twenty-first century: the concept of multiple-component public institutions—the WCD Commission, participating governments, and donor organizations; self-governing, value-oriented organizations—typical of the nongovernmental organizations (NGOs) that participated; and private-sector, market institutions—private engineering firms and private financing organizations.

What may be the most valuable element of this case was Brinkerhoff's detailed listing of the lessons that managers of other public and private-sector partnerships might learn from the experiences of the WCD and the implications those lessons hold for formatting international public policy, including the following:

- Without one agency in control, the context of the partnership must make it possible for opposing interests and policy leaders to meet in compromise in a search for second- or third-best solutions. In today's interdependent world, it is not possible for one actor to control a global policy formulating process.
- Conflict does not necessarily eliminate arriving at a consensus; it may, in fact, contribute to achieving mutual acceptance. The more bitter the conflict,

the easier it may be to bring the parties to the bargaining table and to reach agreement on structural or procedural issues—thus beginning the path toward compromise agreement.

- Democratic processes are necessary for success; representative participation, open discussions, responsiveness and decision making, transparency, and accountability can contribute significantly to successful conversion of conflicting positions.
- "Perception is everything," according to Brinkerhoff. This means that participants in the development process must perceive that the process is proceeding in good faith so that they will retain an incentive to achieve success in the decisions reached during the collaborative decision process.
- Resolution of conflict within the group is an ongoing process, affecting all participants. Resolution of the conflict must remain the paramount objective.
- Partnerships can be an effective method of resolving intersectoral policy formulation where the potential for conflict and lack of trust is strong.

Achieving agreement on cross-national public policy under conditions of growing complexity, with assertive and empowered multiple constituencies that expect and demand to be included in the policy-decision process, has become exceedingly difficult. This case study illustrates how highly diverse groups with conflicting agendas found ways to address their concerns in a meaningful and mutually rewarding way.

A Multicase Policy Example

Using secondary data in a multicase research design, Hall examined how Congress uses short-term program authorizations to monitor and shape public policy. Hall (2008) noted that the practice of evaluating the status of government programs at set intervals (one of several ex ante control procedures available to Congress) allows Congress to steer policy in the way originally intended or changed to meet new demands.

The three cases included in his study included Head Start, mass transit (including congestion management and transit safety), and the Commodities Futures Trading Commission (CFTC). Each was reviewed over five reauthorizations extending over twenty-five years or longer. Both Head Start and the federal mass transit program distribute federal grants to qualified implementing bodies; Congress has used reauthorization to change how federal funds are spent, how much is spent, and who benefits from the spending. The CFTC is a traditional regulatory agency.

Head Start was created in 1965 as an eight-week summer program to help preschool children from disadvantaged families prepare for entry into kindergarten. All services are provided by local suppliers under contract. Over the years, the program was expanded to aid children with disabilities. With continual expansion of the program, Congress mandated U.S. Department of Education regulators to develop standards, evaluate programs, provide technical support, and coordinate Head Start with other federal programs.

Federal funding for local mass transit began in 1964 with passage of the Urban Mass Transportation act. The act provided federal matching grants and loans for acquisition, construction, and improvements of mass transportation facilities and equipment. In 1966, control of the program was transferred from the Department of Housing and Urban Development to the new Department of Transportation. Later additions promoted transit for the elderly, disabled, and rural populations, as well as adding environmental policy restrictions. Areas that violated federal clean air requirements were not allowed to use federal gasoline tax funds for highway construction, but could use the money for mass transit developments.

The reauthorizations that occurred in the operations of the CFTC since its establishment in 1974 focused on changes in the way the commission regulates commodity financial markets. The agency was created when Congress took commodity-trading regulation from the Department of Agriculture and gave it to the new commission. The first reauthorization in 1978 resulted in (1) changes in the structure of the commission, calling for a chairman to be appointed by the president, (2) exclusion of some types of commodity traders from CFTC jurisdiction, (3) raises in the amounts of financial penalties that could be levied, and (4) an expansion of commission power to hold hearings and grant immunity to witnesses. Reauthorization in 1982 increased the rule-making powers of the CFTC, gave it authority to regulate foreign futures trading in the United States, and allowed it to limit speculative futures. In 1992, another reauthorization resulted in a series of technical changes in the regulatory powers of the CFTC.

This case serves as an illustration of how Congress has used the reauthorization process to create a system of comanagement of federal programs and to shape the overall goals and decision rules in agency activities:

> [Congress] is also able to promote research and analysis that will inform the review of these facets of a program during the next reauthorization by funding studies and requiring specific reports to be produced. The agencies are, in turn, able to implement the new legislative requirements over a given timeframe—typically four to six years. (Hall 2008, 375)

Research Focus in Public Policy and Management

Case research on policy issues can address many different aspects of the processes of shaping public policy. Public management case researchers approach policy questions from several different levels, including that of the makers of public policy, the agency or agencies that are or will be charged with carrying out policy, the point of view of citizens and other stakeholders who are affected by the policies, and from the external influences that pressure for the adoption, alternation, or denial of a policy. For example,

- Smith reported in a 1987 multicase study on the use of interrelationships with local power centers by five public transportation authorities for establishing and carrying out policy on regional transportation through public and private service suppliers.
- Bogenschneider prepared a single-case study in 1995 in which she described the role that a series of family-impact seminars can have on the shaping of public policy toward families.
- Matouq reported in a 2000 case study on how China's leaders are shaping environmental policy implementation through ISO 14001–based environmental management systems in an effort to deal with the country's many environmental problems in the heavily industrialized north, including air and water pollution from industry and development, sewage and industrial and chemical wastes, and other local-level environmental degradation.
- Mycoo focused on three sets of questions in a 2005 case study of national potable water policy in the twin-island state of Trinidad and Tobago: global changes in water policies, the history of the islands' government policies toward water as a public good, and a review of new policy concepts that have emerged since the 1990s.

The Courts and Public Policy

Judicial shaping of public policy occurs when legislative decisions are incomplete or do not specify an interpretation of a law or do not address issues the courts believe should be addressed (Gerston 1983). For example, Lee and Greenlaw (2000) examined four cases in which 1998 Supreme Court decisions contributed to policies on sexual harassment in the workplace—an issue that Congress and the president at the time considered of secondary importance. Two of the cases affected public sector organizations; two dealt with sexual harassment in private-sector organizations.

In the first public sector case (*Gerser v. Lago Vista Independent School District*), the Court ruled that a school district is not liable for sexual harassment of a student if supervisory individuals were not aware of the incident and, therefore, were unable to ignore or act to prevent the harassment. In the second public sector case (*Faragher v. City of Boca Raton*), two male supervisors allegedly engaged in offensive touching and made offensive comments to two female lifeguards, who eventually resigned. The city had not distributed its antiharassment policy among its beach staff, and the lifeguards had not reported the incidents until long after leaving their positions.

Lower courts ruled in favor of the city, but the Supreme Court decided that the city could be held liable since the actions occurred in areas under ostensible city jurisdiction. The decision did give the employer the right to defend itself by arguing that it took reasonable action in harassment situations or if the victims failed to report the harassment or file a grievance of equal opportunity complaint procedures.

A Case Study of Failure in Policy Implementation

The failure of the fight to end corruption in the custodial system of the New York City public schools was the topic of a case research study reported in the July/August 2002 issue of *Public Administration Review.* While serving as counsel to the Special Commissioner of Investigation for the school system, attorney Lydia Segal (2002) directed investigations of corruption and malfeasance among custodians and administrators in the city's 1,200 schools.

Public reformers have long contended that corruption in public agencies can be effectively controlled by measures such as improved oversight, increased regulation, internal audits, sanctions, surveillance, structural reorganizations, and performance accountability systems. However, Segal (2002) found these and other controls unable to end corruption in the New York City school custodial system. Decades of entrenched corruption had produced a "deeply corrupt system" that continued to resist reform after more than eighty years of efforts to cleanse the system. The school system custodial unit has an annual budget of nearly a half-billion dollars and a workforce of 8,500. It is the largest and most expensive such system in the United States. A policy of reform was initiated by the state legislature in 1993 and 1994. However, management's failure to implement the control measures enabled in the legislation resulted in failure of all efforts to eliminate corruption in the custodial system.

Segal (2002) employed a three-part data-gathering approach in her research. First, she examined a number of commission findings and published reports that included more than thirty study reports produced by government agencies and nonprofit organizations, hundreds of newspaper articles, and unpublished government documents. The government documents included city and state audits of the system, grand jury reports, investigative reports, and transcripts of secretly recorded conversations with custodians.

Second, Segal (2002) conducted a number of in-depth interviews with senior and midlevel managers at the Board of Education and the custodial system's parent organization, the Division of School Facilities. She also interviewed many school principals, system and government auditors, investigators, and city officials. The third leg of her investigation involved participant observation carried out during her tenure as special counsel for the school district investigation commission. While engaged in that activity, she interviewed many witnesses and informants employed at all levels of the school system.

Segal's case research led her to conclude that one of the main reasons why extensive reform attempts have failed to curtail corruption in the custodial system was a failure of management to identify with reform objectives. One reason for this failure was that top management has become influenced by groups—the *dominant coalition*—with agendas that conflict with the reform attempt. Accordingly, when this happens, the dominant groups "gain power over official decision making and set up an organization's real agenda to reflect their own, not the public, interest. If corruption controls threaten its power, the dominant coalition will seek to block the enforcement of controls" (Segal 2002, 450–51).

The custodian's labor union was cited as one of the organizations that blocked genuine reform of the system. When top management abrogated its responsibility and failed to support the reform mission, it sided with the union against "even the most sensible law enforcement suggestions to reduce abuse." Moreover,

> The reform pitfalls highlighted [in the study] . . . have implications for many agencies battling systematic corruption. An ingrained culture of deviance and management's failure to enforce rules, rather than their absences or inadequacy, for example, can help explain the persistence of corruption in agencies ranging from the New York Police Department, where scandals crest every 20 years or so despite decades of various corruption controls . . . to Medicare programs, where the FBI has been fighting fraud for over a decade with little sign that it is diminishing. (Segal 2002, 455)

The conclusion that some may draw from this case research is that it is futile to rely on traditional redress devices when seeking to reform deeply corrupt organizations. Segal (2002) disabuses this pessimistic view, however, by describing the early successes of efforts to reform the Chicago custodial system. Corruption in that system began to decline in 1995 when the Illinois state legislature passed the Chicago School Reform Act.

That legislation gave a new executive appointed by the mayor wide powers to privatize many services affecting a number of public employee classes. A doubling of the number of inspectors in the school inspector general's office, establishment of a new fraud hotline, and privatization of the school internal audit unit have also helped derail corruption and fraud in the Chicago school custodial system. Stiff penalties are also being handed down for persons convicted or fraud; in 1996, for example, a school facilities director was sentenced to forty-one months in federal prison for extortion and kickbacks.

A Three-Case Analysis of Public Management Reform

Professor Lois Wise of Indiana University carried out a 2002 case research study on forces behind the adoption of new public management reforms that occurred during the 1980s and 1990s in Norway, Sweden, and the United States. In contrast to the more commonly used model of government transformation resulting from economics and market-based forces, Wise employed three social and values-oriented factors as the analysis framework for this study: demands for social equity, greater democratization and citizen empowerment, and improved humanization of public administration; each is defined in Table 11.1.

The drive toward greater efficiency and accountability in government that resulted in adoption of many market-based innovations in the three study countries was also influenced by these three social forces. Of possibly more importance, they

Table 11.1

Social Factors Driving Public Management Reforms

Factor	Meaning and Examples
Demands for social equity	Grounded in theories of distributive justice, this movement has resulted in efforts to promote socioeconomic equality. Programs include equal opportunity and fair compensation for public sector work and laws prohibiting discrimination within and between the private and public sectors.
Democratization and citizen empowerment	This trend influences programs to provide greater citizen access to power and accountability in government. Programs include promoting greater citizen involvement in government decisions, participative decision making and the use of cross-functional and self-directed work teams, and empowerment of employees and stakeholder groups.
Humanization of public service	Humanization in public service refers to programs designed to improve the quality of work life and human relations programs that promote the acceptance and celebration of diversity in the workforce; it also includes such employee satisfaction-centered programs as job enrichment and cross-training, paternity and maternity leaves, and person-friendly human resource policies and practices (such as flexible work schedules).

Source: Wise (2002).

continue to play a role in government reforms. The conclusion that can be drawn from this three-country case study is that multiple factors—not just economic and market-based—contribute to the way that government reforms are shaped. These additional factors were not uniform in their adoption or form in the three countries studied. However, their existence supports the conclusion that a pattern of "expanding social equity" took place both within government and in society in general.

Norway and Sweden appeared to be more successful than the United States in achieving pay equality, while the United States has made greater strides in implementing management of workplace diversity programs. A larger proportion of public sector jobs are held by women in the Nordic countries than in the United States. Humanization in the public sector is a common trend in the three countries, although it was found to be somewhat more developed in Norway and Sweden.

Summary

Case research in public policy tends to focus on phenomena within three broad areas or themes: (1) policies that direct agency actions, (2) policies regarding the production and delivery of government services, and (3) policies on performance monitoring and enhancement of government services. The focus of case research in policy focuses on policy formulation and the changes in management practices and procedures that are employed in implementation.

Case research in public policy focuses on such basic questions as what government should do and should not do, how much it should be involved in society, and how it should be financed. These questions involve politics and the polity. Thus, case research in this area tends to illustrate the influence of politics on the pro and con, success or failure of issues in policy formulation and/or implementation. Case research on public policy addresses many different aspects of policy formulation and implementation.

Changes in policies and practices in public management have been brought about by a number of factors. The two most commonly proposed drivers of change have been economics and market-based changes. Such factors as demands for greater social equity, democratization and empowerment in government and among the polity, and humanization of the public sector have also helped bring about these reforms.

Note

1. *Ex ante* and *ex post* refer to legal bases for policy and legislation. Ex ante legislation focuses on the factors leading up to an action or decision—the antecedents of an issue. Ex post focuses on the results or effects of an action or phenomenon (Sindico 2005).

➤ 12 ◄

Case Research in Performance Management

A worldwide movement toward the use of performance management in both the public and private sectors has been occurring, especially over the past decade. "Performance management" focuses on planned performance and improvement over time. It applies to both organizations and individuals in the organization.
—Howard Risher and Charles H. Fay (2007)

A key theme in much of the public administration case research published during the 1990s and the first decade of the twenty-first century focuses on the shift to policies and practices that have come to be known as public management. Some observers believe that the managerial approach to government has replaced (or is about to replace) the traditional view of government operations in which the bureaucracy is the core concept in public administration. Countries such as Australia, New Zealand, the United Kingdom, Sweden, and Norway are often pointed to as leaders in this movement, with the United States not far behind.

The public management model has spawned a new global view of governance that has been collectively labeled as the new public management (NPM). Under NPM, the processes of performance management are applied both internally and externally (Milward 1996; Lane 2000; Kettl 2005). That is, they apply to both the organization and to individual government workers. The emphasis in this chapter is on case research on performance management activities as adopted in government organizations.

The Framework for Performance Management

The guiding principles of new public management focus on three core activities: (1) performance management, (2) strategic management, and (3) administrative reform. The first of these, performance management, includes comparative benchmarking, performance standards, measurement, and performance-based rewards systems (Ammons and Riverbank 2008). Its core objective is improving government performance and accountability.

Strategic management is the second core concept in performance management. It includes planning the operations of government agencies to reflect leadership's perceptions of such long-term trends as globalization, global warming, human capital planning to adjust to diversity in the workplace, and related environmental factors.

Administrative reform includes changing service delivery approaches by forming networks and collaborations patterned after market-based structures—that is, a greater reliance on contracting out the delivery of public services and selected internal operational activities. This reform is only the latest in a long history of efforts to reform the bureaucracy. Earlier efforts included such change management programs as reinventing government, reengineering work processes, and enterprise transformation that focuses on integration of information and communications technology into agency operations.

Performance management in government also refers to allowing the market (i.e., citizen demand) dictate the level and type of government services provided to citizens and selection of the mode of delivery for those services (Heinrich 2003). Prisons and schools run by private, for-profit businesses, privatization of military base housing, and similar services provided by nongovernment organizations under contract with a government organization are examples of a growing market orientation.

In some governments, the level of resources made available to agency administrators is based on a measurement of stakeholder satisfaction or program effectiveness. Underlying this theme is the revolutionary idea that few government programs are expected to last forever, and thus no government job is a permanent sinecure.

One of the fundamental questions behind governments' adoption of public management principles is, How can we improve the level and quality of the services we deliver to out citizens?

Donald Kettl has been following the public management movement since the first national conference on the topic in 1991. Two of the six core reform components of the public management movement he identified in 2005 are (1) improving services delivery through such devices as benchmarking and performance measurement and (2) decentralizing the delivery of government services—that is, moving delivery from providers' convenience closer to where, when, and how the services are needed and wanted by citizens. Each of these trends is discussed in greater detail in this chapter, with several cases illustrating the level and scope of case research in these practices.

Improving Government Services

Improvements in service delivery reforms focus on strengthening the ethos of service that characterizes the actions of public servants. It involves changing the internal focus on maintaining the stability of the organization by an unwillingness to change that is said to exist in many agencies to an external focus on meeting the needs of citizens and other stakeholders. For some time, big government was seen as unwilling to respond to citizens. Rebuilding and reinforcing the level of service orientation among government workers is a key objective of service delivery reforms. Cases in three approaches to delivery improvements presented in the first half of this chapter focus on such issues as the ethos of public service, continuous product and process improvements, and use of e-learning to improve government workers' qualifications.

By any measure, state government in the United States is big and getting bigger. While local government continues to grow, the federal government is shrinking in size, if not in dollars spent. The 2007 census of governments reported a total of 89,527 individual federal, state, and local governments—more than 2,500 more than the nearly 87,000 reported in the 2002 census. This number included 3,033 counties, 37,381 special local districts (such as library, fire, noxious weeds, mosquito abatement, etc.), 29,122 school districts, and 36,011 municipalities and townships (U.S. Census Bureau 2008b).

State and local governments employed more than 16.1 million full-time equivalent workers in 2006 (latest year available), an increase of slightly less than 2.5 percent over the 15.7 million workers in 2002, when the previous census took place. State and local payrolls grew at a much faster rate, however. The payroll for all state and local government was $60.7 billion in 2006—a more than 13.3 percent increase over the $52.6 billion in 2002 (sums include all state and local administrative, resources, utilities, public safety, and primary and secondary education expenditures).

While employment in state and local governments has continued to grow, civilian employment in the federal government has declined nearly every year since 1989, when the size of the federal civilian workforce peaked at 3.23 million workers. Federal civilian employment bottomed out at 2.69 million civilian workers. In 2006 the number of federal workers (2.7 million) remained roughly the same as it had been in 2002. What small increase did occur may have been largely due to formation of the new Department of Homeland Security in 2002.

Despite holding employment numbers steady, the federal civilian payroll has continued to increase; it was $991 billion in 1989, $1.3 trillion in 2002, and $1.6 trillion in 2006 (U.S. Census Bureau 2008a). With personnel and payroll numbers this large, it should not be surprising that government executives, legislators, managers, and taxpayers continue to be interested in improving the way that governments at all levels do their work.

What to Improve: Efficiency or Effectiveness?

Administrators and legislators trying to improve government services direct their change strategies toward one of two often contradictory objectives: They seek to improve the efficiency of government workers, or they try to improve the effectiveness of government programs. The efficiency approach focuses on producing or providing more (or better) government services with the same or reduced resources.

Because employee compensation continues to be the major cost factor in providing government services, improvement efforts have long focused on improving government efficiency (Frates 2004). This approach includes, but is not limited to, improving the quality of services delivery, during which limiting resources becomes a secondary consideration. Improving customer service has become an improvement goal for many government managers. To measure their progress on improvement initiatives, nearly all government managers have implemented some type of performance measurement program aimed at improving efficiency.

In a continuing series of efforts to improve the effectiveness and efficiency of government, Congress passed the Government Performance and Results Act (GPRA) in 1993. The law requires all federal government agencies to develop strategic plans and establish methods for measuring outcomes. Similar efforts implemented in earlier years failed to accomplish the desired goal of improving services and their delivery. Greater hope was held for GPRA, however, because Congress got behind the program and passed it. The Office of Management and Budget uses the GPRA to shape agency programs. Kettl (2005) predicted that GPRA may have greater staying power than earlier attempts.

Improvements in the effectiveness of government services can take more than one form (Epstein 1982). Government managers may seek to improve their decisions in several areas: policy formulation and implementation, effectiveness of government programs, program delivery systems, and their internal organizations and their interactions with other agencies at the same or different levels. Table 12.1 compares types of government improvement programs, the type of benefits accruing from their achievement, and the form of value received by managers of the agencies that succeed in their implementation.

Benchmarking for Process Improvement

Benchmarking is a core concept in performance management. In government, it is the practice of identifying what leaders in the field are doing and adapting these strategies to provide government services in the best possible way. The president of the Xerox Corporation, the firm that became the leading exponent of this process, defined benchmarking as "the continuous process of measuring products, services, and practices against the toughest competitors or those companies recognized as industry leaders" (Kearnes 1986, 20). This also applies to government organizations and public sector.

Benchmarking goes beyond simply emulating industry or sector leaders. It is a continuous process of research for new ways of doing things: new methods, practices, and processes. It means adopting best practices or adapting their best features and implementing them to incorporate the best of the best into one's own

Table 12.1

Government Improvement Efforts, Benefits, and Types of Value Received

Type of Improvement	Form of Benefit Products	Form of Value Received
Improved policy decisions	Resources are shifted to higher priority community needs.	Reallocated resources result in increased value to the public as their needs are better met by tax dollars; value cannot be expressed in a hard dollar value.
Improved effectiveness of service performance	Government services are made more responsive to needs of service recipients and greater impact on program outcomes.	Recipients gain in value of services as their needs are better met; value cannot be expressed in a hard dollar value.
Improved efficiency of service delivery	More service is provided for the same level of resources committed; can be measured as lower cost per unit of service delivered.	A hard dollar value of increased efficiency can be calculated and expressed as real savings, avoidance of cost increases, or both.
Improved operations	Transformational change is enabled in organizations, with greater employee creativity, effectiveness, and efficiency; can also result in greater employee satisfaction and motivation.	Government operations increase in value to the public as their ability to change and improve is enhanced; difficult to express in a hard dollar value.

Source: Epstein (1982).

organization (Camp 1989). Benchmarking is both the practice of using the performance results of another organization or agency as a standard of performance by which to compare one's own performance and selecting a target goal toward which an organization will strive to achieve or emulate.

Three models of benchmarking have been implemented at one time or another by government managers. The first is the corporate comparative model, common in the private sector. The second is a benchmark-as-target approach that is often written about in the public management literature. The third is a model for the comparison of performance statistics. It is probably the most commonly used model in government (Ammons, Coe, and Lombardo 2001).

The performance statistics model is similar to the corporate model, but the performance standards are never arbitrary. Rather, they are derived from performance targets that are found externally. Examples include such published performance achievements as professional standards, performance averages found in regional or national statistics, or targets set and reached by comparable agencies or units. The target performance objectives are usually set after the collection of statistics for a variety of activities or functions; this approach seldom includes the detailed analysis of work processes that is a core element in corporate benchmarking.

Ammons, Coe, and Lombardo (2001) compared three cases of benchmarking applications in their case on performance management in local government. The projects were the result of the participants' desire for greater reliability of the data they use for comparisons. Two of the projects examined in this multicase study were national, one sponsored by Innovation Groups (IG) and the other by the International City/County Management Association (ICMA). The third, which was instigated locally by a group of North Carolina city managers and coordinated by the school of government at the University of North Carolina–Chapel Hill, targeted participating local governments in that state. The next section includes selected results for each of the three projects.

The Innovation Groups Project Case

The Innovation Groups (IG) is a networking association for cities and counties that focuses on innovation and transformation in local government. The group partners with the ICMA and Arizona State University. In 1991, the IG formed a national benchmarking center to collect performance measurement data from cities and counties. The group compiled the data for other jurisdictions to use for benchmarking comparisons.

The IG staff measured some thirty programs; they prepared measures of resource inputs, outputs, efficiency, effectiveness, and productivity for each program. Participating organizations were charged a $750 fee. Data questionnaires were distributed on diskettes; only about half of the initial seventy-five participating government units returned completed questionnaires. The data collection method was changed to a new Web site, but participants considered the questionnaires to be too complicated. Eventually, they were reduced to a dozen or fewer questions for each program.

When only about thirty jurisdictions were still using the site several years after its introduction, the program was considered too costly for its size and was discontinued. The authors concluded that the program failed because the lack of control over the accuracy of the data during collection and interpretation resulted in doubts about the data's reliability.

The ICMA Project Case

The ICMA Center for Performance Measurement began in 1994 with thirty-four cities and counties with populations greater than 200,000. The program was limited to four core local government services: public safety, fire services, neighborhood services (including code enforcement, housing opportunities, parks and recreation, libraries, road maintenance, refuse collection, and street lighting), and support services (including facilities and fleet management, human resources, information technology, purchasing, and risk management).

A voluntary policy committee of city managers and other managers guided the program direction and scope. This group was later changed to a ten-member steering committee of two members each from each of the four service areas and two fiscal at-large members. Priority was given to identifying and gathering data seen as core determinants of service performance.

As of 2008, the ICMA performance management center was still a going concern (ICMA 2008). From its initial group of forty-four cities and counties, the program has grown to more than 220 communities in the United States and Canada. Data collection produces information for benchmarking and internal performance review comparisons.

North Carolina Local Government Project Case

The North Carolina Local Government Performance Measurement Project was organized in 1995 to provide concerned managers in the seven largest cities in the state with performance statistics and reliable cost data. It was expanded in 1996 to include a county component; a year later a third unit was organized to serve small and medium-sized cities and counties. Eventually thirty-five cities and counties participated in the project. The city project provided data on three services: solid waste collection, police, and street maintenance. The county study included four services: building and environment inspections, emergency medical services, jail operations, and selected social services that focus on children.

Results Assessment

Participants reported that involvement in the programs provided substantial benefits through improved communications with their counterparts in other communities, identified possible alternative approaches to service delivery, and highlighted common problems. Only a few respondents said participation resulted in tangible cost savings or program or service improvements, although four of the ICMA and North Carolina participants indicated their participation resulted in substantial program or service improvements. Finally, the three projects both benefited and suffered from the high expectations of their early participants; results could not come close to achieving the results that planners believed would accrue.

Measuring Performance for Performance Improvement

As shown, performance management in government includes several of the core issues in public management; it is particularly extant in the areas of productivity, market emphasis, and accountability. Performance management begins with stated objectives, includes strategies to accomplish those objectives, and measures progress. It is the idea behind attempts to implement performance-based pay and other incentives among government managers and administrators.

Jeannette Taylor (2006) analyzed the performance measurement systems of government finance departments in Australia and Hong Kong in a two-case comparison study. The systems were evaluated against five criteria often recommended for performance measures: validity, legitimacy, credibility, public accessibility, and functionality. A key objective of the study was evaluation of how well the two governments were able to meet these five criteria.

The performance management system in Australia evolved over a two-phase adoption process. The initial steps were put in place from 1987 to 1997 under a Labor government, which introduced a systematic and centralized approach to performance measurement. A policy requiring department managers to follow centralized guidelines was implemented. The second phase began in 1997 with election of a conservative coalition government. The centralized approach gave way to a policy of a minimal and devolved approach, under which department managers are encouraged rather than directed in their performance measurement processes.

The Australian accrual-based, outcome-and-outputs system was set in place to improve public accountability and the departments' corporate governance. The Department of Finance and Administration (DoFA) encourages rather than directs government departments in their performance measurement efforts. Responsibility for the performance measurement system is shared between the DoFA and the Australian Public Service Commission.

Under the last U.K. governor of Hong Kong, Chris Patten, the government began implementation of a system of performance measurement pledges in 1992 that were modeled after the U.K. citizens' charter system. The objective was to encourage a new customer orientation among government workers in order to improve the quality of public service. This led to development of the Hong Kong Efficiency Unit (EU) program. The performance measurement system is now largely state planned and state managed. The EU's progress toward its goal of promoting measurable transformation in the management and delivery of public services was measured according to a performance measurement framework that follows the Kaplan and Norton (1996) balanced scorecard approach.

A Problem Metric in Florida

In a case study of Florida's methods for making comparisons between the performance of private and government delivery of services, Fernandez and Fabricant (2000) compared the state of Florida's biased method for making comparisons between public and private service providers with a follow-up comparison using random selection of cases for examination. Their analysis concluded with recommendations on ways to avoid such problems in the evaluation process.

The primary objective of this study was to determine the effectiveness of research methodology used by the state to compare the relative efficiency of private versus state agency service providers. Compared were the results of the collection of delinquent child support payments from an absent parent. The initial report indicated the state agency produced a collection rate that was 307 percent greater than that of the private or contracted group. The agency's cost-benefit ratio was approximately 109 percent greater than that of the private contractor.

In the second comparison, however, the state agency had a 19 percent collection rate compared with a collection rate of 22.2 percent for the private firm. Cost-benefit ratios were also better for the contractors, with ratios of 5.27 and 4.56 for the state and the contractors, respectively.

Fernandez and Fabricant (2000) revealed that the study design was fatally flawed. The agency success report was based on a sample that represented the total population of cases, whereas the sample worked on by the private firm represented only those cases that had been delinquent for longer than six months and which the state agency had been working on unsuccessfully for the six-month period. Fernandez and Fabricant suggested that a negative correlation probably existed for the period of time a case was delinquent, and the probability of collecting owed child support was low. Had similar samples been used, the researchers would most likely not have replicated the heavily biased results they produced with the faulty design.

Decentralization Programs in Government

Decentralization changes the center of decisions and management control of the administration of government services. In federal systems, decentralization has involved moving power and responsibility to lower levels of government, nongovernment and nonprofit organizations, and outsourcing with firms in the private sector. Typical of the underlying questions being asked by government managers planning decentralization programs is: Should traditional government services such as urban renewal, education, public assistance, public safety, corrections, and similar activities be managed at the national, state, or local level, by government or nonprofit organizations, or by public or private-sector businesses? Decentralization implementation has also raised questions regarding such actions as giving frontline public managers more power to make decisions. Case research in three closely related themes in decentralization—collaboration, partnerships, and networks—is examined next.

Much case research being conducted in the area of decentralization of government operations has focused on problems encountered informing collaborative structures—a concern that a number of agencies hold in common. Collaboration is one of the main ways that government agencies achieve decentralization. The two key approaches to collaboration in government are partnerships and networks (Kamensky and Burlin 2004; Linden 2002; Schaeffer and Loveridge 2002).

Governments collaborate to bring diverse and often widely distributed expert knowledge and skills together to exercise their joint efforts, resources, and management decision making to provide public goods and services. All members of the group of units contribute to the operation, and all share ownership in the product or service produced. According to Kamensky and Burlin (2004), the focus of their

Table 12.2

Some Collaboration Approaches Found in the Federal Government

Collaboration Models

1. Within a department, such as Agriculture, Defense, or Homeland Security
2. Across departments, such as Justice and Homeland Security
3. Between federal and state governments, such as Transportation
4. Between federal and municipal, such as the FBI and local police departments
5. Between federal, state, and municipal, such as clean water and clean air
6. Between sectors of the economy, such as government and business corrections
7. Between government and nonprofit organizations, such as faith-based delivery
8. Between government, business, and nonprofits, such as welfare and education
9. Between federal agencies and international organizations, such as the WTO
10. Between federal and a single nation, such as drug enforcement
11. Between federal and more than one nation, such as air traffic control

Source: Kamensky and Burlin (2004).

collaborative effort is on producing or implementing a government service. Collaborative models fall on a continuum of arrangements that range from loosely associated groups or individuals with common interest in a topic to formal, contract-based networks or partnerships that reach across separate organizations, levels of government, and sectors of the economy. Table 12.2 lists models of collaboration used in government.

Collaborating Through Networks

The exercise of collaborative effort in any of these approaches may be formal or informal. Networks tend to be the most informal approach, often consisting of loose relationships among diverse organizations. Each member of the network has some voluntary obligation to act on some agreed-upon action. Successful networks display five characteristics in common: shared vision and trust, independent members, voluntary links between members, multiple leaders, and clearly defined roles (Kamensky, Burlin, and Abramson 2004, 10).

Communities of interest and communities of practice are examples of collaborative networks (Snyder and Briggs 2004; McNabb, Gibson, and Finnie 2006). Although they have existed for years, these networks have only relatively recently been recognized as mechanisms for turning raw data into useful information, and then turning information into knowledge. Both types of communities can also be important building blocks in developing a culture of knowledge sharing that helps create learning organizations.

Communities of interest, in which membership and contact are voluntary, tend to be far less formal than communities of practice. In some agencies a community of interest is used as a synonym for a community of practice. However, although their fundamental goals are similar, their functions and organizational benefits are structurally and operationally quite different. Typically, a community of interest is formed by an already existing group—such as a work team or a department or unit—with a vested interest in the delivery of the service. A community of practice is more commonly an informal group of persons, often widely dispersed geographically, who share a passionate interest in the topic, product, or service. The U.S. Army's company commander community of interest is an example of a widely distributed interest group.

A Community of Interest Case

The case study of an early community of interest formed by the Federal Highway Administration (FHWA) is another example of how a community can build on and use information technology tools. Mike Burk, the Highway Administration's senior knowledge officer, helped create one of the earliest and most-often cited best models in the federal government (Snyder and Briggs 2004).

The FHWA recognized that an informal community of interest was forming with federal, state, and local highway and safety personnel using the Internet to share knowledge about highway rumble strips. Rumble strips are the serrated bands installed along the outer edge or center of highway paving that produce a loud rumble noise when driven over. They are designed to let drivers know they are about to drive off the highway or cross lanes into oncoming traffic. They are particularly useful for alerting drowsy drivers before an accident occurs.

Contact between members of the community of interest was more often than not via e-mail or through information available on the lead agency's Web site. For example, the knowledge-sharing activities of the group were supported by the Web site http://safety.fhwa.dot.gov/roadway_dept/rumble/index. This site was created and maintained in a collaborative effort by the knowledge manager for the FHWA's New York division, an FHWA marketing specialist, several highway safety engineers, and an outside consultant. Anyone with an interest in highway construction and safety can access the site for reports from states that have installed the devices, descriptions of the various types available, word on some of their drawbacks, and a short video on the various types of strips and how they are installed.

Communities of Practice

A community of practice is a group of people with like interests, knowledge, concerns, skills, and training who come together in some social situation, such as an informal meeting or conference, to share what they do and don't know. The purpose of these sessions is often to provide an opportunity for members to learn from one another. This sharing of knowledge makes it possible for all members of the community to learn—because of instant feedback, this means that the individual doing the sharing will also learn. Learning by sharing is similar to learning by doing; it may not result in the tacit knowledge of a skill that is forged through years or decades on a job, but it does help avoid repeating the learning failures that may have occurred in the past (Ash and Cohendet 2004).

A community of practice has also been defined as a tightly knit group of members of some organization who participate in a shared task or practice (Wasko and Faraj 2005). The members know each other and work together. They usually meet face-to-face and are continually engaged in negotiating, communicating, and coordinating with each other directly. Interacting in this way, communities of practice are able to perform the following functions for organizations (Snyder and Briggs 2004):

- They develop, collect, and enhance the knowledge assets of organizations.
- Operating as social learning systems, practitioners connect with each other to solve problems, share ideas, set standards, and develop informal relationships with peers and stakeholders.
- They complement the information-transmitting of units in organizations that have the primary purpose of delivering a product or service.
- They typically bridge formal organizational boundaries, thereby increasing the collective store of knowledge, skills, and professional trust and reciprocity.

Collaborating Through Partnerships

Collaborating through the forming of formal partnering agreements refers to governments' use of third-party or nongovernmental organizations to deliver or administer what are considered to be public services. The approach to collaboration has long been a popular way to deliver federal services through local organizations. The approaches used in these partnerships include grants, contracts, and official memoranda.

There are two major types of collaboration memoranda. The first, the memorandum of agreement, is the more formal of the two and is often a legally binding, written instrument between parties in a partnership. The second, the memorandum of understanding, is a document that spells out a level of mutual understanding of something between parties; it is similar to but slightly more formal than a gentleman's agreement. In law, it is a synonym for a letter of intent.

In practice, partnerships can be between agencies on the same level, between agencies or government bodies across levels, between government agencies and nonprofit organizations, or between government agencies and private businesses. The public–private model has been defined as a partnership that works

> together in the provision of service, financing, and development of infrastructure, and the administration of government. [It represents] a cooperative venture between the public and private sectors, builds on the expertise of each partner, that best meets clearly defined public needs through the appropriate allocation of resources, risks, and rewards. . . . The essence is the sharing of risks. (Klitgaard and Trenton 2004, 11)

Thus, for any of the three types of partnerships to be considered to be high-performing, it must be organized in such a way that individual member organizations share authority, resources, and accountability for achieving the mutually agreed upon target objective. For the partnership to achieve sustainability, to be around year after year, it must periodically post significant results. Otherwise, the partnership will be seen as a paper tiger and quickly go the way of the thousands of other failed government initiatives.

Other Drivers of Administrative Reform

Not all of the case research in government reform focuses on traditional themes found in the global NPM movement. In fact, there is a considerable effort under way to stop using NPM as the collective label for the reforms that have been occurring in public management since the 1970s. Critics of the term have concluded that NPM "is no longer new, not clearly defined, and not a useful construct" (Wise 2002, 564). Instead, a number of researchers have turned to a different paradigm, one that focuses on social rather than economic foundations.

Traditional administrative reform is a key element of the NPM movement; this model emphasizes ways to reform government for greater efficiency through the implementation of such market-based operational activities as performance management, performance-based pay, and privatization of services.

Examples of forces other than those in NPM that influence administrative reform include changes in attitudes, opinions, values, and tastes of citizens; effects of economic development and the evolution of social and economic institutions; and the addition, loss, and reinterpretation of knowledge and technology. An example of case research in this model is the comparative study that focused on reforms in government that were shaped by three sets of social values as drivers of administrative changes (Wise 2002).

The stated objective of this case research was to establish the validity of previous research assertions that many threads of administrative reforms have always been present and that forces driving change exist even if they do not occupy the same popularity of NPM-related reforms (Wise 2002). Rather than focusing on the economic and budgetary restraints that are common in many studies of organizational change, Wise focused on social values as drivers of administrative reform.

The values Wise (2002) considered to be particularly relevant to public administration reform were (1) demands for greater social equity, (2) democratization and empowerment, and (3) humanization of government. This case study examined the impact that these related sets of social values have had in influencing government reforms in general, and then compared their influence in Norway, Sweden, and the United States.

Social equity refers to such themes as egalitarianism, welfare, equality, and a just society. It is the force behind the just distribution of public goods and services and the standards of fair and equal treatment. This force has influenced government reforms in the United States since the Progressive Era, and it is common in Scandinavia. It is manifested in policies, laws, and agreements that prohibit discrimination, promote tolerance and fair treatment in public sector employment, and value diversity and more democratic treatment of government workers.

Greater Democratization in the Workforce

The role that the demand for greater democratization in the public workforce, together with the empowerment of government workers, has had on administrative reform is the second of the three social forces discussed in this case (Wise 2002). The benefits organizations enjoy from greater employee participation and commitment have long been recognized. Examples of such benefits that are also common elements in the NPM movement include a flattening of organizations by eliminating management layers; more informal coordination and communication; reduced dependence upon the hierarchy of command and control; and involving staff in determining agency goals, objectives, and strategic planning. Efforts to move more women, minorities, and the disadvantaged into positions of leadership are also part of the NPM movement.

Humanization—considered the most important trend in public administration during the middle of the last century—continues to influence administrative reforms more than sixty years later. Wise (2002) provided this definition and scope of the humanization trend:

> The human side of public administration is linked to concerns for the quality of working life and philosophies that see employees as whole persons with different needs and interests that must be balanced. The human side of public administration emphasizes involvement and greater engagement. It also involves efforts to incorporate democratic values into public administration. (Wise 2002, 558)

Other Humanization-Related Reforms

Beyond public employment, humanization has influenced reforms in employment for all employees and citizens by government enacting legislation that centers on programs to improve the life of citizens at work and away from work. Reforms have included programs that promote skills training and retraining, provision of educational opportunities for all citizens, mandated improvements to the quality of work life through safer work site environments, and many other human resources development advances.

Wise (2002) concluded that the research supported the contention that competing drivers of administrative reform remain in force, even when they do not dominate reform movements. Moreover, the examination of the role of the three social forces supports the argument that many factors contribute to the form that reform movements take in different countries. Wise found similar patterns of expanding social equity in each of the three countries examined; democratization and empowerment have resulted in similar efforts to improve opportunities for women and minorities; and humanization, while existing in all three countries, is more developed in Norway and Sweden than it is in the United States.

Summary

This chapter examined some of the case research on developments shaping the concept of public management, with a focus on two aspects of this trend in administrative reform: improving government service through benchmarking and performance measurement and the decentralization of government services through the use of networks and collaborations. Programs promoting greater humanization of the workplace were also noted as topics for case research.

In addition, the chapter looked at how public management programs associated with the new public management trend have been implemented to increase the efficiency and effectiveness of public workers and public programs. Questions regarding the continued efficacy of the NPM paradigm were also brought to light.

➤ 13 ◀

Case Research in Sustainable Government

Sustainability—meeting the needs of the present generation without compromising the ability of future generations to meet their own needs—is an overarching value that requires best practices at every level of organization. Public sector fiscal sustainability is a crucial part of this definition.
—Jeffrey I. Chapman (2008)

Sustainability has become an important policy concern and strategic planning target for government organizations at all levels. While few would concede that achieving "true sustainability" any time in the near future is not possible, governing units around the globe are implementing policies and programs with the objective of working toward achieving that goal (Agyeman and Evans 2003; Astleithner and Hamedinger 2003; Ulhøi 2004).

While there appears to be no single accepted definition of sustainability, the one used by Agyeman and Evans (2003) follows the commonly used definitions proposed by the World Commission on Environment and Development (WCED) and the International Union for the Conservation of Nature (IUCN 1991): Sustainability is "the need to ensure a better quality of life for all, now and into the future, in a just and equitable manner, whilst living within the limits of supporting ecosystems" (WCED 1987, 36).

In its report to Congress on its strategic plan for 2008–2012, the U.S. Government Accountability Office (GAO) identified seven themes that served as the framework around which its five-year program of work would revolve. Managing advancements in science and technology for achieving sustainability in economic growth and the quality of life was one of those key programmatic themes. Seven functional areas are included within the science and technology theme: (1) managing science and technology to facilitate growth in productivity and the economy, (2) information and communications technology, (3) cybersecurity and personal privacy, (4) data quality and reliability, (5) space exploration, (6) elections and citizen involvement, and (7) humanity and research ethics. The GAO report also described the importance of science and technology to sustainability in these terms:

> Science and technology influence every aspect of life. While information technology is a major force today—linking individuals, organizations, and economies around the world—other kinds of scientific and technological advances are also creating significant changes. Developments in science and technology present great opportunities to improve the quality of life, the performance of the economy and the government, and the relationship of government to citizens. (GAO 2007, 2)

Science and technology was included as one of the key elements of the GAO's focus because it is now, and will most likely continue to be, the single most important contributor to the ability of governments at all levels to achieve their goals of sustainability. International, national, state, and local governments depend on science and technology to come up with solutions for the many constraining factors that are affecting the capacity of governments around the globe to achieve their sustainability goals.

Among these constraining factors are population growth and aging of the population, rising health care costs, unsustainable energy consumption and the continued dependence upon fossil fuels, global climate change, depletion of natural resources, air and water pollution, and growing diversity in the nation's population (GAO 2007).

Science and technology contribute significantly to a society's ability to maintain economic growth. Technology particularly helps integrate that ability into government organizations' operations. Because it can collect, store, and make available knowledge and information in real time, technology makes elements of the organizational culture—its strategies, capabilities, and capacities—available to all personnel at all organizational levels (Hill and Jones 2001). Thus, one of the major justifications for continuing to make substantial investments in new technology is that its application is necessary for achieving sustainable government operations.

Declining Faith in Science to Achieve Sustainability

Science is no longer the "favored child" of the federal government. In the decades following Word War II, 70 percent of the research and development in the world came from the United States. Today, that percentage has dropped to less than 30 percent. Moreover, U.S. funding of basic research has steadily decreased. Although the share of research done by the private sector has increased, business and industry are not willing to fund much pure research (GAO 2007).

Questions of research ethics and scientific misconduct are a major concern in the strategic focus of the GAO. Incidents of poor quality and low reliability data have reduced citizens' trust in the scientific community and the role of government in funding that research. Case research has brought to light the mismanagement responsible for the Challenger explosion, the approval of thalidomide for use by pregnant women, and the Tuskegee syphilis study (and studies like it, considered to be breaches of research ethics).

Assessing Development Sustainability

Developing tools for conducting assessments of the impact on sustainability of decisions before they are made is a growing area of case research in sustainability and
sustainable governance. Except for the fact that sustainability assessments must be
anticipatory and future directed, the design of such tools need not be very different
from traditional environmental assessment and planning studies (Gibson 2006).

Box 13.1 displays eight classes of criteria that should be covered in a sustainability assessment tool. The concepts were collected during a meta-analysis of
published literature on sustainability research.

A Sustainability Assessment Application Case

A practical application of the various criteria used to form sustainability measurements focused on developing indicators in a case study of the urban water system of
Toronto, Canada (Sahely, Kennedy, and Adams 2005). The objectives of the study
were to (1) examine different tools used for measuring sustainability, (2) propose a
framework for understanding infrastructure sustainability, (3) propose sustainability
criteria and indicators for infrastructure systems, and (4) apply selected quantified
sustainability indicators for the urban water system of Toronto.

The study focused on key interactions between the infrastructure and three
systems: (1) environmental sustainability, which includes resource use and waste
products; (2) economic sustainability, including capital, operating and maintenance
costs, and investments in innovation; and (3) socioeconomic sustainability, including accessibility and health and safety. From the environmental point of view, a
more sustainable system is one where resource use and residuals are minimized,
while socioeconomic criteria are met when "costs are minimized while investment
in research and development, technology change and innovation, accessibility,
and health and safety are maintained at appropriate levels" (Sahely, Kennedy, and
Adams 2005, 75). Sustainable engineering targets are reached when performance
is maximized or maintained at acceptable levels.

Four levels of environmental sustainability have been suggested for use in
measuring the sustainability of urban water systems. Measurements on each of the
four criteria were used to subjectively place the Toronto system in the appropriate
level of the environmental scale. The following are the four possible categories
(from highest level of sustainability to the lowest):

- Level A: Environmental and health objectives are met; resource use is efficient;
  waste is minimized; and recycling of (wastewater) nutrients and water are in
  place.
- Level B: Environmental protection standards are met or exceeded, but focus
  remains on compliance and output solutions. Regular monitoring of water
  and wastewater quality exists.

Box 13.1

Basic Components of a Practical Sustainability Assessment

Governments, civil society organizations, and private-sector firms around the world are experimenting with various ways of assessing the impact projects and programs will have on their ability to sustain their operations. Many are turning to "triple bottom-line" assessments, with social and ecological factors given the same importance as that traditionally given to economic factors. This emphasis on sustainability reflects a growing consensus that the increasingly interconnected world can no longer support current conditions and levels of degradation of the biosphere. Therefore, environmental impact statements that are required as cost-benefit analyses are increasingly including sustainability assessments as well.

After conducting a meta-analysis of sustainability activities in the public and private sectors, Gibson suggested these eight classes of generic criteria for inclusion in sustainability assessments:

1. Ensuring the long-term integrity of the socioecological system, includ-ing protection of irreplaceable life-support functions.
2. Maintaining human livelihood and growth opportunity without compro-mising future generations' opportunities.
3. Maintaining *intra*generational equity by ensuring that today's choices do not exacerbate gaps between the rich and poor in health, security, growth opportunity, and other factors.
4. Maintaining *inter*generational equity so that future generations will be able to live sustainably.
5. Maintaining resource availability and efficiency (doing more with less) while reducing threats to socioecological systems so that sustainable livelihoods are available for all.
6. Maintaining socioecological civility and democratic governance through more open and better informed discussion, deliberation, and collective responsibility.
7. Taking precautionary action and adapting to rapidly changing condi-tions and requirements, to avoid irreversible damage to the foundations for sustainability.
8. Applying principles of sustainability immediately to gain mutually sup-portive benefits and multiple gains.

Source: Gibson (2006).

- Level C: Minimum standards for environmental protection and health stan-dards are met.
- Level D: Objectives for environmental protection and health and adequate supply are not met; environmental monitoring stands at minimal level.

Using this four-factor classification system, Toronto's urban water system was rated as falling into the B-level of environmental sustainability. This decision was based on an assumption that environmental and energy use norms then in place were in fact sustainable. The researchers pointed out that the case research was not intended to be a comprehensive assessment of the sustainability of the Toronto water system, but instead serve as an example of a process that could be used to select appropriate indicator metrics. The authors concluded with a call for more interdisciplinary research and more comprehensive studies related to sustainable urban infrastructure.

The Human Side of Sustainability

Sustainability is not just about ensuring that financial and physical resources will be available to government so it can do its job (Liebowitz 2004; Nigro and Kellough 2008). It is also about engendering a commitment to human capital development, including ensuring that public employees have the skills and knowledge they will need. It is about cooperation instead of competition between public labor and management. It is also about restoring citizens' trust in government, in their elected and appointed public leaders and employees—as well as returning to an ethos of public service. It is about valuing public servants and providing the same workplace environment enjoyed by workers in the private sector.

Maintaining the human relations policies necessary for human resources development and retention was the topic of a city government case study by Secret and Swanberg (2008). They conducted a series of focus group interviews to identify work–family concerns of line and supervisory workers in a midsized southeastern U.S. city. In terms of its theoretical foundations, the study was rooted in a work–family spillover model and an organizational analysis framework. After reviewing the extant literature, Secret and Swanberg came up with five research questions to guide their focus group interviews:

1. What are the personal circumstances and expectations related to work–life issues of the city employees?
2. What is the nature of the work environment?
3. What links connect home and work for the employees?
4. What influence does the organizational culture and philosophy of the city government have on the work environment?
5. What changes in organizational resources, structure, and culture might improve their work–family conditions?

The research findings reinforced conclusions that municipal employees face the same types of challenges as private-sector employees in managing their work and family responsibilities. Employees indicated that flexible work schedules, supervisory support, and an organizational culture responsive to employee needs would best help them meet their challenges. Employees defined a "family-friendly" culture as one in which the work environment reflects and endorses a nurturing family system.

Secret and Swanberg (2008) also found that municipal employees maintain a high level of commitment to voluntary work in their community, and that there was a strong demand for elder care. Employees sought a system that would allow them greater flexibility and involvement in caring for elderly members of their family. Finally, in a recommendation similar to the ombudsman system, respondents urged that a work-family advocate be employed to help supervisors create and maintain a more family-friendly workplace culture.

Sustainability in State and Local Governments

Chapman's (2008) case study of sustainability in state and local governments focused on the long-term ability of a government to consistently meet its financial responsibilities. A sustainable government is one that meets the needs of present citizens and stakeholders without curtailing its responsibility to meet the needs of future generations of citizens. In a government that is sustainable, its philosophy becomes "an overarching value that requires best practices at every level" of the government organization. To achieve the goal of sustainability, governments must begin by ensuring fiscal sustainability. Chapman (2008, S115) defined fiscal responsibility at the state and local government levels as "the long-run capability of a government to consistently meet its financial responsibilities. It reflects the adequacy of available revenues to ensure the continued provision of service and capital levels that the public demands."

Chapman (2008) reviewed five structural pressures that apparently restrict the ability of public sector managers to establish future sustainability for their jurisdictions in both expenditures and revenue: (1) demographic changes (particularly the aging baby boom generation); (2) suburbanization trends that are exacerbating urban sprawl while placing excessive demand for public services; (3) increases in the mobility of people and businesses, with many citizens now working, shopping, and seeking entertainment in different jurisdictions, together with the increasing mobility of capital; (4) the shift from the consumption of goods to that of services, which are often not included in the state and local sales tax base; and (5) the growing importance of e-commerce, which has further eroded the sales tax base.

Three Forces Pressuring Governments

As these pressures reduce the dependability of tax revenues for state and local governments, they also make it more difficult to develop programs and policies that ensure sustainability for future generations. Chapman (2008) examined the impact of these pressures on three programmatic areas: Medicaid, pensions, and infrastructure.

The growth path of Medicaid spending is not sustainable under existing policies. Moreover, it might become the most likely cause of sustainability problems that state government budgets will face in the future. It is predicted that Medicaid spending will grow from 7.3 to 8.3 percent per year for the next several decades.

Spending on pensions for the thousands of baby boom public employees who are now becoming eligible for retirement is growing at a rate faster than total population growth. And, because state contributions to pension funds in the past were often tapped as a ready source of funds by cash-strapped governments, many public pension programs are seriously underfunded. In addition to pension-funding problems, many state and local governments are facing a number of other retiree-related costs, including medical and prescription drug costs; dental, vision, and hearing costs; life insurance; and long-term care and disability benefits.

The high cost of repairing and replacing much of the physical infrastructure is another sustainability concern facing public managers. Some federal grants and aid will be available for a portion of the work needed, but the largest proportion of work will be needed on facilities for which federal funds may not be available. Infrastructure refers to roads and bridges; railroads and airports; water and waste-water distribution, collection, and treatment facilities; solid waste disposal sites; physical plants and offices; and similar facilities.

Some Possible Solutions

Chapman (2008) recommended a number of short- and long-term solutions for achieving greater government sustainability. These are grouped into three broad classes of actions: revenue solutions, expenditure solutions, and administrative and management solutions. Revenue solutions include making adjustments in existing revenue sources, including sales and property taxes. Unfortunately, Chapman concluded, "tinkering with" such adjustments alone cannot solve fiscal sustainability problems. Other potential or partial solutions included tinkering with the sales tax alone, the property tax alone, or with fees and user charges. The final possible revenue solution was developing new sources of revenue, such as privatization, sale of roads or bridges to private firms that institute tolls for the use of the facilities, and new taxes on e-commerce and services.

Expenditure solutions are limited by entitlements, special interest group pressures, citizens who are content with existing circumstances, and political pressures. However, some small changes might include changes in pension contributions and greater employee contribution to health insurance and other benefit programs. Another set of changes might range from changes in age-related benefits and public services to benefits and services that are income based.

Administrative and management solutions include improving and simplifying tax laws (eliminating current loopholes) as a way to smooth out revenue streams so that economic downturns do not result in years when tax revenues drop dramatically. In addition, an important recommendation is that all state and local governments establish and maintain rainy day funds.

Chapman (2008) concluded that what may be the most difficult reform public managers will have to make is to "change the deep belief of most residents that there really is such a thing as a free lunch."

International Sustainability Case Research

It is clear that case research in sustainability is recognized as a global rather than a national or local problem. Researchers in many different countries are studying the problem from many different points of view. Three examples are included here.

The first is a case about the role of the government of Denmark in forming policies for sustainable development. The author of this case, Ulhöi (2004), is a member of the business administration faculty at the Aahus School of Business. The second case was written by a team of researchers led by He, from the College of Environmental Science and Engineering at China's Nankai University. He and colleagues' (2006) study looked at sustainability management of declining groundwater resources. The third case examined obstacles and opportunities for implementing sustainability as a new form of governance in Vienna, Austria (Astleithner and Hamedinger (2003).

Government Agency and Sustainable Development in Denmark

Ulhöi's (2004) case study was based on a policy on development that once focused on the potential negative effects of environmental restrictions on the competitiveness of business and industry, and was transformed into a policy of development that balances economic interests with those of the environment. As the twentieth century was coming to a close, the Danish Ministry of Trade and Industry joined with the Ministry of Environment and Energy to forge a policy that called for environmental issues to be considered a strategic asset for Danish industry.

The Danish government's Green National Enterprise Strategy (GNES) was launched in 2001 with the mission of taking a more proactive role on environmental issues and conflicts. The GNES was the product of a precedent-setting partnership between members from the business community and sustainability interest groups. The challenge facing the partnership was to see whether it was possible to incorporate environmental restraints into the market. The rules and regulations proposed under the market-based GNES focused on self-regulation rather than traditional command-and-control regulation. At the writing of the case (Ulhöi 2004), it was still too early to evaluate the effectiveness of the program.

Water Sustainability Management in China

Policies for maintaining sustainable economic growth—particularly in light of such issues as global warming and declining energy and other natural resources—have become thorny issues affecting national governments. China is often pointed out as a nation with potentially insurmountable environmental problems in the face of maintaining its three-decades-long path of economic growth and prosperity. However, a closer look at the record suggests that China's leaders are concerned with sustainability issues and are beginning to take steps to ensure continued economic growth.

China has undergone two major transformations since the economic reforms that began in 1978. First was the phenomenally successful shift from a command-and-control economy to a market-based economic system. The second has been the equally successful shift from a rural to an industrial, highly urbanized society. Neither of these transitions has been without cost, however. On the positive side have been annual growth rates that have averaged 10 percent or more per year for over two decades. Much of the Chinese population has enjoyed significant improvements in the quality of life.

What are less admirable, however, are the tremendous pressures this growth has had on the environment and degradation of the air the Chinese breathe and the water they drink. These pressures are at the point now where they have the capability of severely undermining the sustainability of China's long-term economic growth.

A group of faculty and graduate students from Nankai University in northeastern China have published results of a case study they conducted on the challenge of managing groundwater resources (He et al. 2006). Water tables have dropped significantly as a result of withdrawing too much of the underground water for agriculture and urban consumption. Land surfaces are subsiding, and in many locations, saltwater is encroaching into many of the more than 3 million wells in the region. Accordingly, the research team concluded that

> China faces the following serious problems: (1) inadequate, unevenly distributed, and contaminated raw water resources; (2) insufficient supply of [water and wastewater] treatment infrastructure; (3) and uncoordinated management policies. All these contribute to water pollution and acute water shortages—one of the most serious environmental challenges that China faces. (He et al. 2006, 388)

The Case of Urban Sustainability in Vienna, Austria

The city of Vienna, Austria, acceded to the Charter of Aalborg in 1996, thus agreeing to abide by the global sustainable development plan, Agenda 21, which was signed in Rio de Janeiro, Brazil, in 1992, and Local Agenda 21 (LA21), which was agreed to in Aalborg, Denmark, in 1994 (see Box 13.2). At the same time Vienna city officials agreed to implement LA21, they also adopted the Vienna Climate Protection program (KliP)—a master plan that focused on changes that implementation of LA21 would make necessary in city government.

Astleithner and Hamedinger (2003) selected the changes in the structure of the Vienna municipal government required by the sustainability program as the focus of their case study. They described a new urban governance that recognized the need to organize cooperation processes while at the same time establishing stakeholder bargaining systems that were cooperative and nonhierarchical. These changes needed to be established according to the new "discourse and communicative" model of democracy that reflects the new public management governance model.

As of the writing of the case, the authors found that Vienna—actually, the whole country of Austria—was not moving as rapidly as other European states, particularly the Scandinavian states, Germany, and the United Kingdom. They suggested that

Box 13.2

Sustainable Development in the European Union

The 1992 Earth Summit in Rio de Janeiro, Brazil, adopted Agenda 21, a plan of action to stimulate progress toward sustainable development. Agenda 21 recommended that governments draw up national sustainable development strategies (NSDS). A 1997 Special Session of the UN General Assembly set a target date of 2002 for their adoption. In 2002, the World Summit on Sustainable Development in Johannesburg, South Africa, recommended a plan that urged countries to make progress in forming their NSDS and to begin implementation by 2005.

Representatives from eighty regional organizations met in Aalborg, Denmark, in May 1994 for the EU (European Union) Conference on Sustainable Cities and Towns. The delegates adopted the Charter of European Cities and Towns Towards Sustainability—more commonly known as the Aalborg Charter. The key initiative of the charter was for each district to draw up a local plan, called Local Agenda 21 (LA21), for implementing sustainability governance.

The European Council agreed on a strategy for sustainable development, based on the principle that the economic, social, and environmental effects of all policies should be examined in a coordinated way and taken into account during decision making. To evaluate implementation and progress, the Sustainable Development Strategy foresees the development of a set of sustainable development indicators. As outlined at the Aalborg Conference, the main requirements for sustainability plans for European towns and cities are the following:

- Responsibility of cities and towns for sustainability
- Acceptance of the notion and principles of sustainability
- Sustainability as a creative, local, balance-seeking process
- Movement of the urban economy toward sustainability
- Social equity in urban sustainability
- Sustainable land-use patterns
- Sustainable urban mobility patterns
- Responsibility for the global climate
- Prevention of the poisoning of ecosystems
- The role of citizens as sustainability key agents and community involvement
- Instruments and tools for urban management toward sustainability

Sources: Astleithner and Hamedinger (2003); Joas and Grönholm (2004); Organisation for Economic Co-operation and Development [OECD] (2004a).

one possible reason for the slow adoption of the sustainability provisions in Vienna was the size of the city—a population of 1.8 million in 2003. A strategy suggested for coping with the size problem was to create a master plan and deal with issues that affect the entire city before moving forward with proposals that impact only one or a few districts of the city.

Summary

This chapter looked at some examples of the type of case research being conducted on issues pertaining to governments' role in establishing and maintaining a sustainable level of operations in a global environment of energy and natural resource shortages, air and water pollution, the perils of toxic waste, and declining financial resources for dealing with these challenges of sustainability. Case research has been carried out at all levels of government, as well as in the arena of international agreements and partnerships.

The chapter closed with three international examples of case research on sustainability issues: a look at a new government-sponsored, market-based environmental protection policy in Denmark, a study of sustainable management of underground water resources in northern China, and a case analysis of the adoption of Agenda 21 urban sustainability programs in Vienna as an example of a new public management initiative as a new model of governance.

➤ 14 ◄

Case Research in Technology Management

Congressional policymakers are concerned about potential inefficiencies and inefficacies in the operation of the federal government, particularly as it relates to decisions regarding information technology (IT) investments. These concerns have increased as federal IT spending has grown to approximately $70 billion annually.
—Jeffrey W. Seifert (2008)

The impact of technology on government operations has long been a topic of intensive study by academic and practitioner researchers. Today, governments are particularly concerned over the high cost of replacing old "legacy" systems. Administrators support the view that a core purpose for applying the products of science and technology in government agencies and organizations is to help organizations achieve higher performance. To accomplish this goal, they are endorsing the view that new technology purchases should meet four key operational objectives: (1) to gain operational and financial efficiency; (2) to achieve greater quality in government-provided programs and services; (3) to design and implement innovative processes; and (4) to improve agency responsiveness to clients, customers, legislators, and other stakeholders. Each of these purposes provides excellent opportunities for case research.

The Office of Management and Budget has identified a number of agency operations that are common to many departments and agencies. Among these are financial management, grants management, case management, human resources management, federal health services, and information security. In the past, each individual agency has maintained a staff and invested in information technology for performing its services. This same pattern occurs in most state and many municipal governments. The goal of technology management initiatives is to shift the bulk of these back-office activities from each individual department or agency to consolidated or shared service centers that perform the services for more than one department.

Consolidation is not as simple as it might seem. To achieve success in their efforts to attain greater consolidation, agency managers recognize that implementing new or different technology is not a simple task for administrators in any organization. A number of limiting factors restrict the ability of managers to integrate new technology into agency operations.

These limitations include the high initial cost of technology and its implementation; penalties associated with selecting the wrong technology system; the time needed to fully implement a technology change; and the high cost of training and/or hiring new staff to operate the system. Case research is, therefore, often the method of choice for research intended to warn other users of the difficulties associated with a given technology.

For example, a case study by Cooper (2000) reported that commonly held beliefs that information technology (IT) can enable radical organizational change, reengineering, or other transformations of organizations and work processes are seldom shown to be entirely true. Organizational inertia typically inhibits such change, which results in acquisition or development of IT that maintains or even reinforces the organizational status quo.

Technology is often used in ways not planned for or endorsed by its suppliers (Orlikowski 2000). Errors—in the form of misperception or lack of understanding, or by intent through sabotage, inertia, or innovation—often distort the intent of new technology. Its users may ignore, alter, or work around its initial technological properties; users may expand or change the properties of the technology by adding peripheral devices, new software, or data.

The manner in which technology is put to work is an artifact of the way its users understand its properties and function. That understanding is influenced by both internal and external circumstances. A mental picture of the technology is built up from the descriptions and demonstrations provided by such external sources as suppliers, other users, and opinion leaders. The technology's marketers, journalists, consultants, champions, trainers, managers, and "power users" all contribute to this picture through what they say about the technology, its use, and its value.

Even with all the right steps taken and each of the important preconditions in place, science and technology often do not produce the great improvements in organizations that supporters claim will result from implementation, as more than one researcher has noted: "The potential of information technology to loosen the hierarchical stranglehold on organizational practices, creating networked and lateral relations that can usher in new organizational forms and practices," is much overrated (Orlikowski 1991; Cooper 2000). The case research story in Box 14.1 illustrates the way that technology is transforming government.

Cases on Technology in Government

A large number of case studies have been conducted in the area of information technology, including multiple studies that analyze how the many expensive IT-related

---

Box 14.1

The Benefits of Technology in Government: The Case of Australia

Steve Alford, general manager of the business strategies branch of the National Office for the Information Economy, has provided a number of examples of how the application of technology has helped to transform government in Australia. Among the biggest changes that were enabled by technology was the increasing use of public–private and trans-level partnerships, and implementation of a (market-modeled) purchaser–provider system between government and stakeholders. According to Alford (2002), these developments have changed the way in which the Australian government carries out its business; it is also changing the way government administrators do their work. There are now more knowledge workers, far fewer process workers, more intelligent systems online, and greater use of paid and volunteer intermediaries in the delivery of government services.

Three examples of technology-driven changes in the work of government in Australia described by Alford (2002) are the following:

1. *Business Entry Points* (www.business.gov.au), which are single points of access for all government services of interest to businesses that bring together information from multiple agencies and multiple levels of government, including transaction services.
2. *E-tax Web site,* which is part of a process designed to push work out from within the tax department to intermediaries and to taxpayers themselves. Greatly simplifying the tax system is one of the results of the initiative.
3. *Australian Jobsearch* Web site, which provides information about job openings throughout the country.

What Alford (2002) described as perhaps the main benefit accruing from the growth of e-government in Australia was the transfer of government services to a level closer to users of those services, with wider distribution—and doing so with fewer people and at lower costs. He concluded with a call to acknowledge that "e-government is not just another channel for government; it's about making a better government, a better transformation, and a better service to customers."

Source: Alford (2002).

---

problems have been resolved by administrators in government agencies and departments. These case studies offer important guidance for other administrators when they run into the same or similar difficulties in their technology initiatives.

This instructional character of case research is particularly valuable in several types of management problems. First, case research provides great insight when research and theory are to some degree still in their formative stages. Adoption of enterprise resource management systems in government agencies and implementation of e-government programs at the state and local level are examples. The case method is considered to be appropriate for capturing knowledge held by government workers and developing theory from that knowledge:

> The [learning] process in which practitioners are engaged is necessary for knowledge to accumulate. It is incumbent upon the scientists to formalize this knowledge and proceed to a testing stage. Before this formalization takes place, case studies could be employed to document the experiences of practice. (Benbasat, Goldstein, and Mead 1987, 370)

Second, case studies that analyze other administrators' experiences and the actions taken have been shown to be exceedingly valuable. Cases make it possible for administrators to study technology issues as they occur in a natural, recognizable situation. Case descriptions of applications of new, cutting-edge technologies make it possible for administrators to learn about advances in technology and other operational tools as they are happening.

The story of an implementation allows the researcher to delve into and answer the *how* and *why* questions of interest to other administrators:

- How did an agency manager effectively introduce new information or communications technologies?
- What problems did the implementation team encounter? What strategies did they employ to surmount those problems?
- Was the project on budget and on time? Did cost and time overruns occur?
- What key issues were not considered before going ahead with the program?

Early Examples

Benbasat, Goldstein, and Mead (1987) were among the early researchers examining case research in technology applications. In a meta-analysis case study, they evaluated a sample of case research reports taken from information systems journals against a set of characteristics chosen from a larger list identified in five leading papers on the theory underlying case method research (Table 14.1).

Benbasat, Goldstein, and Mead (1987) evaluated the cases against the following four questions selected from the larger list: (1) Can the phenomenon be studied outside of its natural setting? (2) Must it focus on contemporary events? (3) Is control or manipulation of subjects necessary? (4) Does the phenomenon enjoy an established theoretical base? The researchers examined case studies reported in a total of five journals and published conference proceedings, eventually selecting these four case studies as best illustrations of the strengths and weaknesses in case study research: (1) Dutton (1981), (2) Markus (1981), (3) Olson (1981), and (4) Pyburn (1983).

The Dutton (1981) case is particularly relevant because it involved the city of Tulsa's adoption of a fiscal impact process model and its eventual rejection. The purpose of the study was an examination of the interpersonal, organizational, politi-

Table 14.1

Selected Characteristics of Technology Case Studies

Item	Characteristic
1.	Phenomenon of interest is examined in a natural setting.
2.	Data are collect by multiple means.
3.	One or a few entities (person, group, organization) are examined.
4.	The complexity of the unit is studied extensively.
5.	Cases focus on the exploration, classification, and hypothesis stages of the knowledge-building process; investigator has a receptive attitude toward exploration.
6.	No experimental controls or manipulation is involved.
7.	Investigator may not specify the set of independent and dependent variables in advance.
8.	Results derived rely heavily on the integrative powers of the investigator.
9.	Changes in site selection and data collection methods could take place as the investigator develops new hypotheses.
10.	Case research is useful in the study of *why* and *how* questions because these deal with operational links to be traced over time rather than with frequency or incidence.
11.	The focus is on contemporary events.

Source: Benbasat, Goldstein, and Mead (1987, 371).

cal, and technical limitations as they impacted implementation of the model. The case included a variety of data-gathering methods: newspaper accounts; government reports, memos, and documents; more than twenty unstructured interviews with individuals who participated in the process; and telephone interviews that preceded and followed site visits. Dutton concluded that the political environment contributed most to the city's failure to implement the innovative process.

Wireless Technology for the City of Philadelphia

Jain, Mandviwalla, and Banker (2007) developed an administrative case study of the city of Philadelphia's efforts to implement a municipal wireless network (MWN). The researchers suggested that Philadelphia's experiences might provide useful guidelines for other municipalities when selecting and implementing information technology, while also illustrating how information technology can be used to promote social and economic change. They defined an MWN as a wireless Internet access network formed with the participation of a local government.

Their case report was divided into three sections: The first section provided a discussion of the emergence of wireless networks as new information technology infrastructure. Section two was a detailed analysis of the Philadelphia wireless project. This section described the several phases of the project while also emphasizing important milestones in the process. The third section included the expected conclusion and a summary of lessons learned and a number of issues of interest for future researchers in this budding technology.

The data were gathered in a series of 12 focus groups that involved 120 key stakeholders in the city's MWN program, contact with a city project task force, interviews with private contractors (vendors) and participants in MWN projects in other communities, and an analysis of an earlier pilot project carried out in a single Philadelphia neighborhood.

The city of Philadelphia covers approximately 135 square miles and contains nearly 660,000 households. Prior to implementation of the wireless system, some 40 percent of the city population reported that they were nonusers of the Internet; only 45 percent had Internet access at home, compared with the U.S. rate of 70 percent; both of these measures of participation were below the national average.

The Philadelphia MWN case is also an example of a successful collaboration between the public and private sectors. The system as designed required an initial investment of $10 million. A request for proposals resulted in applications from twelve private-sector firms. The final contract went into effect in February 2006, with complete installation expected to take two years. The winning bidder covered the entire $10 million cost of building and operating the network over the entire 135 square miles of the city. Upon completion, the firm would own the system and have the right to sell retail access to individual and commercial end users.

The contractor agreed to set a special price for low-income and disadvantaged citizens, pay the city $2 million for the rights to build the network, and pay rent for the use of city-owned power poles and lampposts. After the second year of operation, the contractor would pay the city 5 percent of its revenues to a new civic organization to be known as "Wireless Philadelphia." That organization was to be used to expand use of the Internet among low-income and disadvantaged citizens—reducing the "digital divide" that existed in the city.

Two lessons can be taken from this case. First, it provides a successful model for administrators considering their own community-wide wireless networks. Second, it serves as an illustration of how local governments are collaborating with private-sector firms to provide services the government body does not have funds to implement on its own. The case authors offered this conclusion:

> By outsourcing all of the key technical, service, and management elements of the project, the city stayed away from activities that are typically outside its scope of expertise. Essentially, what the city government did was to monetize its passive assets such as lampposts and other rights-of-way properties. It had created a new source of income without investing anything. (Jain, Mandviwalla, and Banker 2007, 1001)

When Technology Fails

Reasons why implementation of a major IT investment program failed to achieve hoped-for transformation objectives were described in a case study published in

MIS Quarterly. Cooper (2000) described the experiences of an organization during the installation of an imaging IT system. The technology was initially acquired to improve work processes for storing, indexing, and retrieving images of documents and to make a single document available to several people at the same time. Also, work in progress can be automatically distributed, together with an audit trail of changes made to the document. In addition to these work process improvements, the senior manager in charge of the project wanted to use the technology to radically change his departments by altering or eliminating departmental boundaries, job descriptions, and work flow. The effectiveness and efficiency goals for the system were achieved, but the organizational changes were not.

Cooper (2000) attributed the problems with achieving the IT-enabled organizational engineering goals to several factors, among which were worker inertia, lack of an appropriate organizational climate, and lack of appropriate communication regarding the potential benefits that the technology could provide. Although many of the requirements for a change were in place—full top management support, significant user participation, and a powerful champion—creativity-fostering elements such as reward structures for risk taking were not in place.

Cooper (2000) had access to all documentation concerning the project, including meeting minutes, interoffice memos, and proposals and presentation materials. He also conducted fifteen personal interviews with employees who (1) represented all areas affected by the project and (2) had been closely involved in the decision-making processes.

Cooper's case analysis weighed the organization's experience of only partially successful adoption of the new technology against this set of eight theoretical creativity constructs:

1. Knowledge: Evidence supports contention that success of implementation can be improved by providing greater knowledge of potential IT capabilities, and the work tasks and process to which it is to be applied.
2. Cognitive factors: Creative IT development can be constrained or enhanced by providing individual creativity improvement techniques or tools.
3. Intrinsic motivation: Providing tasks that increase autonomy, provide opportunities for professional growth, and are seen as enjoyable by group members can improve development and acceptance of new technology.
4. Extrinsic motivation: Providing motivation through reward structures such as increased pay and advancement, and rewarding risk taking regardless of whether it is successful.
5. Group tasks: Technology adoption can be improved by ensuring that clear development goals are matched with considerable flexibility in the process by which they are achieved.
6. Group norms: Ensuring that group norms foster clear roles and responsibilities, cooperation, and trust can improve adoption.
7. Group diversity: Worker diversity through job enrichment, cross-

training and related worker empowerment programs improves adoption processes.

8. Group problem solving: Finally, improvement in adoption can be achieved by the use of systems analysis and design methods commensurate with high levels of uncertainty, together with group creativity improvement techniques.

The research revealed that the climate needed for smooth adoption did not exist at the organization. One of the reasons for this is the policy that required adoption of technology that produced the fewest disruptions possible and which most closely matched existing work processes and procedures—"a system that took as little user effort as possible to develop, had the least disruption to user daily activities, and mimicked their current systems" (Cooper 2000, 263–64). As a result, the program seemed designed to support business as usual rather than the desired transformational change.

Removing Discretion in the Netherlands

Bureaucracies in large-scale public agencies have been undergoing a fundamental transformation in many parts of the world (Bovens and Zouridis 2002). The old model of large numbers of street-level "window clerks" delivering services one customer at a time in face-to-face interaction is being replaced by rule-based, faceless interaction and computer decisions based on data provided by citizens via the Internet. In many public service categories, advanced information and expert systems are replacing case managers and eliminating the discretionary power that once allowed them to rule in contested situations.

It is important to remember, however, that the circumstances in which information and communications technology can effectively replace traditional street-level workers are not appropriate in all service delivery situations. Rather, they work only in those situations where there is routine handling of large numbers of nearly identical formal transactions.

Two successful applications in which rule-based, digital decision-tree situations have effectively replaced discretionary decision-making powers by low-level public employees were described in a public agency technology case study in the Netherlands (Bovens and Zouridis 2002). The two services were the processing of applications for student loans and grants, and the enforcement of traffic regulations through a system of fixed cameras in traffic locations, fixed schedules of fines for violations, and automatic billing and follow-up on fines.

In both of these scenarios, technology first transformed the old street-level bureaucracies into *screen-level* bureaucracies in which citizens interacted with public servants via a computer screen. Subsequently, however, these and similar screen-level systems were replaced by what the authors described as *system-level* bureaucracies, where public employees are no longer involved in the collection of application information or the processing of forms. Because of the need to continually improve the efficiency of the system, customer service workers are being replaced by programmers and other information and communication technology personnel.

The Student Loan System

The old practice of negotiating with street-level caseworkers to determine eligibility and award amount for grants and loans for higher education was replaced with a technology-based system in the mid-1990s. Under the old system, street-level workers determined who got what financial support and why; decisions were made by individual caseworkers based on their perception of the individual student's economic situation and academic abilities and qualifications.

By the 1980s, caseworker discretionary power had largely been replaced by accept or reject decision recommendations produced by computer software. By the 1990s, the legacy single-purpose "stovepipe" software systems that were designed and implemented in the 1980s were being replaced and interconnected so that all applicant information would be available for use in the decision process.

After several additional efforts to improve the system, public employees were no longer involved in handling individual cases; instead, they focused on improving links between systems and information processes. Applicants now enter their information directly into the system, usually via the Internet. Decision and award amount rules are built into the programs, and decisions are made accordingly. Customer contact, while still considered important, has been relegated to providing of application assistance and information to applicants by help desk staff; transactions are now fully automated.

Enforcement of Traffic Regulations

Enforcement of traffic regulations was managed through the practice of hand-issuing tickets by policemen who observed a violation and who, in many cases, collected the fine on the spot. If the violator paid the fine, criminal proceedings were avoided. If the driver did not pay, the case was transferred to the office of the public prosecutor. Further failure to pay might result in the case being transferred to a higher court. At each step, the amount of the fine is increased.

In the new technology-based system, the processing of traffic violations has shifted from local police departments and minor courts to a new computer network created specifically to manage the process. Criminal law has been replaced by administrative law. Cameras record license plate numbers of violators. The data are fed into the network, where case files are processed and fines are sent to offenders without any human intervention and no criminal actions involved. Most of the fines are paid immediately or after one or more computer-generated collection messages. Offenders can appeal to the public prosecutor, but few such appeals occur.

In both of these examples, the nature of work in public organizations has been dramatically changed by the introduction of information and communications technology. The following changes are taking place at the upper levels of public organization management:

> Contacts with citizens no longer take place in the streets, in meeting rooms, or from behind windows, but through cameras, modems, and Web sites.[Technology] has come to play a decisive role in the organizations' operations. It is not only used to register and store data, as in the early days of automation, but also to execute and control the whole production process. Routine cases are handled without human interference. Expert systems have replaced professional workers. Apart from the occasional public information officer and the help desk staff, there are no other street-level bureaucrats [as defined by Lipsky 1980]. . . . The process of issuing decisions is carried out—virtually from beginning to end—by computer systems. (Bovens and Zouridis 2002, 180)

These changes in the organization of public institutions will also make major changes to the nature of work that is carried out in government agencies as well as the skills and knowledge base of the workers charged with the responsibility to perform the agencies' mission. At the systems level, three types of workers will be needed to replace the disappearing caseworkers: (1) technology workers familiar with systems design, legislative procedures, legal policies, and systems management; (2) public management specialists who are skilled in controlling the production and delivery of public services; and (3) skilled communicators, such as public information officers and help desk workers, individuals trained to resolve complaints and misunderstandings, and those with legal training in the management of contracts with external providers.

Bovens and Zouridis (2002) provided suggestions and recommendations that may help readers of the case if they must deal with the same or similar public management situations. The authors did this by recommending three categories of innovations that could aid in making changes to a systems-level bureaucracy.

First, senior administrators and legislative bodies should insist on greater supervision of IT purchasing and implementation. Systematic reviews of architecture plans and proposals would help in this area; IT supervision could even become institutionalized over time, functioning as part of regular audit reviews.

Second, the frustrations that often occur as a result of removal of human contact during the transaction might be resolved through introduction of hardship clauses and panel reviews into the decision process under the rigid, rule-based system.

Third, greater accessibility to expert systems could be accomplished by permitting citizens and interest organizations to access electronic forms, decision trees, and checklists used in the organization's decisions. This accessibility could result in greater democratic control of system-level bureaucracies, while at the same time keeping system designers alert to problematic elements of the process.

Measuring the Impact of Technology on Performance

One of the biggest issues in technology management in government for years has been determining the level of improvement in performance that may or may not result from an investment in information technology. Researchers have struggled to find a metric that effectively measures the impact of any particular technology on performance within an agency. Many studies at the economy level have revealed a negative relationship between technology and performance. At the industry level, the results have been mixed, whereas at the organization level, many studies have found a positive relationship between performance and technology.

From their analysis of the literature for a case study of the application of technology in a health care organization, Devaraj and Kohli (2003) concluded that the more focused the study, the better the chance to determine the impact of a technology on performance.

For this reason, they suggested that a more appropriate way to measure the impact of IT is to focus on the use of the IT rather than the investment. Moreover, despite a number of problems associated with the approach, usage studies in the past have continued to collect data through the self-reporting of IT use; Devaraj and Kohli (2003) controlled for these difficulties by monitoring of the *actual* use of IT instead of using the self-reporting method (their emphasis).

The research design involved examination of various financial and nonfinancial measures of performance in eight hospitals over a three-year period (Devaraj and Kohli 2003). The technology involved was implementation of decision support systems (DSS), which are designed to help managers improve organizational effectiveness and productivity. In the eight hospitals included in this study, the systems were used for such purposes as analyzing contracts with insurers; comparing costs of expected services and payments; and identifying areas where operational improvements could be made, mortality rates reduced, and cost cutting might be appropriately applied. The researchers only examined hospital-provided DSS reports to ensure that they were measuring only actual usage of the systems.

The eight-hospital case analysis resulted in strong support for the hypothesis that usage of this particular technology provided significant economic and noneconomic benefits. Devaraj and Kohli (2003) found that DSS usage had a strong, significant relationship with the measures of hospital performance.

Summary

Science and technology have been key contributors to the economic growth of the United States for many years. Scientific advances have greatly improved the quality of life for most Americans while also driving much of the gains in productivity in industry and government. The increasingly complex and competitive environments in which government organizations must function while continuing to improve everything they do have required public managers to transform their organizations in many ways. Helping to make these changes possible have been the considerable investments being made in information and communication technology.

However, the implementation of these new technologies appears to have more often reinforced the organizational status quo than it has contributed to significant organizational change. The IT problem facing public managers, then, is determining which factors contribute most to their ability to carry out the organization's mission with the greatest possible efficiency and effectiveness. This chapter looked at how some managers are using case research to address issues in the management of IT in the organizations and agencies of government and concluded with a review of a multicase study on the impact of technology on organizational performance.

➤ 15 ◀

Case Research in National Security Issues

September 11, 2001, marked the advent of a new kind of terrorism
radically different from the isolated threats posed by pockets of
national or regional terrorist: international terrorism, of unpredictable
magnitude, against which no country can claim to be protected.
— Organisation for Economic Co-operation and Development (OECD 2004b)

As a consequence of the terrorists' attacks on September 11, 2001, Congress and the president began steps to improve the nation's ability to prevent further attacks and speed recovery from possible future attacks and other disasters. The Bush administration issued the first *National Strategy for Homeland Security* in July 2002 (http://www.dhs.gov/xlibrary/assets/nat_strat_hls.pdf). Updated in October 2007, the document included a plan to strengthen homeland security through greater cooperation and partnering of federal, state, local, and private-sector organizations. It also identified twenty-two federal agencies with some degree of responsibility for security measures. The five largest agencies, along with their employees and payrolls as of December 2006, are listed in Table 15.1.

To combine and coordinate these diverse areas of responsibility, the Department of Homeland Security (DHS) was created by the Homeland Security Act of November 2002 (U.S. Government Accountability Office [GAO] 2008a). When DHS became operational in March 2003, it brought several agencies under the direction of a new cabinet-level office.

The GAO conducts annual audits for all federal agencies. In these audits the GAO identifies progress made in various management functions. In addition, it also carries out analyses of departments' progress in achieving their mission. These performance reports are presented to agency managers, the White House, the appropriate congressional oversight committees, and the public.

GAO investigators examine progress and adherence to required standards, identify successes and areas where work remains to be accomplished, and publish their results for other managers to review to aid in carrying out their own management

193

Table 15.1

Five Largest DHS Agencies and Their Employees and December 2006 Payroll

Agency	Total Civilian Employees	Full-time Civilian Employees	Civilian Payroll (millions)
U.S. Coast Guard	7,522	7,403	$44.66
U.S. Secret Service	6,578	6,441	44.33
Bureau of Customs and Border Protection	43,640	46,148	244.75
Federal Emergency Management Agency	26,944	7,410	133.23
Transportation Security Agency	56,829	46,806	213.28
All Other Agencies	28,236	27,735	187.13
Total DHS	169,749	138,953	$867.34

Source: U.S. Census Bureau (2007).

initiatives. The following discussion of the DHS was taken from published GAO reports. It is included here to bring to light the many opportunities for case research in federal, state, and local security and emergency management operations.

Delivering DHS Programs

Much of the work of DHS is carried out through grants to state and local governments and through contracts with private-sector and nonprofit organizations. As with all federal organizations, the department conducts its operations through management programs in five key functional areas: acquisition, financial transactions, human capital, information technology, and buildings and facilities (real property) management. Through effective management in these areas, DHS is able to focus on achieving its key mission areas of border security; immigration enforcement and immigration services; aviation, surface transportation, and maritime security; emergency preparedness and response; protection of critical infrastructure; and science and technology (Table 15.2).

Partnerships and Coordination

To achieve its underlying mission of maintaining a safe and secure nation, DHS works closely with other federal agencies, state and local governments, private and nonprofit organizations, and international partners. Examples of such cooperative efforts include the partnership DHS has with the Department of Transportation to improve security with surface transport firms and organizations, cooperation with airlines to make air transportation secure, cooperation with the shipping industry for inspecting containerized cargo, and collaboration of the Federal Emergency

Table 15.2

Management Functions of the Department of Homeland Security

Management Function	Major Mission Function
Acquisition management	Border security
Financial management	Immigration enforcement
Human capital management	Immigration services
Information technology management	Aviation security
Real property management	Surface transportation security
	Maritime security
	Emergency preparedness and response
	Critical infrastructure and key resources
	Protection
	Science and technology

Source: GAO (2008a).

Management Administration (FEMA; part of DHS) with state and local governments for disaster response and recovery.

DHS Grants to State, Local, and Tribal Governments

The federal government uses homeland security grants as its primary method of supporting state, local, and tribal governments' capabilities for emergency preparedness and response to terrorist attacks and natural disasters (GAO 2008b). More than $19 billion in grants for planning, equipment, and training has been awarded since 2002. FEMA was given responsibility for allocating and managing these grants after passage of the Post-Katrina Emergency Reform Management Act of 2006.

In its role within DHS, FEMA provides local government with the threat assessments conducted by the DHS, validates infrastructure data, reviews local security investment plans, provides technical assistance to local governments on preparing their grant applications, and holds post-award conferences to collect process feedback. The system that DHS uses to determines the scale and scope of its grants to state and local partners is based on its assessment of the risk of potential terrorist or natural disaster to the region (GAO 2008b). *Risk* is defined as the product of *threat* times *vulnerability* and *consequences* $(R = T \times (V + C))$.

One of the major problems FEMA and the DHS are having with the grant process is that red tape and bureaucratic obstacles are making it difficult to get its grants to where they are needed in a timely and expeditious manner. Many state and local regulations sometimes cause delays of months before the local agencies can spend the grant money. In some cases, state legislature approval is required before county, municipal, or special district agencies can accept the federal grant. When the state legislatures are not in session, more months may be added to the process. DHS has obligated some $20 billion in emergency preparedness and response grants from 2002 through 2007. However, as of January 2008, about $7 billion had still not been spent.

State Coordination

To coordinate federal and state efforts, beginning in 2002, individual states established their own offices or divisions of homeland security and/or emergency management. In most cases, these were not an additional bureaucratic layer of government but rather a coordinating office. Typically, the offices were established within existing departments of public safety or were attached to the local governor's office.

An informal review of the home pages of some of these state-level programs reveals a number of common features. For example, all included some version of the then-current DHS-distributed threat condition; some offices were set up to function at the state level alone; others also included threat conditions for aviation in or entering U.S. airspace. All programs included a number of links to other information, such as home preparedness, immigration and travel, press releases, and more information.

Many state homeland security Web sites also included a mission statement and other strategic management themes. Some examples of mission statements in a random selection of state security and emergency preparedness offices are displayed in Table 15.3.

Homeland Security at the State and Local Level

The homeland security program in Alabama is typical of these state programs (State of Alabama 2003). Alabama was the first state to create a state cabinet-level Department of Homeland Security, enacted into law on June 18, 2003. The Alabama DHS is organized into four major functional areas: borders, ports, and transportation; science and technology; information management and budget; and emergency preparedness and response. Since its inception, the Alabama DHS has administered more than $100 million in federal homeland security grants.

Homeland security and disaster preparedness and response have become important activities at the local as well as the state and federal levels. The nation's largest cities and most populous counties are taking advantage of DHS grants and awards to expand and modernize their security and emergency preparedness units. Examples include Chicago, where the Office of Emergency Management and Communications team coordinates the city's disaster mitigation, preparedness, response, and recovery planning and implementation programs (City of Chicago 2006). Houston maintains an office of public safety and homeland security as a division of the mayor's office (City of Houston 2009).

In another example, the city's Division of Emergency Services manages San Francisco's homeland security activities (City of San Francisco 2009). The division is a unit of the city's Department of Emergency Management. The division

Table 15.3

Missions of Selected State Homeland Security Offices

State	Mission Statement
Alabama (State of Alabama 2003)	The mission of the Alabama DHS is to work with federal, state, and local partners to prevent acts of terrorism in Alabama; protect lives and safeguard property; and if required, respond to any acts of terrorism occurring in Alabama. To accomplish this mission, the Alabama DHS works closely with both public and private-sector stakeholders in a wide range of disciplines: law enforcement, emergency management, emergency medical, fire services, public works, agriculture, public health, public safety communications, environmental management, military, transportation, and more.
Alaska (State of Alaska 2008)	The mission of the Office of Homeland Security is to be the single, statewide focal point for coordinating the state's efforts to prevent terrorist attacks, reduce Alaska's vulnerability to terrorism, minimize the loss of life or damage to critical infrastructure, and recover from attacks if they occur.
Oklahoma (State of Oklahoma 2008)	Duties of the Oklahoma Office of Homeland Security are to: • Develop and implement a comprehensive statewide homeland security strategy. • Plan and implement a statewide response system. • Administer the homeland security advisory system. • Coordinate, apply for, and distribute federal homeland security grants. • Implement national homeland security plans.
Pennsylvania (State of Pennsylvania 2007)	The department's mission is to manage the commonwealth's overall protection framework and oversee implementation and continual evaluation of the Commonwealth Critical Infrastructure Protection Program. This comprises a fivefold mission: • Identify critical infrastructure, key resources, and significant special events. • Assess risks (consequences, vulnerabilities and threats). • Determine the gaps in capabilities to respond. • Partner with federal and commonwealth agencies and municipality, county, and private-sector entities to develop strategies to mitigate the risk. • Prioritize and implement risk-based protective programs.
Tennessee (State of Tennessee 2008)	The Tennessee Office of Homeland Security has the primary responsibility and authority for directing statewide activities pertaining to the prevention of, and protection from, terrorist-related events. This responsibility includes the development and implementation of a comprehensive and coordinated strategy to secure the state from terrorist threats and attacks. Further, the office of Homeland Security serves as a liaison between federal, state, and local agencies, and private-sector [organizations] on matters relating to the security of our state and citizens. [Responsibilities include:] • Awareness—Identify and understand terrorist threats within Tennessee. • Prevention—Detect, deter, and mitigate terrorist threats to Tennessee. • Protection—Safeguard our citizens, their freedoms, property, and the economy from acts of terrorism. • Response—Assist in coordinating the response to terrorist-related events. • Organizational excellence—putting the safety of citizens first.

develops and maintains emergency operations planning for both the city and county of San Francisco, and it coordinates regional response planning with ten Bay Area counties and the cities of Oakland and San Jose.

Homeland security planning in Los Angeles County and city is managed by the Sheriff's Department Office of Homeland Security (Los Angeles Sheriff's Department 2009). The department is also responsible for security and safety on 80 miles of coastline and more than 800 square miles of ocean within the county limits. The country's busiest port, San Pedro, is in Los Angeles County.

As these few case studies illustrate, the states have been largely left to their own resources and priorities for deciding how to best implement local homeland security and emergency preparedness programs. Problems dealing with federal, state, and local interface in homeland security were brought to light in this case study on the role of local law enforcement in terrorism prevention and response.

A Case on Problems with Security Grants

Problems that local law enforcement administrators face as they begin to implement federal programs in terrorism prevention were the subject of a case study conducted by the Department of Criminology at the University of South Carolina. The chief difficulty revealed by the research was that while the states have been given extensive responsibility for carrying out activities in the war on terrorism, they have received few specific directions or guidelines for carrying out those tasks and how best to spend federal grant money (Pelfrey 2007).

The role that local law enforcement agencies are expected to exercise was spelled out in Homeland Security Presidential Directives (HSPDs), two of which were announced in 2003. HSPD 5 dealt with procedures and responsibilities primarily of federal level agencies in the management of "domestic incidents." HSPD 8 dealt with the steps that state and local organizations were expected to administer for national preparedness. This role included steps to ensure "the existence of plans, procedures, policies, training, and equipment necessary at the federal, state and local level to maximize the ability to prevent, respond to, and recover from major events" (Pelfrey 2007, 314).

The tasks and responsibilities of local agencies were further identified in guidelines issued by the U.S. Office of Domestic Preparedness in 2003, but they did not include steps or procedures for assessing or auditing state and local actions. Additional confusion emerged in the failure to recognize the distinction between prevention of and response to incidents—focus areas with distinctly different goals, objectives, procedures, and processes.

Semiannual Surveys

Pelfrey used survey data for his 2007 case. The data were collected in 2004 during one of the semiannual surveys of South Carolina's nearly 290 law enforcement agencies.

Survey questions addressed such issues as agency preparation for dealing with terrorism, homeland security, levels of preparedness, training programs, and funding requests. Responding agencies included 135 police departments, thirty-two sheriff departments, and four state agencies, one of which was the state highway patrol. Survey findings revealed that while many agencies had taken significant strides in achieving terrorism preparedness, a number of problems remained, including the following:

- Less than half of the responding agencies had developed a policy for handling terrorism threats or events.
- A minority of agencies had held any type of terrorism prevention training or response exercises; what exercises that were held did not always involve emergency medical services.
- Very few agencies had appointed an emergency management coordinator, instead assigning the task to the agency's existing chief officer.
- The federal government had still not determined how funds should be allocated and which agencies should be the most prepared to handle a terrorism event, as well as how the hierarchy of federal, state, and local enforcement agencies would function in the event of a terrorism event.
- Federal, state, and local funding is widely available, but generally includes little in the way of guidelines in how the money should best be used. Most local agencies are using the funds to purchase equipment and material.

Although this case report (Pelfrey 2007) did an excellent job of describing the scope of the problem faced by local law enforcement agencies, it provided little in the way of guidance for enforcement agency administrators, elected officials, and local government managers about what might be done to rectify the discrepancies revealed in the South Carolina survey. In this way, the case was descriptive, not prescriptive. It identified a problem but did not provide a remedy.

The Homeland Security Alert System

The next example is a case study by Shapiro and Cohen (2007) of a multi-jurisdictional government system: the U.S. terrorist alert system that was instituted just six months after the September 11, 2001, terrorist attacks in New York, Pennsylvania, and Washington, DC. The newly formed U.S. Department of Homeland Security (DHS) began using a new color-coded terrorist alert system known as the Homeland Security Advisory System (HSAS) in 2002. This color alert system was one of three arms of a DHS system for alerting government organizations and emergency and safety responders to the likelihood and potential severity of a terrorist attack. The three-part system included dissemination of threat information using the color-coded threat level system; assessments of vulnerability; and a threat communications system for governments, public safety responders, and the public (DHS 2008).

In any multilevel alert system such as the HSAS, the alert level is raised for any of these three reasons: (1) to prevent an attack; (2) to deter, divert, and defer an attack; or (3) to lessen the effects of an attack that cannot be prevented. Despite the good intentions of the color-coded alert system, it apparently not only failed to achieve its objectives, but it also quickly became what was described as a total failure.

Shapiro and Cohen (2007) reported in their case study that the agencies and organizations that the system was designed to assist either did not understand what they were supposed to do when the code was raised or lost their trust in its effectiveness. Within just a few years after its implementation, distrust of the system among state and local government emergency response planners resulted in the nearly total disappearance of the system in state and local homeland security planning.

The Color-Coded Warning System

The core of the HSAS system was a five-level, color-coded warning system. This terrorist alert system was designed to serve as a quick and easy-to-understand means of informing all agencies and organizations that needed to know the likelihood and potential severity of a perceived terrorist attack in any part of the nation. Based on the alert level, responders would then be able to determine what preventive and reaction posture to adopt. The advisory system ranks terrorist danger on five levels of risk; each risk level is assigned a color code and label (Table 15.4).

Risk is defined by DHS as a product of the probability of an attack and the potential severity or level of damage to critical infrastructure and loss of life. However, a major problem surfaced when the distinctions assigned to gradations of risk were not further defined. Responders were unable to differentiate between a high and a severe risk, for example. This naturally resulted in a lack of clarity in what actions responders needed to take when the level of alert shifted to a higher or lower level of risk.

This obscurity between threat levels, together with a perception that the increases in warning levels were being used for political reasons, resulted in a severe drop in responders' confidence in the system after just two or three years of operation. When no attacks occurred after DHS raised the alert level from yellow to orange or from orange to red during the months prior to the 2004 election, it resulted in a perception that DHS was using the system as a way of improving the public's approval of the Bush administration—further increasing distrust of the system.

Three Major Weaknesses

Shapiro and Cohen (2007) determined that there were three major weaknesses in the HSAS. First, contradictions in the system reduced its credibility among government and private users. This, in turn, could have resulted in unexpected or unplanned reactions by participants. Second, the system did not consider any incor-

Table 15.4

Color-Coded Levels of Terrorist Threat in the HSAS Warning System

Color Code	Threat Level	Description
Red	Severe	Severe risk of terrorist attack
Orange	High	High risk of terrorist attack
Yellow	Elevated	Medium risk of terrorist attack
Blue	Guarded	General risk of terrorist attack
Green	Low	Low risk of terrorist attack

Source: DHS (2008).

rect assumptions made by responders. Their reactions to changes in the system were not consistent because the system did not include clearly defined actions for each alert level. And third, the system's complexity could have resulted in unexpected responses. As structured, the HSAS made it impossible for planners to predict any secondary effects caused by or resulting from a change in alert levels.

The complexity of the system made it particularly difficult to manage in large metropolitan areas. Shapiro and Cohen (2007) identified at least seven different types of participants affected by an alert system: federal government agencies, state agencies, local government agencies, the media, business and industry, private citizens, and, of course, the terrorists. A geographic unit may include many different organizations from each of the groups. The authors used the New York metropolitan area as an example. An incident there would involve the terrorists, at least four federal agencies, four states, thirty-six counties, many small cities, at least nine local television stations, upwards of a hundred or more radio stations and newspapers, thousands of firms, and millions of citizens.

Shapiro and Cohen (2007) suggested an alternate system to replace HSAS. It would supplement a very basic color-coded alert system with specific instructions for different regions and respondent types. The color systems would be used for simple functions that would be suitable in any emergency. Supplemental instructions would include highly specific actions, for example, to increase the guard force at designated infrastructure localities. In addition, the requirements for defining each level would need to be clearly specified, with costs of reacting calculated for each risk and potential response. The proposed alternative system would have these four advantages:

- It would reduce the need for public negotiations over compliance during a crisis—activities that could provide useful information to terrorists.
- By negotiating actions possible for each level of alert in advance, confusion and repetition would be greatly reduced.
- Advanced negotiations would bring to light many potential problems and reduce the impact of wrong assumptions.

- Advanced negations would also help organizations to resolve possible incompatibilities in action plans and thereby reduce system complexity.

Shapiro and Cohen wrapped up their review with the following conclusion and recommendation:

> A functional alert system must sufficiently increase the beliefs about the value of protection, and it must generate predicable outcomes that match the purposes for an alert. The current alert system in the United States fails at both tasks. . . . No one with whom we spoke in researching this article believes that the HSAS has been effective. Given the failure of the HSAS, the time has come to take on the challenge of creating a better system. (Shapiro and Cohen 2007, 153–54)

International Security Case Research

Protecting against terrorist attacks and outside intervention in the internal affairs of nations has become a major concern of governments around the globe. As a result, a number of researchers are focusing their attention on these issues. Two international cases on national security issues are included in the following pages. The first is a global case study on how an international organization is working to control money-laundering activities that threaten their internal financial systems and how they have expanded their actions to identify and stop the global movement of funds to support terrorist activities. The second case is one in which the small states that were once a part of the former Soviet Union are finding themselves facing the growing use of intimidation as a tool of Russian foreign policy.

Fighting the New Wave of Terrorism

The terrorist attack on New York City's World Trade Center and the Pentagon on September 11, 2001, was only the first in a series that included attacks in Central Africa, Bali, Casablanca, Madrid, Saudi Arabia, Pakistan, Turkey, London, India, Chechnya, and other former Soviet States. This wave of terrorism—traced primarily to the Al-Qaida network—has resulted in a huge drain on the time, people, and physical resources of federal, state, and local governments. The counterterrorist strategy of the UN Financial Action Task Force (FATF) was selected as an "ideal case study for effective measures in response to the particular challenges of the funding of global terrorism" (Gardiner 2003, 326).

In this case study, Gardiner (2003) identified three key features of the new wave of terrorist activity. First, terrorist activity had taken on a global character, with connected terrorist cells in the Middle East, Africa, Asia, and south and central Europe. Second, the rate of terrorist incidents has increased since 9/11. Third, evidence suggests that terrorist groups have modified their organizations' structures and widened their support base to cope with global counterterrorist actions. Controlling terrorist organization funding operations was the focus of this case study.

The FATF strategy has three primary objectives: (1) denial of assets to terrorist groups; (2) acquiring and disseminating knowledge of terrorist threats; and (3) achieving strong national compliance with global and regional plans, procedures, and principles. Ensuring compliance with the goals and programs of the global partnership is, of course, a heavy burden on the already resource-strapped operations of state and local government organizations.

Gardiner's (2003) research into what was being done in the fight against terrorist activity involved a case study of FATF, which was established in 1989 at the G8 Summit in Paris to examine money-laundering trends and techniques, review what actions nations had already taken, and determine what still needed to be done. A year later, the original membership of sixteen industrialized countries came up with a set of forty recommendations on money laundering, which are now considered the international standard in combating illegal transfers of money. The original forty recommendations covered criminal law, national regulations, and international cooperation. A core process in cooperation is national monitoring and recording of cross-border money flows. As of 2007, FATF had grown to include thirty-one member nations and two international organizations

The recommendations were revised in 1996, 2002, and again in 2003. After 9/11, the mission of FATF was expanded to include putting an end to the financing of terrorist activities. Eight special recommendations specifically dealing with stopping terrorist financing were adopted in 2002; a ninth recommendation was added in 2004. The nine special recommendations include making money laundering and financing terrorism illegal; giving investigative agencies authority to trace, seize, and confiscate criminally derived assets; sharing relevant information among member states; expanding anti–money-laundering provisions to include other remittance systems; and ensuring that nonprofit organizations cannot be used to finance terrorism activity. As a result, FATF is now in a leading position in the global fight against money laundering and other terrorist activity financing mechanisms.

Assessing the overall success of FATF has been problematic for several reasons. First, it is difficult to determine whether member nations are complying with antiterrorist and anti–money-laundering provisions because they are members of FATF, or if they are doing so regardless of the provisions. Second, principles and recommendations are not prioritized. Furthermore, no scale of degree of compliance exists, and no measure of rates of prosecution or scale of penalties exists. Most disconcerting is the fact that international enthusiasm for the antiterrorist program is waning as memory of the events of 9/11 fade into an increasingly distant past and new issues and concerns grab the attention of public managers and political leaders.

A Case of Security Threat in Latvia

As this book was being written, King and McNabb (2009) were finalizing a security-focused policy case study based on research undertaken in 2007–2008 during their assignments as Fulbright Senior Specialists in Latvia. They studied of the role of Latvian citizens and noncitizens (Russian and other Soviet-era émigrés remaining in Latvia) in shaping national security policies in the aftermath of the 2008 Russian invasion of Georgia. King and McNabb found widespread belief that Russia's pretext of defending Russian citizens in two Georgian provinces was really a military offensive and an internationally dangerous excuse for the rebirth of Russia's expansionist foreign policies.

The authors explored four possible political objectives of Russia that are perceived by many Latvians as constituting a threat to Latvian independence:

- Restoration of military security by Russian-led forces and the disestablishment of all NATO connection in Latvia, thereby increasing the ability of ethnic Russians to regain control of the Latvian state
- Regaining greater economic influence by Russia—if not total control—over Latvia as a strategically important neighboring territory
- Conversion of Latvia into a binational (Latvian and Russian) de facto, if not de jure, client state, with Latvian foreign relations controlled from Moscow
- Diminishment of ethnic Latvian identity and roles in schools, the economy, and international relations, with an increase of funding for Russian-language public schools

King and McNabb (2009) began with a review of recent attitudes and behaviors evident in the changing Latvian relationships with the East and the West. Latvia's position as a crossroads state between the East (Russia) and the West (the European Union [EU] and NATO block countries) has influenced the policies of this small but important Baltic Sea state. The case study reviewed responses by Latvian political and government leaders and influential citizens to a perceived decline in Western power and a concomitant resurgence of Russia's imperial aspirations.

Expediency or Appeasement

Latvia's political leaders find themselves forced to choose between a policy of expediency or one of appeasement. A policy of expediency implies flexibility, that is, the ability to evolve with changing external dynamics, whereas a policy of appeasement is a policy of one path, a road without recourse. Once an appeasement takes place, a nation or an individual is committed to sinking or swimming with the decision. The authors suggest that current events have made inevitable the policy of expediency that Latvia is trying to follow.

Latvia has long been part of Russia's strategy to gradually restore its influence over the former parts of the Soviet empire, as well as its prestige elsewhere in the world (Ozoliņa and Rikveilis 2006; Tabuns 2006; Treņins 1998). Latvia's independence, first proclaimed in1918, lost in 1940, and restored in 1991, has always been shaped by external and invasive forces. A small country unable to provide an adequate defense against aggression, Latvia adjusts its foreign policies to changing circumstances, with the resulting decisions of political expediency. However, recent geopolitical events may render such a policy incapable of protecting Latvia's independence in the future. The dramatic adjustments in Russia's foreign and military policies that occurred during the presidency of Vladimir Putin have the potential to greatly influence the shape of Latvia's internal and external relationships.

Latvians are sensitive to recent expressions of benevolent attitudes such as the visits of heads of states of Western powers to the country, on the one hand, and statements that can be interpreted as potentially damaging to the status quo, on the other hand. Examples include the reassuring visits to Latvia by U.S. presidents Bill Clinton and George W. Bush. Conversely, the proposal recently made by U.S. senator Charles Schumer in *The Wall Street Journal* has had an alternate and highly disturbing impact on public attitudes. Senator Schumer advocated the strengthening of American influence in Iran with Russian support and a simultaneous surrender of American interests in Eastern Europe to a Russian hegemony (Greenwald 2008). Lucas (2008) is another example of the point of view that the small Baltic states represent a weathervane in East–West relationships.

The responses to external changes by citizens of the Baltic States, however, are not likely to be uniform. To a large degree, they depend on feelings of security held by the population in each country. In the Baltics, feelings of insecurity are most pronounced in Latvia, which has the largest mass of unassimilated Russian immigrants who remained in the country after the collapse of the Soviet Union. These Russian loyalists are supported in their actions by former residents of the Belarus and Ukraine regions of the Soviet Union.

Russian Baltics Strategy

Elaborate plans to bring Latvia back into the Russian fold have been presented by Vyacheslav Altukhov, chairman of an advisory committee serving the Russian embassy in Riga. The multitiered plans announced by Altukhov include the restoration of Latvia as part of the Russian empire. If achieved, it would result in Latvians having less autonomy than that of the Finns in the Duchy of Finland before World War I. Altukhov's sample five-year plan includes the following schedule:

- 2008: Establish a Latvian TV channel with exclusively Russian programming.
- 2009: Make Russian officially the second state language in Latvia.
- 2010: Change the structure of the legislature to provide proportional Russian representation.
- 2011: Require a Russian prime minister in a binational state.
- 2012: Provide for double, Latvian and Russian, citizenship for all permanent residents in Latvian territory.

This plan, reminiscent of the Sudeten German claims before World War II, was confirmed during the first Conference of Russian Organizations, which is composed of representatives of Russians hostile to Latvian independence. The conference was billed as the most important Russian gathering in Latvia after the ineffective Interfront meetings in 1991.

The plan also requires the restructuring of the Latvian constitution and laws related to citizenship, education on all levels, as well as the status and use of state language. As a first step, Russian ambassador Aleksandr Veshnyakov urged the conferees to campaign for local municipal voting rights to all persons residing in Latvia, regardless of citizenship.

Such voting would pass the control of the city of Riga from Latvians (40 percent of residents) to ethnic Russians and other external minorities. Interestingly, the head of the Russian Orthodox Church in Moscow was critical of the conference as harmful to church unity and good international relations.

Latvian economic relationships with Russia reflect the political priorities of Russia in dealing with countries that were ruled by the Soviet Union. At best, they represent both ongoing business as well as new business opportunities in a unstable political environment. They are shaped by (1) increased Latvian dependence on Russian energy resources, (2) use of Latvian transportation systems and ports for transit trade for Russian foreign traders, (3) unproductive Russian private investments in Latvia, and (4) uncertain import–export bilateral trade of processed food and industrial products. The more important and strategically significant an economic relationship element, the more it has been subordinated to political considerations.

In contrast to Western nations, the economic programs of Russia are still determined by the ruling elite. Although Russia is no longer a superpower, it retains a militarily and economically powerful influence in all the bordering states of the former Soviet Union. In this context, one of the problems in assessing Russian influences is that the West, more specifically the EU, is in many respects rather a fluid and contested entity (Lehti 2007).

To prosper economically, Latvia needs both the East and the West. Expecting a new Atlantic alliance with the advent of the new century, Latvians hoped that American influence in Europe would increase, and that the EU itself would adopt a stronger, more unified approach in building economic and political relationships with Russia. Such developments were expected to show a trade expansion (already accounting for most Latvian trade) with the West as well as more normalized imports from Russia and other countries that were formerly parts of the Soviet Union.

Summary

This chapter began by examining some of the case research carried out on the problem of developing and managing programs for the prevention of terrorist attacks on the United States and its overseas facilities. Following this was case research on how to react to and manage safety and security issues in the event of an attack—an issue of concern to all levels of government. Because DHS is the lead agency for most antiterrorist activity, the first section focused on cases pertaining to one or more aspects of DHS and the nearly two dozen existing federal offices and agencies with some degree of responsibility for security that were combined to form the new cabinet-level department.

The preparedness process and procedures of DHS and its state and local partners were also described, followed by a look at the DHS grant system and its associated problems. The last section examined some of the case research on the antiterrorist activities and responsibilities of state and local government agencies.

The final two cases discussed in this chapter were studies on international security issues. The first was a study of an international organization formed to fight money laundering and the international movement of finances in support of terrorist activity. The second was a study on attitudes and opinions of political and governmental leaders in the small Eastern European state of Latvia, which must shape its internal and external policies with regard to possible reactions from the perceived return of expansionist policies by its neighbor Russia.

➤ 16 ◄

Case Research in Emergency and Disaster Management

> *Recent natural disasters, the spread of severe acute respiratory*
> *syndrome (SARS) from China in 2002 and the persistent threat of*
> *an influenza pandemic,* and the 2001 attack on the World Trade*
> *Center all highlight the need to plan for a coordinated response*
> *to large-scale public health emergencies. They also underscore*
> *the importance of the federal role in planning how to protect the*
> *American public, the nation's critical infrastructure, and the disaster*
> *responders involved in rescue, recovery, and cleanup activities.*
> — U.S. Government Accountability Office (GAO 2008c)

The chapter examines case research in the structure and workings of several federal, state, and local emergency and natural disaster preparedness programs. The chapter begins with a study in which existing theories of disaster and emergency management are discussed and a new theory is proposed. Although this study does not qualify as case research, it is included to provide readers with a structural model to follow for using case research to propose or test a theory. By substituting real cases for the hypothetical ones described in the study, a new theory can be introduced in the same way that it occurs in this study.

This section is followed by a brief review of the history and various programs and policies of the Federal Emergency Management Administration (FEMA). The third section focuses on case research on state and local government and nonprofit organization preparedness programs.

Emergency and disaster planning is a highly developed practice in many parts of the world, although response capabilities differ significantly. Disaster relief is expensive, and not all nations can afford to maintain and distribute relief

---

*This threat has now taken a more serious turn; on June 11, 2009, the World Health Organization declared that the A(H1N1) strain (swine flu) outbreak constituted a pandemic.

supplies, nor are they able to respond quickly with emergency medical care and infrastructure repair.

A Theory of Disaster and Emergency Management

In a multicase study of paradigms currently shaping research on disaster management, McEntire et al. (2002) concluded that the predominant theoretical approaches to the study of disaster management all fail in some way or another to provide sufficient guidance for emergency preparedness policymakers. Instead, the authors suggest a new model that they perceive as being better suited for helping scholars and practitioners to understand and reduce disaster damage. The existing models and McEntire et al.'s proposed new model, comprehensive vulnerability management, are shown in Table 16.1.

Three of the framing paradigms currently dominant in disaster research are (1) the disaster-resistant community, (2) the disaster-resilient community, and (3) sustainable development and sustainable hazards mitigation. These are examined as cases in this study. A fourth model, invulnerable development, is also proposed as a research paradigm and policy guide.

As a replacement for all four of these disaster scholarship and planning paradigms, McEntire et al. (2002) proposed the comprehensive vulnerability management model. The biggest advantage of this model is that it is holistic; that is, it integrates all activities involved in the reduction of emergencies and disasters. This paradigm represents an effort to identify and reduce all disaster vulnerabilities.

Invulnerable development refers to a process that exists to reduce the quantity, the frequency, and the extent of damage that results from emergencies and disasters. This occurs through mitigation capacity building and the reduction of liability. The process uses the following three steps:

- Altering cultural attitudes about disasters
- Linking development to reductions invulnerability
- Building and improving emergency management institutions

The Federal Emergency Management Agency

The Federal Emergency Management Agency (FEMA) was established in 1979 by President Jimmy Carter with two objectives: The first was to provide disaster relief and prevention and to lessen the damage and suffering that result from such large-scale disasters as earthquakes and hurricanes. The second was to function as a coordinator of civil responses to a nuclear attack. Loosely associated with the second mission was to plan and coordinate responses to national security threats. Box 16.1 touches upon some of this agency's recent problems in dealing with natural disasters.

Under President Ronald Reagan, the first mission objective was considered to be less critical, and as a result, the emergency and disaster preparedness arm of the agency

Table 16.1

Paradigms in Comprehensive Emergency Management

Paradigm	Definition	Examples of Activities
Disaster-resistant community	This model helps communities to minimize their vulnerability to natural hazards while maximizing application of the principles and techniques of mitigation to their development and/or redevelopment actions.	Mitigation activities include hazard and vulnerability analyses, prezoning methods, land-use planning, communication education, and stricter building codes and regulations.
Disaster-resilient community	No agreed-upon definition exists, but the term is implied to mean the ability to recover or bounce back to normalcy after a disaster occurs; a measure of how quickly a system recovers from failures.	Quick repair/redevelopment is planned for economic, emotional, and cultural infrastructure; may include more than the physical sciences and engineering. Sociologists, economists, anthropologists and psychologists may play a role.
Sustainable development and sustainable hazards mitigation	Sustainable development is what meets the needs of the present without compromising the ability of future generations to meet their needs; sustainable hazards mitigation may have a close association to the disaster-resilient model.	Sustainable development is the interaction of the environment, development, poverty, quality of life, and disaster planning. Hazards mitigation involves better land-use planning; building codes; loss insurance; and better prediction, forecasting, and warning systems.
Invulnerable development	Development undertaken in ways that reflect environment, economic, and social vulnerabilities of societies.	Decisions and actions are designed and implemented to reduce risk and susceptibility and increase resistance and resilience to disasters.
Comprehensive vulnerability management	A holistic and integrated system of activities directed toward the reduction of emergencies and disasters by diminishing risk and susceptibility and building resistance and resilience.	Decisions and policies are made based on careful and continued assessments of the liabilities and capabilities of the physical, social, and organizational environments.

Source: McEntire et al. (2002).

received far fewer resources. The second mission was given far greater attention; one example was the formation under FEMA of the Civil Security Division, which provided training for more than a thousand police in riot and political disturbance control procedures. In 1982 a presidential directive required FEMA to coordinate with the military; FEMA personnel then developed an effective telecommunications network that was taken over by the military and intelligence community.

Box 16.1

How FEMA Stumbled after Katrina

Charles Perrow, Yale University sociology professor emeritus, provided the following insightful analysis of why the Federal Emergency Management Agency (FEMA) performed so poorly in hurricane relief.

The focus of FEMA under President Clinton was on preparedness and natural disaster emergency relief. This focus was shifted to combating terrorism after 9/11. The resulting loss in disaster relief capabilities left the agency unprepared to meet the challenges of hurricanes Katrina and Rita. A few of the unnecessary problems that resulted were described by Perrow:

> Following Katrina, trucks with no supplies drove aimlessly past "refugees" who were without water or food or protection from the sun. Reporters came and went, but food and water and medical supplies did not. The Red Cross was not allowed to deliver goods because it might discourage evacuations. . . . Evacuation by air was slowed to a crawl because FEMA said the post-9/11 security procedures required a (prolonged) search for more than 50 federal air marshals to ride the airplanes, and to find security screeners. At the [departure] gates, inadequate electric power for the detectors held things up until officials relented and allowed time-consuming searches by hand of desperate and exhausted people. . . . Their only food, emergency rations in metal cans, was confiscated because it was thought that cans might contain explosives. . . . Volunteer physicians watched helplessly; FEMA did not allow them to help because they had not been licensed in the state.

> Perrow offered this partial explanation for these and more failures of FEMA: After being absorbed into the Department of Homeland Security, the agency lost the necessary ability to be flexible and innovative. In the absence of experienced leadership and a clearly defined emergency response mission, midlevel managers on the spot fell back on following the rules and going by the book. "Rather than being flexible and innovative, even when the challenge [was] overwhelming, these personnel appeared to revert to rote training, insistence upon following inappropriate rules, and an unusual fear of acting without official permission."

> *Source:* Perrow (2006).

Under President Bill Clinton, many of the earlier emergency preparedness responsibilities were returned to the agency. One particular success was the establishment of proactive programs to minimize damage from future disasters. Examples included government purchase of flooded lands to prevent future redevelopment, thus halting the cycle of development-flood-redevelopment and its associated costs.

Under President George W. Bush, an emphasis on privatizing many of FEMA's services and programs became a policy directive. After 9/11, the agency was merged into the new Department of Homeland Security. This again forced the agency to focus its attention on antiterrorist activities and responses to terrorist attacks, with preparedness for disaster relief again curtailed. Thus, FEMA was unable to respond effectively to such widespread natural disasters as hurricanes Katrina and Rita. The results of the weakening of its initial mission capabilities were made patently clear for everyone to see.

Case Research on Disaster and Emergency Management

Prior to the September 11, 2001, terrorist attacks on the World Trade Center and the Pentagon, few public health professionals had devoted much time to preparedness for dealing with such emergency situations (Glick et al. 2004). However, after the attacks, preparedness became a top priority of public safety and health organizations. This section describes four case research studies in which some aspect of disaster or emergency planning and/or implementation is addressed. The first is a single-case study that focuses on local emergency planning. The next section describes the experiences of two different organizations as a result of Hurricane Katrina. This is followed by a multicase study of emergency management programs in Florida counties.

Disaster Management Case Research Examples

The first single-case study is concerned with a local public health community: the emergency preparedness activities of the Charlottesville, Virginia, health department. This post-9/11 program was described in a 2004 case study (Glick et al. 2004).

Disaster Management Planning in Charlottesville

Charlottesville, with a population of 45,049 and another nearly 80,000 residing in the county, is the home of the University of Virginia's (UVA) medical school and a 529-bed academic medical center. A 176-bed community hospital, the local public health department, and numerous nearby health-related agencies are tied into the preparedness network. The city is located just 110 miles southwest of Washington, DC, and 162 miles west of the Norfolk, Virginia, U.S. Navy Base. It is a primary backup location for casualties in the event that either of those high-priority locations suffers a terrorist attack.

The UVA health system participates in the National Disaster Medical System and employs a Hospital Emergency Incident Command System for emergency management. The system defines roles and responsibilities, and uses a common language for all emergency responders. Preparedness for a terrorist attack was defined as the following:

Preparedness for a terrorist attack includes personal, professional, or community knowledge and plans to prevent or alleviate a disaster. In addition, it requires interdisciplinary efforts that encompass the best skills of all health professionals working together. To be prepared to respond in a timely manner requires creation of public–private partnerships that include public health and hospital personnel; emergency-response personnel, including police and fire departments; laboratory and pharmacy resources; mental health support; and community volunteers. (Glick et al. 2004, 267)

FEMA requires that all jurisdictions receiving federal funds for emergency management have annual emergency operations plan exercises. One of these drills took place in Charlottesville in 2004, with more than 400 professionals participating in a combined exercise involving a simulated illegal dumping of toxic chemicals and a terrorist group hostage-taking scenario.

The description of that exercise serves as the chief knowledge-building function of this case. In addition to helping participating agencies learn where additional attention is needed, the emergency drill experiences described in the case can serve as an information source for other emergency-response networks.

Two Cases on Emergency Response

Hurricanes Katrina and Rita resulted in the loss of hundreds of lives and billions of dollars in damage to the American Gulf Coast. Particularly hard hit were the states of Louisiana and Mississippi. This section presents excerpts from two widely different cases on damage from Katrina.

Saving Animals in New Orleans

The first of these two case studies describes the experiences of a New Orleans non-profit organization before, during, and after Hurricane Katrina. This well-written and informative case study on one of the few success stories to come out of the 2005 flooding in New Orleans can serve as a model of emergency preparedness and disaster response that other agencies will find valuable. Rizzuto and Maloney (2008) described the actions of the Louisiana Society for the Prevention of Cruelty to Animals (LA/SPCA) before, during, and after the emergency. The local animal shelter was one of the many civil organizations destroyed by floodwaters after Hurricane Katrina struck the Gulf Coast in August 2005.

Prior to the disaster, LA/SPCA was the largest animal welfare agency in the state and the only animal shelter in New Orleans. It operated with sixty-five paid staff members, hundreds of volunteers, and an annual budget of $3 million. This case describes emergency preparedness actions taken by LA/SPCA management before the hurricane, actions that it followed during the flooding, and action steps that were taken after the flood during the initial cleanup and early rebuilding.

Although many organizations failed to meet the challenges set out for them—

including the initial response failures of FEMA—the LA/SPCA stands out as one of the disaster's few successes. Floods caused by breaches in a number of levies destroyed the animal shelter along with Lower Ninth District of New Orleans. However, the fast action of the LA/SPCA before the hurricane hit the city enabled the staff to save all the animals in the shelter.

A Three-Stage Response

The case describes the actions of the agency during three response phases of the disaster. The first stage consisted of preplanning and emergency preparedness before landfall (August 26–28). LA/SPCA began planning its animal rescue and recovery operation four decades before Hurricane Katrina hit New Orleans. Lessons on what not to do were driven home when Hurricane Betsy hit the city in 1965. Then, the shelter did not have a plan that called for early evacuation of animals in its care. As a result, when the shelter flooded, many animals were lost.

In 2005, however, the shelter placed its emergency plan into operation days before Katrina hit shore. The plan mandated emergency evacuation of all animals seventy-two hours before the landfall of any Category 3 or higher storm. Katrina, originally a Category 5 storm, had been downgraded but remained a Category 3 storm. Therefore, three days before the storm hit, the staff evacuated all animals to shelters in Houston, Texas.

The second stage involved operations during the crisis, August 29 through October 15. Because it was the only animal shelter in New Orleans, the LA/SPCA was to be the lead emergency-response agency for animals in local emergency plans. However, many of the agency's staff and volunteers also lost their homes in the flooding. The staff became both emergency responders and an affected population.

The LA/SPCA lost more than 75 percent of its staff during this period; many were evacuated along with thousands of other New Orleans citizens. Remaining LA/SPCA staff and volunteers had to rescue thousands of stray animals left in the devastated city. Rescuers had to operate in an environment marked by "violence, anarchy, fires, and toxic floodwaters" (Rizzuto and Maloney 2008, 79). A location some sixty miles west of the city was designated as the center for animal rescue activities, resulting in what was described as the "largest animal rescue in U.S. history," with something like 15,000 animals rescued.

The third stage occurred from October 2005 through August 2006. In this, the stage identified as a crisis of legitimation, the agency implemented four strategies: Increase animal placement, improve a temporary shelter structure during construction of a new shelter (to be occupied in 2007), build new work structures (including procedures, policies, job titles and descriptions, etc., in response to high rates of stress and employee turnover), and continue to improve planning and crisis preparation. The permanent staff was increased to forty-five employees during this period.

Lessons Learned by LA/SPCA

Following the tenet introduced by Pearson and Clair (1998, 74), "What is yet to be learned and disseminated by researchers and managers regarding crisis management is of vital importance to organizations," Rizzuto and Maloney (2008, 83–84) concluded their case report with five recommended strategies for organizations involved in crisis and emergency preparedness planning:

- Extend the planning horizon to include other organizations. LA/SPCA's planned operations were hurt because of failures or inadequate planning by other organizations. Strive for optimal self-sufficiency and limited dependence on other organizations.
- Develop crisis contingencies and conduct exercises with contingency circumstances. Form crisis management teams for critical operations such as communications, decision making, rescue and recovery, and internal staff and team support; establish a system for knowledge collection, sharing, and archiving.
- Make sure that leadership is in place across the organization. Leadership cannot occur only at the highest levels; all employees must know when and how to lead by making quick and autonomous decisions in emergency situations.
- Develop and maintain the employee–employer commitment that is needed to maintain mutual trust among staff. This commitment resulted in the heroism and self-sacrifice of members of the staff during the 2005 rescue mission of the agency.
- Build an organizational culture that accepts change. Managers must show that they value innovation, are willing to accept new tasks and procedures, and can change behaviors. An important goal of this strategy is emergence of a learning organization that embraces change as an opportunity.

Hurricane Disaster Management in Public Utilities

Disaster and emergency planning and implementation are not just a concern for government agencies, as this case about a large public utility attests. Although the organization described in this case (Ball 2006) is an investor-owned public utility, the impact on public welfare caused by disruption of utility service is such that it is included as an example of the damage a disaster can cause. Moreover, because utilities are often highly regulated by state and local governments, private utilities are seen as quasi-government agencies (McNabb 2005). This case study of the benefits of preplanning and disaster-response training for utility employees focuses on damage to electric power generation and distribution facilities in the Gulf Coast caused by Hurricane Katrina (Ball 2006).

Hurricane Katrina hit the Mississippi-Louisiana state line on the morning of August 29, 2005; it was the worst disaster in the eighty-year history of Southern Company's Mississippi Power subsidiary. All of Mississippi Power's nearly 200,000 customers lost power; nearly two-thirds of the transmission and distribution system was damaged or destroyed; all but three of the company's 122 transmission lines were down; more than 300 transmission towers were damaged. Nearly 65 percent of the distribution system facilities were damaged; 9,000 poles and 2,300 transformers were lost.

Total cost of restoration of the Mississippi system was estimated to exceed $250 million—the most costly in the company's history. Overall, the total of all losses in 2005 dollars from the hurricane was estimated at $125 billion— the most expensive natural disaster in U.S. history. The next most expensive loss may have been the damage caused when Hurricane Ike—the then largest Atlantic hurricane on record— came ashore in the center of the county's oil production sector in September 2008. That damage was estimated at over $27 billion (NOAA 2009).

Restoring Power after Katrina

A case study of the planning that made relatively rapid recovery by Southern Company possible, prepared by the senior vice president of Transmission Planning and Operations, was posted on the National Academy of Engineering Web site a year after the storm (Ball 2006). Each of the power company's five operating subsidiaries developed detailed disaster-recovery plans that identified specific responses and resources. Every year before the start of the hurricane season, employees undergo storm-damage training to ensure that every aspect of the recovery plan, including recovery assignments, is understood by all workers.

Examples of preplanning activities for Mississippi Power included lining up personnel, material, and logistics for the projected storm-damaged service area. This included nearly 3,000 line workers and 1,750 tree trimmers. Arrangements were made to have nearly 4,800 beds available in mobile sleeper trailers, military and college facilities, tents, motels, and company buildings. Portable toilets, showers, and waste facilities were set up at predetermined staging sites, three days before the storm came ashore. The company had spent nearly $7 million in setting up activities even before the storm damage began.

A number of lessons were learned from the disaster and incorporated into plans for future disaster responses. Among these were to plan for the worse to happen, but be prepared for the damage to be even greater than anticipated, and plan in advance to coordinate and seek support from federal, state, and local government agencies.

Multicase Studies of Emergency Management

The next two cases deal with widely different aspects of disaster and emergency activity. The first is an analysis across sixty-seven selected counties in the state of Florida to evaluate differences in spending growth for emergency programs (Choi 2004). The second is an analysis of the lack of communication and rescue coordination among government agencies, private firms, and volunteer rescue groups at a railroad accident in the United Kingdom (Smith and Dowell 2000).

Growth in Emergency Spending in Florida Counties

Local governments have long been considered to be the most appropriate and effective organizations for rapid response to natural (floods, fires, earthquakes, ice storms, etc.) and other types of disasters (including but not limited to toxic waste spills and terrorist attacks) (Comfort 1985; Waugh 1994; Choi 2004).

County governments are often singled out as the best structured for this purpose. Counties are also usually of the best size and scope to lead regional planning, policy making, and disaster and emergency program implementation. Just as counties differ widely in size and financial strength, however, their ability to lead in emergency planning and response varies. One of the chief factors that limits this ability is the amount of resources counties earmark for emergency and disaster activities.

In an effort to identify antecedent factors affecting emergency-response effectiveness, Choi (2004) examined economic, political, institutional, and demographic characteristics in a multicase study involving sixty-seven counties in Florida. Florida was chosen for the study for several reasons. First, in the several years prior to the study the state had experienced a number of natural disasters, including hurricanes, floods, and wildfires. The great majority—78 percent—of the state's residents live along the coast, resulting in more people at risk than any state in the nation. Since Hurricane Andrew caused extensive damage in 1992, the state has implemented more emergency management activities and programs than any other state.

In this study, Choi (2004) found that growth in county spending on emergency management could be explained by five factors: the structure of county government (council-manager forms spend less on emergency management functions but more on public safety programs), changes in property values, the vulnerability to natural disasters, and population growth and density.

Rescue Coordination Failure Across Agencies

Smith and Dowell (2000) reported on their multicase study of interagency coordination issues in three emergency and disaster response agencies in the United Kingdom. The triggering event was the response to a small-scale 1995 railway accident, with the analysis focusing on decisions on how to transport casualties from the isolated location to a hospital.

The two-train collision occurred in the rain at an isolated location, with the track high above a roadway and the only access to the site by foot up a steep, slippery slope. Three options were discussed to move the approximately thirty accident victims to a hospital: (1) carry them by stretcher down the slippery slope; (2) carry them along a rough path along the track to an overpass where they could then be transferred to ambulances; or (3) call for a third, emergency evaluation train (some sixty minutes away). In this latter case, the injured could stay warm and relatively comfortable in the railcars. The first option was discarded at the advice of medical staff as being too dangerous. The second option was tried with the badly injured driver of the first train, using volunteer stretcher bearers. It, too, proved too difficult. Someone called the railway company to ask if a rescue train was available. One arrived an hour later, with no one knowing who ordered it.

Smith and Dowell (2000) described the lack of coordination between involved rescue agencies as a "persistent problem" in the management of disaster responses. These agencies include emergency services (police, fire, ambulance) and local and national government agencies, private-sector organizations, and volunteer groups (in this case, local mountain rescue groups).

The core of the problem in such situations, apparently, is that despite the good intentions and good performance of the individuals involved, when no one seems to be in charge, some things get overlooked while duplication of effort occurs elsewhere. This is particular problematic when the persons on the scene have multiple options, with the ramifications of each not clearly understood.

Decision making at the site of the U.K. train accident was restricted to persons at the site; regardless of their rank, individuals not at the site did not attempt to direct actions. The problem with the circumstances at the site was that it was not clear who should make what kinds of decisions. In such situations as this the following occurs:

> Each disaster gives rise to the formation of what can be called an incident organization; that is, a temporary configuration of otherwise disparate resources drawn from many agencies. Within the incident organization, those distributed people, technologies and procedures concerned with directing resources can be identified collectively as the disaster management system. The problem of inter-agency coordination lies in the interaction between the structure of this emerging disaster management system, and techniques of individual and team decision-making. (Smith and Dowell 2000, 3)

Disaster Management after a Tsunami

Cuddalore, the district and regional center in Southeast India, has the dubious distinction of being one of the most disaster-prone areas of all the Indian subcontinent. This multihazard district is subject to cyclones, floods, droughts, earthquakes, and, periodically, devastating tsunamis. A brief look at one of those disasters is the last case to be included in this chapter.

The latest megadisaster to strike Cuddalore occurred on December 26, 2004, when tsunami waves poured ashore after a 9.1 Richter scale earthquake on the floor of the Indian Ocean. In just a little more than seven hours, shores around the Indian Ocean were devastated. In Cuddalore alone, 618 people died; the lives of more than 97,000 people of the region were affected in some way—many were left homeless in a matter of minutes. More than 80,000 people received some type of medical attention, and some 24,000 people had to flee their home villages with nothing.

The extent of the tsunami damage and the coordinated relief efforts of the Indian and local government agencies, volunteers, and many nongovernmental agencies was the subject of a 2006 case study by Anu George, an Indian Administrative Service (IAS) officer in Cuddalore. The IAS, originally the Indian Civil Service under British rule, became the IAS when India achieved its independence; the IAS manages both the national and state public administration for the entire country. The case describes in detail how the Indian government and district administration managed relief and rescue operations following the tsunami, including protecting against misuse of the global outpouring of sympathy in the form of financial and other aid.

Many nongovernment agencies (NGOs) also rushed to the aid of the victims of the tsunami. A major task of IAS administrators became managing the work of these and other groups and individuals. The case report included a list of important lessons that anyone involved in a similar situation would benefit from. They are paraphrased here:

1. Some NGOs and individuals with high-profile media attention may have to be tolerated for their nuisance value; in some cases, the attention they commanded in the media outshone the steady work of the district administration.

2. NGOs, like all large organizations, tend to be bureaucratic. The bigger they are and the greater their reputation, the more bureaucratic they can be. Often, they are the first to reach a disaster site, but their rigid structure makes their progress slow.

3. Be wary of agencies wanting to spread their aid too thin. Restoration should be structured to protect against efforts that are provincial or political.

4. Most NGOs need a local person to listen to their stories, even it entails a "trip down memory lane."

5. In whatever they do, voluntary agencies need to be given center stage. Often what they do depends on what they are asked to do. It is usually better to request specific items rather than simply asking for help. For example, it is better to request a toolbox with a specific set of boat-building tools, with the total cost for a specific number of tool sets, than it is just to say "we need tools for our boat carpenters."

6. Never let any help that shows up go away. Every cent is important; everyone can do something. Give organizations like NGOs choices and call later to remind them you are waiting to hear from them. Often it is a call from you that results in an action; it makes them feel that their effort is important to the total effort.

7. Be prepared to broker peace between various agencies or NGOs working in a village.

8. The follow-up has to continue until the end of the delivery stage of the restoration. NGO coordination meetings are valuable at this time because they can help to exercise friendly pressure on the groups to deliver what they promise.

George (2006) concluded the case report with the important reminder that disaster management involves sound administration and a sound system in place that can respond positively when the need arises. As with many of the cases examined for this report, "Ultimately what we need in addition to warning systems and communications equipment are people who can manage the situation against all odds. This together with training and preparedness can go a long way in making this world a better and a safer place to live" (George 2006, 21).

Summary

To increase understanding of the emergency and natural disaster programs and policies of the federal, state, and local governments, the chapter examined case studies on how five states have reacted to federal mandates to form their own security and emergency preparedness and response planning and administrative offices.

The second half of the chapter focused on examples of case research in emergency preparedness and response among state and local organizations. The first case described a city-county program to improve health department effectiveness. The second case described the experiences of a nonprofit animal shelter organization—a program considered to be one of the few emergency preparedness and response actions in the wake of Hurricane Katrina and subsequent flooding of much of the city of New Orleans. A case on how utilities preplan and prepare for disasters such as Hurricane Katrina was also discussed, as were cases on emergency management programs in Florida counties, disaster response mistakes at a railway accident site, and the 2004 Indian tsunami.

➤ 17 ◄

Case Research in Social and Health Services

*Growth in health-related costs serves as the primary driver of the
fiscal challenges facing the state and local sector over the long term.
Medicaid is a key component of their health-related costs. . . . States
and localities are facing increased demand for services during
a period of declining revenues and reduced access to capital. In
the midst of these challenges, the federal government continues to
rely on [the state and local] sector for delivery of services such as
Medicaid, the joint federal-state health care financing program for
certain categories of low-income individuals.*
—Stanley J. Czerwinski (2008)

Social and health services provided by federal, state, and local governments are
designed to provide benefits and programs such as education; food safety and nutrition support; health care; subsidized housing; and other programs for improving the
health, life, and living conditions of the nation's children, disabled, disadvantaged,
elderly, and poor. All of these programs are mirrored to some degree in state and
local governments, where the services are actually delivered. For the first time since
1983, however, in 2008 and 2009 state and local governments were spending less
on social welfare (adjusted for inflation and need). This drop was largely due to
a steep decline in federal grants to states and local governments, which occurred
mostly because of changes in the Medicaid program (Gais and Dadayan 2008).
How, when, why, and by whom these services are delivered to the public and the
nature of the services themselves are targets for case research.

The U.S. Department of Health and Human Services (HHS) administers the
federal programs that deal with health and welfare. HHS manages more than 300
programs with nearly 65,000 employees and a 2008 budget of $707.7 billion. These
social services programs designed to enhance the total well-being of the entire
society swallow nearly a quarter of the entire U.S. federal budget.

Health and Human Services administers more grant dollars than all other federal agencies combined (HHS 2008). Because almost all of its services are provided to target clients through contract with states, counties, municipalities, faith-based, and other nonprofit organizations and private firms, HHS programs have a tremendous impact on the economies of most state and local governments and the well-being of their citizens.

A short list of some of the major programs of the HHS include health and social science research; prevention of disease; assuring food and drug safety; administering Medicare and Medicaid; financial assistance for low-income families; improving maternal and infant health; Head Start, faith-based, and community initiatives; preventing child abuse and domestic violence; services for older Americans and Native Americans; and medical preparedness for emergencies and terrorist activity.

The social services supported by HHS are provided through state and local governments through three main management approaches: (1) directly, using government workers; (2) indirectly, using grants and contracts awarded to private nonprofit, faith-based, and private-sector firms for providing services to eligible individuals and groups; and (3) indirectly through vouchers that are delivered to eligible citizens who then use the vouchers to purchase services from approved public- or private-sector providers (Savas 2002).

Social Services at the National Level

Case research on social services at the national level tends to focus on policy issues rather than the methods or means of delivery of the services, whereas at the state and local levels, case research tends to focus more on applications and delivery of social services. Therefore, this chapter will concentrate on case research at the state and local levels.

Social Services at the State Level

Departments of social services are often the largest agencies in state governments. For example, the more than 19,000 employees of the North Carolina Department of Health and Human Services administer programs with impact from birth to old age on nearly every citizen of the state through its prenatal programs, child development, and rest home regulations and health and welfare programs in between. The department is organized into three main divisions: medical assistance; social services; and mental health, developmental disabilities, and substance abuse services (North Carolina Department of Health and Human Services 2008).

The 5,200 employees of the Nevada Department of Health and Human Services administer a diverse set of programs that are organized into five divisions: services to the aged and aging; child and family welfare; health services, including food and drug and medical facilities; health care financing and policy, including Medicaid; and mental health and development services, including substance abuse, welfare, and support services (Nevada Department of Health and Human Services 2006).

North Dakota, with approximately 2,000 employees and a biannual budget of $1.9 billion, has one of the smaller state human services departments (North Dakota Department of Human Services 2007). Services provided include the care of the disabled by the Department of Mental Health, Retardation and Hospitals; child protective and social services provided by the Department of Children, Youth and Families; health programs at the Department of Health and the Department of Human Services; financial assistance and social services provided by the Department of Human Services; and pharmaceutical assistance and home health care at the Department of Elderly Affairs.

The administrative functions of human services in Rhode Island are organized into five departments: Children, Youth and Families; Elderly Affairs; Health; Human Services; and Mental Health, Retardation and Hospitals. These departments annually serve 284,000 Rhode Island citizens; the departments' budget exceeds $2.3 billion, which represents 41 percent of the state budget (Rhode Island Department of Human Services 2005).

Welfare Reform and Privatization in Mississippi

The Personal Responsibility and Work Opportunity Reconciliation Act (PRWORA) of 1996 allowed the states great discretion in the way they would assume responsibility for implementing elements of this welfare reform program. The experience of the state of Mississippi with welfare reform was the subject of a 2002 case study by Breaux et al. Mississippi chose to privatize elements of the program by contracting with private and nonprofit organizations for delivery of two of its three chief functions.

By the time the PRWORA bill was signed into law, the federal government had given permission to any state that wished to experiment with reforms and improvements to their welfare systems. Forty-three states took advantage of the opportunity, and welfare reform began to take shape. Incorporating the best of those experiences, the final program that was finally enacted into law followed most of the provisions in a model developed by just three states: Mississippi, Oregon, and Wisconsin. Mississippi had implemented a pilot study in welfare reform (Work-First) in 1994, fully two years before passage of the federal law. Mississippi's WorkFirst plan made receipt of welfare benefits contingent upon fulfillment of a work requirement. After passage of PRWORA, Mississippi implemented its pilot program statewide. However, the new system also included significant provisions for privatization.

Temporary Assistance for Needy Families

The new system replaced the state's Aid to Families with Dependent Children (AFDC) program with Temporary Assistance for Needy Families (TANF). Under

AFDC, once clients met eligibility requirements, there were no time limits or work requirements needed for benefits. Under TANF, however, strict work requirements and time limits were imposed. Accordingly, state human services personnel found the missions of state human services agencies changed from providers of benefits to facilitators of transition to work programs.

The TANF program in Mississippi was based on three components: First was establishment of *client eligibility.* State Department of Human Services (DHS) personnel at local human services offices made these decisions. The eligibility workers also determined whether the client was exempt from the work requirement. The state eligibility determination system was divided into six management districts. Every county in the state also had a DHS director who reported to one of the six local district directors.

Transfer to the Second Component

Once established as eligible, clients were then transferred to the second component: *case management.* At this stage such barriers to work as child care and transportation needs were evaluated. As a part of the case management system, each client was required to sign a contract that spelled out his or her responsibilities for remaining eligible. Case management services were provided by workers referred to as Case Management Entities, or CMEs.

Case management services were contracted out in twelve districts of the state. The Mississippi Department of Economic Development—a carryover from the earlier Job Opportunity and Basic Skills (JOBS) program—negotiated the contracts and managed contractor performance. Each of the twelve districts had its own director. CMEs received high salaries and had fewer job skill requirements than the DHS workers in the first component of the system—a point of contention among state workers.

Transfer to the Third Component

After case management, the client was referred to the third component of the program: regional job placement contractors (JPCs). Placement services were divided into nine different districts, with each district having its own director. Job placement contracts were managed by the state Department of Human Services. JPCs placed clients in jobs and determined needs for (and provided, if necessary) job-readiness training. Both the case management component and the job placement component were contracted out to either private or nonprofit organization service providers in the various districts.

Achieving success in the program required close cooperation of representatives from the three component parts of the system—a level of cooperation and coordination that was seldom reached, according to the case researchers. It did not take long for the complex system to unravel. A large number of clients passed quickly through the system at first, resulting in an inflated success rate. When the number of clients dropped, the success ratio also dropped. Because contractor contracts called for payment by the number of clients served, their income dropped significantly, and they sought renegotiation of their contracts. When the client load fell, they were left with the hardest-to-serve clients and demanded to have their contracts revised. Many jobs provided were low-quality, low-paid, service-oriented positions, another point of contention.

More Problems Surface

Another problem was the availability of jobs in the various districts. Placements in jobs depended on the numbers of jobs available in communities—a rate that differed dramatically across the state. The availability of suitable placement contractors with the desired quality and experience in providing needed services varied significantly between private and nonprofit provider organizations. The authors summed up the problems that occurred in the system this way:

> In sum, the TANF story in Mississippi is one of a pattern of complex contractual relationships in a multi-actor principal–agent relationship that were not adequately monitored. Furthermore, the incentives in the contracts were often at odds with the goals of DHS and, perhaps, with the larger goals of citizens. The inability to co-align goals . . . among citizens, government, and the various contracted entities created an implementation structure that courted mediocrity, if not outright failure. (Breaux et al. 2002, 99–100)

Two years after the complex public–private partnership was established, the problems in managing the system forced an end to the privatization experiment. All private and nonprofit job placement contractors had left the system, and DHS was managing all three components of the system itself, although personnel shortages required it to use some personal-services contracts (with five-day cancellation clauses) with individuals for provision of job-readiness training. Performance-based contracts had been replaced by hourly rate or flat fee payments for services. By bringing the three components of the system in-house, DHS regained direct performance monitoring authority. The researchers concluded their report with the caveat that such complex structures for public–private partnerships and contractual systems require public managers to decide which program goals take precedence over others while arriving at a balance between administrative control and political expediency.

Social Services at the Local Level

Case research on social services issues and programs at the local level often deals with issues that have to do with activities and programs in operation at the point of delivery. An example of this type of case research is the 1988 case developed by Glenda Laws of York University. The case focused on three researcher-formed questions as they related to the case of Toronto, Canada.

The first examined was the ways in which organizations in the social services community had reacted to social problems that had arisen as a consequence of changes outside of the city's boundaries. Chief among these external forces included restructuring of the national, regional, and local economy from a manufacturing to a services focus, with reductions in the size and focus of the private sector.

The number of citizens living below the poverty level and thus in need of some level of social assistance was a consequence of this restructuring. It also included a shift of the nation's resources away from social services to such other sectors, thereby reducing the resources available to assist the growing in-need population. As a consequence, a trend toward privatization of services had occurred.

The second question addressed in the case was an examination of the ways in which the privatization of social services could affect the delivery of social services in local communities. Privatization was defined as a process that involves transfer of the responsibility for delivery of social services from the public to organizations in the private sector, including private for-profit enterprises and traditional nonprofit and faith-based organizations.

Widespread Growth in Privatization

At the time of the case, privatization was occurring in many different areas of public service, including public transportation operations and facilities, public utilities, and social services. This was also a period of widespread growth in the global public management movement and privatization of many state-owned public enterprises.

The case then examined four consequences of privatization that could impact a local economy: (1) a loss of government jobs, (2) competition within the private sector for government contracts for providing the services, (3) growth in regulation and funding of local private-sector organizations by local governments, and (4) the local reaction to privatization.

The third component of the study was an examination of some of the changes then occurring in social services in metropolitan Toronto. The region had been under considerable pressure to "rationalize" public services and reduce expenditures across the board. The distribution of citizens in need of social services had shifted from central Toronto to several suburban areas. The "suburbanization" of poverty was accompanied by greater demand for food assistance, affordable housing, and health services in those regions. A result was development of additional food banks, emergency housing, and other services by a host of private-sector organizations. A need for some coordination of public and private services became apparent and was met by establishment of a coordinating board by the city of Toronto.

Two broad sets of sociopolitical forces were determined to be major contributors to the local emergence of social problems in Toronto: first, the extent of reactions to economic restructuring in the locality (the greater the impact of economic change, the greater the need for social services) and, second, the form that restructuring of social services takes in the region (how and whether these greater needs are met by the public sector, through privatization, or through a combination of both). In Toronto, privatization was the selected means of answering social services needs.

Case Research at the Local and Rural Levels

Volunteer delivery of emergency medical service (EMS) in rural areas and small communities was the topic of a case study report by Norris, Mandell, and Hathaway (1993). At the time of the study, volunteer EMS organizations with approximately 180,000 members provided EMS to close to 30 percent of the American public. Rather than studying the larger system of volunteer EMS, the authors focused on a single issue of EMS delivery in Wicomico County, Maryland. The predominantly rural county had a population of 74,000 residents, with about 60 percent of the total living in or near the town of Salisbury, the county seat.

Three Conclusions

Norris, Mandell, and Hathaway (1993) drew three conclusions from a review of the empirical literature. First, volunteer EMS units are common in rural areas; in fact, many such areas would not have EMS if it were not for volunteers. At the time of the research, at least 18 percent of reporting local governments used volunteer organizations for their EMS.

Second, reliance upon volunteers for EMS is probably much higher than the study suggested. A few examples supporting this conclusion were reports that 92 percent of all ambulance service in New Jersey was provided by volunteers in nonprofit organizations; 74 percent of Pennsylvania's emergency medical technicians were volunteers; 66 percent of EMS in Alaska was provided by volunteers; in Iowa, as much as 70 percent of EMS was provided by volunteers; and all counties in Maryland, including the heavily urbanized areas of suburban Baltimore and the Washington, DC, area, use volunteer EMS providers.

Third, many EMS organizations were reporting increasing difficulty in proving adequate service, particularly during workweek daylight hours. Reasons suggested for the difficulty included (1) a decline in volunteerism in general and (2) the rapid growth in demand for EMS due to local growth and an aging population. All volunteer organizations in the case study county were reporting difficulty in maintaining adequate service because of this inadequate volunteer coverage.

EMS was provided by volunteer fire departments in rural areas of the county and by professional EMS members of the Salisbury Fire Department. Each of the seven rural departments received annual stipends of $20,000 from the county for providing EMS; the county reimbursed the Salisbury Fire Department for any EMS they provided outside of the city limits (a total of $147,000 the year of the study).

Other than the state certification required of all EMS providers in Maryland, at the time of the study there was little regulatory oversight exercised by any level of government. However, some coordination of service was possible through the channeling of all emergency calls through an area-wide 911 center.

Deciding on an EMS System

Two types of EMS were available in the county: advanced life support (ALS) and basic life support (BLS). Experience had shown county administrators that in almost all cases, it was advisable to respond to all emergency medical calls with ALS service. The problem was a lack of adequate daytime ALS coverage because of a shortage of ALS-certified volunteers.

A committee of volunteer EMS providers recommended that the county fund a solution by purchasing "chase vehicles" to be staffed by paid professionals to provide ALS coverage during weekday daylight hours. The annual cost of the service was expected to be in the neighborhood of $200,000. The committee did not support this argument with any empirical data, however. Therefore, before authorizing the expenditure, the county called for an independent review of the issue. The case described results of the review in detail.

Research Findings

Norris, Mandell, and Hathaway (1993) collected data in several ways. First, a series of in-depth personal and group interviews were conducted with members of county government, the 911 Center, volunteer fire companies, the Salisbury Fire Department, the Maryland EMS governing body, and local hospital emergency personnel. Second, the study team conducted telephone interviews with all volunteer EMS providers. Finally, the researchers examined secondary data that included aggregate records of EMS calls over the preceding six years and a detailed analysis of a sample of EMS calls during the twelve months before the start of the study.

Interviews revealed that all affected organizations concurred that a serious problem with ALS service on weekday daylight hours existed. Analysis of aggregate data revealed wide differences experienced by EMS providers; the greatest jump in calls (an increase of 63.6 percent over the preceding six years) occurred in Salisbury. The city was responding to more calls than were all the volunteer fire departments combined. Detailed examination of the sample revealed the problem to be more severe than local officials had expected. Nor was it just a daytime, weekday problem; it was a problem twenty-four hours a day, seven days a week, 365 days a year.

Recommendations

Norris, Mandell, and Hathaway (1993) examined nineteen alternatives before presenting its list of potential solutions to the problem of inadequate ALS coverage.

Those recommendations ranged from no action at all (immediately rejected) to two sets of solutions that would provide a range of improvement in the level of service—at varying increases in cost. The first set of alternatives centered on the volunteer departments and the Salisbury Fire Department providing "enhanced mutual aid" to one another, with no chase vehicle purchase. The second set of alternatives included sixteen variations, all of which involved purchase of one or two chase vehicles. Variations in this set of alternatives also included use of either paid or volunteer ALS personnel. A "hypercube queuing model" statistical analysis gave researchers data needed to predict the impact of the alternatives on ALS coverage.

Norris, Mandell, and Hathaway (1993) concluded their report with three findings. The first of these has implications that extend far beyond Wicomico County, and which could prove beneficial to other public managers before taking any action on recommendations based on the opinions of even the most well-intentioned individuals: No matter how "intuitively or politically appealing, unexamined claims" of a crisis seem, those claims may not be factually true. Thus, uncritical acceptance of such claims may only result in a poor, overly expensive, or inappropriate solution. In Wicomico County, case research did in fact show the claims of a crisis to be correct. More important, the most cost-effective alternative established in the findings gave elected officials justification for taking action to resolve a pressing health services problem.

Case Research in Health and Human Services Management

The 800-pound gorilla of public management in the early years of the twenty-first century is the aging of the baby boom generation. This phenomenon affects decisions at most areas and levels of government, although the greatest impact may be the effect increasing numbers of retirees are having and will continue to have on health care systems. The high costs of medical insurance make health care already far beyond the reach of huge numbers of citizens.

Denhardt and Miller (2000) touched upon this issue in a short teaching case they developed for city human resource managers dealing with the issue of paying for health benefits for city employees. Administrators of a city of 37,000 residents believed that the city could no longer afford to self-insure employees' health insurance benefits. The difficulty was that no commercial insurance plan provides the same coverage scope as the existing plan. The risk of losing catastrophic care coverage was the greatest worry of the city's employees.

Contracting Human Services in Kansas

Problems and pitfalls experienced with the privatization of five human services in the last half of the 1990s in the state of Kansas were discussed in a case study by University of Kansas researchers Johnston and Romzek (2000). They pointed out that contracting for social services holds a "broad array" of challenges, some of which are political and fiscal, while others are associated with program and contract design, implementation, and performance management. The following are key requirements for state contracting for services delivery described in their case:

> Good contracting requires a clear understanding of costs, understandable and clear statements of the scope of work, clear specifications of performance expectations, and defined obligations on the part of the contracting agency and contractor. Contracts need clarity regarding the contract deliverables, including contractor reports to facilitate state monitoring of cost and performance. While all players involved in state contracting know these conditions are central to success, they are not always able to meet these terms for social service contracts. (Johnston and Romzek 2000, 9)

The contracting of social services occurred after the 1996 Kansas State Legislature adopted a policy of reducing the size of state government—and particularly the state's Department of Social and Rehabilitation Services (SRS)—through one or more of the following processes to be administered by the Kansas Performance Review Board: privatization, elimination, retention, or modification. Johnston and Romzek (2000) referred to this movement as the political forces driving the contracting process.

The five contracted services reviewed in the case represented different approaches to state contracting for social services; all were forms of state efforts to alleviate problems associated with poverty. They included work-related programs stemming from passage of PRWORA and programs related to delivery of Medicaid health care and other services to the state's poor and aged. Five contracted programs examined in this case study are described in the following sections.

Medicaid Case Management Services for the Elderly

Key goals of this reform were consolidation of all services for the elderly and creation of a single point of entry to state health and social services. Cost savings were to occur through increasing home- and community-based services while minimizing use of expensive skilled nursing facilities. Responsibility for the Medicaid case management services for the elderly was transferred from the SRS to the Kansas Department on Aging, while the SRS continued to be the designated contact agency with the federal Medicaid program (Medicaid funding to the states is managed by the U.S. Health Care Financing Administration within the U.S. Department of Health and Human Services).

Medicaid Managed-Care Services by HMOs

In 1994, the legislature mandated that most of the state's nonelderly and nondisabled Medicaid populations were to receive health care services though a managed care health maintenance organization (HMO) program by July 1, 1997. As the deadline arrived, only seven of the state's 105 counties were covered by more than one HMO—and this lasted for only one year. By December 1998, only one financially shaky HMO continued to contract with the state.

Administration and Oversight of Medicaid Managed Care

Privatization and cost-control requirements of the sate legislature also resulted in contracting many of the administrative and oversight activities associated with Medicaid-managed care. A major contract was signed with Blue Cross/Blue Shield (BCBS) of Kansas (also the state's Medicaid fiscal agent), and a smaller contract with the Kansas Foundation for Medical Care (KFMC). BCBS is responsible for claims and data administration, management of client and provider enrollment, information systems and administration, and customer services such as grievance procedures and toll-free hotlines. KFMC helps monitor HMO contracts by analysis of HMO performance.

Agreements with Providers for Preparing Clients for Employment

Passage in 1996 of PRWORA resulted in a heightening of activity in this area. Because the state emphasizes work first, contracts in this area focus on providers that provide training for short-term, job-specific skills. These contracts, which are monitored by local area offices of SRS, are with local schools, colleges, and social service organizations (e.g., Goodwill). At the time of the case research, the state was unable to determine how many agreements were in existence, with estimates ranging from 5,000 to 8,000 provider agreements. In contrast to Medicaid programs, dollar amounts for these services were very small, and they offered more provider choice, more flexibility, more goodwill, and a closer connection between area office staff and contract agency personnel.

A Comprehensive Employment Preparation Master Contract

This is the exception to the decentralized work-first training programs; it involves a single contract between the state and the firm of Curtis & Associates to supply a comprehensive employment preparation service across an eleven-county segment of the state.

Research Method

The data for the Kansas case study were gathered in a series of seventy-five personal interviews conducted over a two-year period. The researchers employed a semistructured interview guide, in which all respondents answered a list of questions designed to address key issues including (1) respondents' assessment of their understanding of the contracts and (2) performance oversight features, such as state and agency capacity to manage the contracts. To supplement the interview data, the researchers reviewed administrative and legislative documents related to the contracts and the contracting process.

Case Findings

The researchers reached these eight key findings from analysis of their interviews and document analyses. Table 17.1 includes the findings and selected comments from the descriptions provided by the authors.

Recommendations for Other Government Agencies

As with many case research studies, Johnston and Romzek (2000) concluded with a number of recommendations for other agency managers planning to implement initiatives for contracting out of social and other government services:

- Take enough time to consider the design of the program, the needs and concerns of agency and contractor staff, cost factors, and contractor responsibilities.
- Avoid the one-size-fits-all approach.
- Negotiate in advance performance expectations for the agency and contractor.
- Thoroughly review all costs.
- Find and evaluate multiple providers who are financially and administratively able to provide the service.
- Agencies and contractors must examine and project financial consequences of contract proposals that shift risks from the government to the contractor.

Summary

Because of the great size of social and health services provided by federal, state, and local governments, much case research is conducted in this field by researchers in the health services as well as the public administration field. These case studies include such programs in health education; food safety and nutrition support; health care; subsidized housing; and other programs for improving the health, life, and living conditions of children, the disabled, disadvantaged, and elderly. Services and programs managed at the federal level are mirrored to some degree in state and local governments, where the services are actually delivered. Case research can be found in all of these services and programs and at all levels of government.

The U.S. Department of Health and Human Services (HHS) manages more than 300 programs with nearly 65,000 employees and a 2008 budget of $707.7 billion. These services programs swallow nearly a quarter of the entire U.S. federal budget.

All U.S. states and most regional governments have social and health services organizations that are similar to their national-level agencies; similar organizations can often be found in most counties and in some municipalities. This chapter looked briefly at the structure of social and health delivery systems and included several cases that illustrated the many kinds of case studies done at the federal, state, and local levels.

Table 17.1

Findings of the Kansas Social Service Contracting Study

Findings	Comments
1. Despite their participation in the decision process, often neither the state agency nor the contracting organization is prepared for the changes required under the contract agreement.	Common themes across the programs studied included contractor surprise at government regulatory requirements, information systems problems, resistance to change among some agency staff, and coordination problems such as scheduling weekly meetings and missed phone calls.
2. Genuine goodwill often exists between the state and most contracting organizations.	A sense of shared mission existed among policy professionals; words like "team" and "partnership" were common; agency staff and contractor personnel shared common commitments to serving targeted populations.
3. Neither state agencies nor contracting organizations are able to accurately project program costs.	State policy reformers found it hard to accurately project costs for the contracted costs; they did not have good initial figures on the real cost of providing the services, partly due to cross-subsidies often existing in state program administration. The state's one-size-fits-all approach did not work in real life.
4. The need for training in contract management and monitoring is often underestimated.	Contract management training is particularly important in an environment devoid of provider competition. In such cases, contract managers are in an especially weak position with regard to contract reinforcement. Also, development of performance measures was very slow.
5. Contracting decisions and implementation process are influenced by political considerations.	Most contracting decisions are made in response to political requirements to contract out as many social services as possible. Much of the contracting activity results from legislative dissatisfaction with the SRS, which is seen as being too large, unwieldy, and insufficiently accountable to the legislature.
6. Contracting problems appear when only a few service providers are available.	For most of the contracted services, just one or two potential providers existed. Pressure to contract out forces the state to contract with agencies whose capacity to provide the service has not been sufficiently determined.
7. Contracting relationships can create problems of accountability.	Contractors face high costs in complying with regulatory and reporting demands. Reliance on advanced information systems to reduce costs and increase accountability is an unreliable strategy; nearly all parties report serious difficulties with information systems.
8. Contracting with advocacy organizations may be too successful.	Advocacy organizations are likely to use highly successful outreach procedures to maximize services to needy clients, resulting in more demand than planned for.

Source: Johnston and Romzek (2000).

➤ 18 ◀

Case Research in Public Infrastructure

If we are to believe the news media and the political rhetoric, we are
in the midst of an infrastructure crisis.
—Robert Bruegmann (1993)

The United States needs to develop a national infrastructure
investment plan that will meet its needs over the next 40 plus years
with respect to water, energy and transportation.
—Robert L. Reid (2008)

A critical and costly problem facing governments at all levels is how to meet the growing demands upon the nation's infrastructure while at the same time refurbish and repair the infrastructure that is rapidly disintegrating. It is a problem that has been simmering for close to forty years or longer—and it is one that needs immediate attention. The August 1, 2007, collapse of the Interstate 35W bridge across the Mississippi River in Minneapolis signaled the need for action in ways that no one could miss. That collapse resulted in thirteen deaths and 145 people injured.

Bruegmann spoke of the causes of the problems facing government managers and the actions government needs to take in his 1993 article on infrastructure management:

> American investment in infrastructure lags behind that of every other industrialized country; deferred maintenance on highways, water systems, and public transportation hinders our productivity; and inadequate funding for new systems jeopardizes out place in the world economy. . . . We need a massive infusion of capital to coordinate all our infrastructure needs, including repair of highways, bridges and tunnels, and to plan new schemes, including high-speed intercity train lines, waste- and water-treatment systems, and data-transmission networks. (Bruegmann 1993, 7)

Despite the warning of observers like Bruegmann (1993) and others like him, not enough is being done to solve the problems associated with the decay of our public infrastructure. Instead, our infrastructure system remains "woefully broken" (Katz 2007). Public spending on infrastructure has been declining for decades, even while economists and engineers have been writing about the dangers of the problem at least since the 1970s (Crain and Oakley 1995). The message that they have been trying to communicate is simple: much of the public infrastructure of the country is falling apart; do something about it soon, or there will be more tragedies like the Minneapolis bridge across the Mississippi.

A Long-Standing Problem

This crumbling of the country's infrastructure did not come about overnight; government managers have been aware of the problem for many years. Much of the nation's roads, bridges, tunnels, railroads, water and wastewater systems, electricity grid and distribution systems, dams, levies and inland waterways, telecommunications systems, airports and ports, and similar facilities are all collapsing or, at best, obsolete. And, unless our governments do something soon, the infrastructure will soon be so far gone that it will mirror the infrastructure of a third world country in just a few decades. The editors of the *Economist* magazine do not hold any punches in their understanding of the problem: "America's tradition of bold national projects has dwindled. With the country's infrastructure crumbling, it is time to revive it" (*Economist* 2008).

Although the problem exists in every state, and despite the size of the problem and critical nature of the failure to act on it, little research on the subject appears in the public management literature. Apparently, what has been missing is a national commitment to dealing with the problem—something like the national vision that supported construction of the nation's Interstate highway system in the 1950s (Charan 2008).

Public administrators may to want to pass off the infrastructure problem as a problem of the engineering department. But the engineers can't do anything unless policymakers authorize the plans and come up with funds for construction. Engineers typically have little training in public administration. Neil Grigg, professor of civil engineering at Colorado State University, made this point in his case study on water quality in distribution systems:

> Practicing civil engineers recommend that students receive training in nontechnical areas, especially management. However, the concept of "management" does not fully capture the need for training for civil engineers involved with public sector projects, which feature government processes, public involvement, and institutional issues that may be new to them. For example, a civil engineer may work on an infrastructure project that features shared or multijurisdictional responsibility in a governmental setting that involves policy, politics, and law, all topics not normally studied in management courses. . . . In particular, engineers should be able to analyze issues relating to the "art of government" (Grigg 2005, 152)

A Big Problem Getting Bigger

Although few would disagree with the argument parodied by Bruegmann (1993), apparently little activity has been expended to rectify the problem. Twelve years after Bruegmann's article, the American Society of Civil Engineers (ASCE) released a report card on the state of the infrastructure in the nation that gave it a cumulative grade of D. The state of roads, drinking water systems, and other public works had declined even more from the overall D+ they received in 2001. Grades ranged from C+ for solid waste to a low of D– for drinking water, navigable waterways, and wastewater; the drinking water grade declined from the D it earned in the earlier report card. Only two categories improved: aviation received a D+ from their earlier D. The grade for the nation's schools advanced to a D from the D– they earned in 2001.

ASCE president William P. Henry was quoted in the release as saying, "Americans are spending more time stuck in traffic and less time at home with their families. We need to establish a comprehensive, long-term infrastructure plan as opposed to our current 'patch and pray' method to ensure a better quality of life for everyone" (Dixon and Buhrman 2005, 1). Henry predicted that it would take an investment of $1.6 trillion over the next five years to repair the country's crumbling infrastructure.

Things have not changed much for the better for the country's infrastructure—at least in the perception held by citizens. After the August 1, 2007, collapse of the Interstate 35W bridge in Minneapolis, U.S. House of Representatives Transportation and Infrastructure Committee Chairman James Oberstar (D-Minn.) warned that of the nation's some 600,000 bridges, nearly 80,000 were rated "functionally obsolete" and should be replaced immediately (Gordon 2007). The forty-year-old Minneapolis bridge was constructed of the same design as a bridge over the Ohio River that collapsed in 1967, killing forty-six people.

Coming up with the huge sums needed for repairing and replacing the nation's public infrastructure is certainly a big reason why much of the work keeps getting pushed aside. Citizens call on their governments to meet many other needs, all of which compete for part of a declining pool of public funds. This means that the politics has to be considered in any examination of variation in infrastructure investments.

Analyzing data from all states except Alaska, Crain and Oakley (1995) evaluated a wide variety of factors in their analysis of the politics of infrastructure investment, including gubernatorial term limits, the stability of one party's control in the state legislature, the volatility of the state electorate, initiative status, the budget cycle (annual versus biennial), exclusion of capital expenditures from the operating budget, the percentage of the state budget spent on welfare, state bond rating, private capital per capita, and gross state product per capita.

While not case research, the Crain and Oakley (1995) study is mentioned here for two reasons. First, it provides a wealth of possible topics for case research, and second, it provides additional support for the need for public administrators to give greater attention to the problem of decaying infrastructure in their jurisdictions. In the absence of federal support, more of the funding for public infrastructure will have to come from state and local sources.

The Importance of Infrastructure to the Economy

Modern economies depend on infrastructure that allows goods, people, information, and energy to flow throughout the nation and, increasingly, the world. This infrastructure—ports, roads, communication networks, power lines, communications systems, and many others—represents an important input into a nation's economy. The poor quality and inefficient infrastructure has become a major issue in the United States.

Economic advances and population growth in the United States, Europe, and newly developed countries have resulted in dramatic growth in demands on the infrastructure. These demands are partly due to continued economic growth and can also be traced to successful deregulation in industries that are heavy users of infrastructure. Since 1980, for example, vehicle traffic on U.S. roads has nearly doubled; passenger-miles of air traffic have increased by 150 percent; and demand for energy is fast outpacing supply. To cap it all, existing roads, bridges, passenger terminals, port facilities, electric power transmission lines, and other infrastructure components have—or soon will have—reached their maximum capacity. The consensus is clear: We must begin immediately to invest the trillions of dollars that are needed to repair and upgrade the nation's infrastructure.

A Call for Greater Federal Support

In July 2008, the U.S. Chamber of Commerce announced it was expanding efforts to get Congress to allocate additional resources for repairs and improvements to the nation's infrastructure. In support of its position, the Chamber brought up the following selected points (U.S. Chamber of Commerce 2008):

- Decaying transportation systems cost the economy more than $78 billion each year in lost time and fuel.
- The United States needs to invest $225 billion per year over fifty years to maintain and enhance surface transportation systems.
- Transit funding is declining even as ridership is increasing faster than any other transportation mode. (U.S. transit systems earned a D+ rating from the ASCE in 2005.)
- The cost of airline delays due to congestion and an antiquated air traffic control system is expected to triple to $30 billion by 2015.
- By 2020, every major U.S. container port is expected to at least double the volume it was designed to handle.

- U.S. railroads will need nearly $200 billion in investment over the next twenty years to meet expected freight increases.
- No new refineries or nuclear facilities have been built in the United States since the 1970s. The nation's refining capacity has actually declined; in 1981, there were 324 refineries with a capacity of 18.6 million barrels per day in the United States; in 2005, there were just 132 refineries with a total capacity of 16.8 million barrels per day.
- While electricity demand has increased by about 25 percent, construction of transmission lines has decreased by about 30 percent.

Infrastructure Financing

Finding ways to finance efforts to correct the problems of the nation's crumbling infrastructure is a major concern for organizations at all levels of government, and particularly critical for local governments. Much of the major infrastructure has been funded either directly by the federal government or through the grant and pass-through process.

A majority of this pass-through funding has been distributed to urban agencies—a not-unexpected occurrence because of the population concentrated in urban areas. This has left many smaller or lower-level jurisdictions scrambling for ways to finance the infrastructure improvements for which they are responsible. In many cases, the problems are closely connected, requiring close collaboration and cooperation of multiple levels of government and a variety of agencies.

Pagano and Perry (2008) examined the infrastructure investment and fiscal policies that now face policymakers and public managers at the federal and city levels. They also looked at some of the trends in public management that are compounding the difficulties associated with infrastructure investments. They examined such trends as the decentralization and fragmentation of government and financial institutions—shortly before the 2008 global credit crisis that has made the costs of municipal borrowing for infrastructure projects far higher than normal.

Other policy trends included a need for local government policymakers to negotiate with neighboring jurisdictions for collaborative participation in projects that affect more than one district, city, county, or government agency, and a trend for more public–private partnerships in the design, development, and often the operation of infrastructure projects. Because of these and related factors, finding the money to finance infrastructure projects is just one aspect of a complex problem: "What appears to be little more than organized chaos has evolved over decades into the complex, if not always rational, system of infrastructure finance and governance in which cities and other local governments find themselves today" (Pagano and Perry 2008, 22).

Funding at the Local Level

Although local government officials cannot effect or control changes in the inter-governmental grant and regulatory infrastructure system, they are able to exercise significant influence in a number of important related areas. For example, local government officials are able to influence the following policies (Pagano and Perry 2008):

- Intergovernmental cooperative and collaborative agreements on regional infrastructure policies can be undertaken.
- In an era of political decentralization and market-focus actions such as greater use of fees and privatization, local government officials are in a position to bridge the gap between the interests of system users and taxpayers.
- By exercising budget reform, the capital and operating budgets of local governments can better illuminate the future costs that will occur from infrastructure decisions made now, as well as the effects of infrastructure investment obligation that are not met, including the real cost of deferred maintenance.
- Revenue generation through the sale of assets or lease-back programs can help pay for the maintenance of existing infrastructure. Facilities such as water and wastewater treatment plants, introducing tolls on roads and bridges, and leasing other transportation facilities are examples.
- Fully funding the community's infrastructure needs for both initial construction and long-term maintenance may be the most important of the policy issues facing public policymakers.
- All infrastructure investment proposals must include full disclosure of the present and future costs of infrastructure assets—including full assessment of sources of revenue to fund future costs.

Funding at the State Level

State governments have found a number of new financing tools for funding infrastructure projects. A key development has been the emergence of federal policies that now allow states to impose tolls on highways and bridges constructed with federal aid. This includes the ability to charge adjustable user fees for nonqualifying vehicles in high-occupancy vehicle lanes during nonpeak hours. In addition to the new toll and user-fee initiatives, there are several financing tools available to the states (*PA Times* 2008):

- *Congestion pricing:* Congestion pricing refers to charging higher fees or tolls as a means of rationing scarce road space during high-volume periods. It is also a source of revenue that can be used to fund transit, road maintenance, or other infrastructure needs.
- *Vehicle miles-traveled tax:* The vehicle miles-traveled tax may supplement or possibly replace existing fuel taxes by encouraging consolidation or elimination of some unnecessary trips. A related program is mileage-based vehicle insurance.

- *Debt financing:* Innovations in project finance provide greater flexibility for states to fund new construction. These include design-build-operate contracts with private-sector organizations.
- *Public–Private partnerships:* public–private sector partnerships (PPPs) are another potential source of capital for new projects. PPP leasebacks are an example.

Case Research on Infrastructure Issues

While possibly not considered to be a "sexy" issue, the nation's infrastructure is clearly an issue that more and more public managers are finding themselves being forced to deal with. A problem is that many public administrators do not become directly involved in infrastructure decision making (Gospodini 2005). Possibly because of this, public administration graduate education programs often fail to give the subject much importance in their curricula.

As a result, case research on infrastructure issues is difficult to find in professional and academic public management literature. Rather, it seems to be considered an engineering problem and often shunted off to engineering journals. Some of the examples of case research on infrastructure included in the following sections were taken from engineering and planning journals.

A Case on Infrastructure Development

In many of the larger cities of the developing world, increasing numbers of poor citizens find themselves forced to eke out a living in substandard housing and without basic services. Driven by growing population and lack of economic opportunity in the rural countryside, an influx of people to rapidly growing urban and suburban slums has exceeded the ability of local governments to provide the infrastructure needed for human habitation.

Trethanya and Perera of the Asian Institute of Technology used the case research method in their 2008 study of the environmental impact of informal infrastructure development in the Bangkok metropolitan area. In their view, the development of fundamental infrastructure is one of the essential requirements for urban growth. The population of the Bangkok metropolitan area grew from 1.6 million in 1958 to more than 5.6 million in 1999. To gain better control over growth in urban fringe areas that is occurring outside of formal development planning, the authors recommended implementing a system of environmental assessment for what they labeled as all "non-prescribed infrastructure development projects."

Coping with Unplanned Urbanization

Coping with the problems caused by this unplanned and uncontrolled urbanization has become a major problem for public administrators in these regions. Some of the problems with urban population growth in developing countries that public managers in these cities must deal with include the following:

- How to provide adequate urban infrastructure and services
- Lack of decent housing and settlements
- Inability to provide adequate security
- Questions of land tenure
- Land-use planning that is either ineffective or unenforceable
- Political pressures that can influence land use and unsafe development
- A lack of long-range plans for development
- Urban economic development that occurs outside of regional plans
- Air, water, and soil pollution
- Uncollected solid waste or improperly handled liquid and solid wastes
- Abject poverty and the many social ills that poverty incubates

At the time of this case study, environmental assessments were required for only major infrastructure projects and those implemented by national organizations. Trethanya and Perera (2008) proposed that small projects and fringe area administrative bodies require environmental assessments before any infrastructure development projects can be implemented. Doing so, they concluded, would be an important "first step towards bringing an environmental management culture to the organizational level of local government."

Case Research on Infrastructure Damage

Case research that provides meaningful lessons for public managers can be carried out on hypothetical data as well as on real data from factual sources. This was illustrated in a case study that examined estimated costs of damage that might result if a magnitude 7.0 earthquake centered on St. Louis, Missouri, had occurred in 2004 (Tirasirichai and Enke 2007). The case study looked at both the direct and indirect costs caused by such disasters. The researchers used a Federal Emergency Management Agency (FEMA) model to estimate the direct financial cost to repair the damage caused by the hypothetical earthquake. They followed this estimate with an analysis of indirect costs to the local economy resulting from disruption to the transportation system that would follow from damage to area bridges. The stated purpose of the study was to illustrate for policymakers the need to consider indirect as well as direct costs when making both pre- and postdisaster infrastructure decisions.

This direct cost portion of the study focused on costs to repair or replace earthquake-damaged bridges in the St. Louis metropolitan area highway system. Direct economic loss refers to the physical damage resulting directly from a natural disaster. It includes damage to buildings, roads and bridges, production and commercial facilities, indoor property, and the like. The FEMA model measures these costs by estimating the costs for replacement or repair.

Evaluating Indirect Costs

The indirect cost portion of the case study then evaluated the indirect costs that would resulting from forced changes to the traffic patterns of the region caused by bridge damage. Indirect economic loss refers to the consequences of the damage caused by the disaster. In this study, indirect loss was defined as "any loss that extends beyond the direct physical impact, such as income loss, business inventory losses, etc." Indirect loss was also described as any loss that resulted from the "multiplier or ripple effect" that occurs through the economy, and which is traceable to the resulting traffic bottlenecks and detours. Business interruption and the costs of temporary unemployment were also described as part of the indirect losses (Tirasirichai and Enke 2007, 368).

The direct losses projected for the hypothetical earthquake were estimated to exceed $1.3 billion. Clearly, this is large enough to capture any policymakers' attention. However, the damaged bridges alone were expected to result in an additional loss of $705 million over the first 500 days following the disaster; the bulk of the loss ($684 million) would be expected to occur during the first 365 days of the postdisaster period.

The authors used these estimates to warn public managers about the inadequacy of traditional methods of damage estimates, which pay too much attention to direct costs and too little attention to the indirect costs. The danger was described in the following way:

> At times, policy-makers focus only on the physical damages, or direct losses [of a natural disaster]. Naturally, these direct losses are easy to notice and observe since they are directly caused by the incident. However, they are only part of the total losses caused by the disasters. Policy-makers tend to overlook the subsequent indirect losses that are characterized with more ambiguous causes and uncertain loss amounts, compared to direct losses. . . . These indirect consequences are also important and significant. (Tirasirichai and Enke 2007, 368)

A Case on Collaborative Infrastructure Development

The question of public utility infrastructure became a particularly pressing concern of public administrators in the first years of the twentieth century as waterborne diseases in local utility systems in the United States and Canada, and gross malfeasance in the electrical energy industry resurfaced (Fox-Penner and Basheda 2001). Although the focus of concern on management malfeasance has faded somewhat on the part of utility regulators, they are still concerned over problems with aging water and wastewater systems; obsolete generating, transmission, and delivery infrastructure; high and growing demand for more power and water; and worries over water and power shortages caused by global warming.

By 2008, however, calls for restructuring, unbundling of the energy industry, more deregulation, privatization, wholesale and retail competition, and outsourcing have been placed on the back burner—supplanted in the minds of legislators and administrators by concerns over the breakdown in nation's economy. At the local level, however, the concerns are still very real. The case study discussed later in this chapter dealing with a small water and sewage treatment system by McNabb and Barnowe (2008) exemplifies that concern.

Governance Issues

Governance in the public utility industry is more complex than it is in most industries. For example, ownership in the electricity and natural gas sectors is shared by two very different enterprise forms, public and private ("investor-owned") systems. Water and wastewater systems are more typically public enterprises, but must function under heavily licensed and controlled federal, state, and local government oversight. In addition, the issue of water rights, particularly in the western states of the United States, is among the most litigious of all resource "ownership" issues (Keohane and Nye 2000).

In most urban areas, power is provided by private enterprises, although a few municipalities still control their own power distribution networks. The investor-owned power utilities serve about 75 percent of the national population. Most of the municipal systems and public utility districts (PUDs) purchase most of their power from federally owned enterprises such as the Bonneville Power Administration. Until recently, they were guaranteed special low rates and preferential access to federally produced power; now those preferential rights are disappearing under pressure from private utilities facing shortages of supply and very high costs of producing peak period power by small gas-fired turbines.

Water and sewage treatment systems are seldom privately owned in the United States, although some privatization of water systems has occurred. In semirural and rural areas, the retail delivery of power is often provided by consumer cooperatives, which serve less than 25 percent of the population. Small cities usually own and operate their own water and sewage systems, although in the smallest communities, water may be provided by a local cooperative or private water district. In rural areas, private water wells and sewage septic systems prevail. Private ownership of water systems by domestic and foreign corporations is common in much of Europe (Dysard 2001; Heller, Von Sacken, and Gertsberger 2001).

A Case on Infrastructure Improvement in Shelton

In the early years of the twenty-first century, the rural community of Shelton, Washington, found itself in the same shape as hundreds of similar communities: It was running out water. The main industries of Shelton are timber and lumber manufacturing and shellfish farming and processing. Its aging wastewater facilities were badly in need of repair and expansion to meet local demand; neither service could satisfy new service demands by growth in the region. Shelton is located on an arm of Puget Sound, some 100 miles southwest of Seattle.

Water in and near the community is supplied from wells, some of which are owned by the city. A variety of small, independent water districts serve various regions of the county, although in the recent past, several smaller districts turned the operation of their installed systems over to a reluctant county utility department. In most of the rural areas, water is provided by private wells and sewage service by septic systems. Solid waste service is provided by private refuse collection firms. Electric service in the county is provided by two PUDs, and liquid petroleum gas is available from several private firms.

Population in the county grew rapidly during the last half of the 1990s and the first few years of the 2000s. The population of the county was 49,405 in 2000 and 54,600 just seven years later, a growth rate of 10.52 percent. Over this same period, Shelton's population grew by 9.4 percent, from 8,442 in 2000 to 9,236 in 2007. The rural nature of the area and numerous recreational facilities, combined with its relative proximity to the cities of Tacoma and Olympia (the state capital) and several large military facilities, have made the region both a popular bedroom community and a site for second homes. It has also become a popular location for retirees, many of whom spend their summers in the region and winters in the Sun Belt.

The City of Shelton entered into an interim intergovernmental agreement with the following stakeholder organizations: (1) the Port of Shelton, which operated a former U.S. Navy auxiliary airport and industrial park in the service area; (2) the State Department of Corrections (SDC), which operated a correctional facility in the service area; (3) the local county's small utility department; (4) the State Patrol, whose officer training academy was located in the area to be served by the project; and (5) the public utility district (PUD) that provided electricity to that portion of the county. Other stakeholder organizations, including local Native American tribes, federal and state environmental protection agencies, and fish and wildlife agencies, signed on as tangentially involved participants. The city utilities department was named the lead agency in the collaboration (Golat 2005).

In the Urban Growth Zone

All of the facilities to be served by the expanded system were located in the state-mandated Urban Development Area Zone for Shelton and Mason County. Development area plans are required of all communities in the state in order to control urban sprawl and ensure that future growth is guided by regional planning.

The agreement called for a $42 million expansion of city sewer and water distribution lines to serve the state correction center, State Patrol training academy, and port-operated industrial park. It also included expansion of the city's sewage treatment plant to be able to meet the new and growing demand; sinking of new wells and installing new water treatment facilities; and remodeling and upgrading existing sewage treatment facilities, including a wastewater treatment and sludge collection and removal facility at a city-owned site near the center of service demand. Construction of the new facilities was to be financed through a mix of grants, loans, and bonds. Each primary participant was to pay a proportionate share of construction costs and normal usage rates.

As lead agency, the city utilities department was responsible for record keeping and recording, and oversight on program planning and construction. The city established two special business funds and accounts for the regional project, with each fund having four "customers": the city, port, Training Academy, and Corrections Center. Private consultants were hired to conduct the necessary environmental analysis and construction planning.

In a classic multiorganizational infrastructure development agreement, no one agency is automatically deemed to be superior or subordinate to others, and no central participant provides guidance and control. In this case, the city assumed the role of lead agency with the approval of the other agencies. Reasons for this were clear: No other agency had the utility management experience of the city. In addition, the development program constituted a request by the other agencies for expansion of existing city-owned water and wastewater services infrastructure.

Revisions to the Plan

The expansion did not proceed as planned. Before construction of the system could begin, both the port and the county withdrew from the collaborative agreement; their withdrawal also meant they would no longer pay their agreed upon share of the cost of construction.

This case example of a jurisdiction-based water treatment facility met the requirement for providing most of the benefits of the model as described by Agranoff and McGuire:

> Jurisdiction-based activity emphasizes local managers taking strategic action with multiple actors and agencies from various governments and sectors. . . . Bargaining and negotiations are important instruments of jurisdiction-based management. Bargaining by local managers within programs of vertical (state or federal government) or horizontal (metropolitan, regional, or intersectional) origin provide alternatives to unilateral concessions, resulting in a "mutually beneficial solution" [to problems that extend beyond a single agency's jurisdiction]. (Agranoff and McGuire 2003, 675)

Summary

The rapid decaying of the nation's infrastructure—the roads and bridges, railroads, ports and airports, electric power production and distribution facilities, and other physical facilities that make large-scale civilization and economic growth possible—is an area of public management that is not receiving the attention it deserves from the public management community. It is, rather, perceived to be either someone else's problem, such as the state or federal government, or an area of public management that is best left to the engineers and planners.

This chapter looked at some examples of the case research that is being conducted in this critical area of public management. The focus of this research is often comparative, as the multicase examples included here illustrate. Moreover, the large numbers of case research reports describing issues in other nations show that the problem is indeed global, and one which the nations of the world must address collaboratively.

➤ 19 ◄

Case Research in Public Transportation

The national objectives of general welfare, economic growth and stability, and the security of the United States require the development of transportation policies and programs that contribute to providing fast, safe, efficient, and convenient transportation at the lowest cost consistent with those of other national objectives, including the efficient use and conservation of the resources of the United States.
—U.S. Department of Transportation (2003)

Public transportation in the United States has a long history of successful cooperation and collaboration between federal, state, and local government. It starts at the top, with the U.S. Department of Transportation (DOT) developing and managing policies designed to promote safety and efficiency in air, road, rail, and marine travel and transportation. Established in 1966, the department and its nearly dozen agencies are responsible for highway planning, development, and construction; urban mass transit; railroads; aviation; and the safety of waterways, highways, and oil and gas pipelines. Many of these aspects of public transportation depend on a publicly provided infrastructure in the form of roads, maintained waterways, air traffic control, pipelines, major hydroelectric dams and transmission networks, and related system components.

Beginning with passage of the Safe, Accountable, Flexible, and Efficient Transportation Equity Act of 2005 (SAFETEA), the U.S. federal government reversed a longtime trend of decline in federal support for transit research (Marshment 2007). The act was noteworthy for two reasons: first, it was the largest surface transportation bill every passed in the United States, and second. it contained more targeted projects than any bills that preceded it.

Policy and funding may come from the top, but the responsibility for providing transit services falls to local governments. Public transportation—passenger bus systems, commuter and urban rail transit systems—represents a mixed form of governance. While most systems are owned and operated by local government

251

agencies, they are guided by federal and state regulatory bodies. Even the operating systems represent a complex mix of ownership, including special districts, city systems, systems managed by special districts or counties, and for-profit organizations. Public management case research in public transportation has not kept pace with the rapid changes taking place in the industry. New York rail transit official Louis J. Gambaccini[1] brought attention to the problem more than thirty years ago:

> I submit that the major issues in transportation research . . . are not in hardware, operations or productivity. They are in the much more complicated areas of institutional interactions, intergovernmental coordination, intermodal coordination and market split, land use planning and controls, and economic and physical sketch planning for the future. Rhetoric? Idealistic? Pie-in-the sky theory? No indeed. (Gambaccini 1977)

Availability and Structure of Transportation Systems

Public transportation in one or another form is available in virtually all large cities and towns and in something like 60 percent of all rural counties in the United States (Brown 2004). About two-thirds of the rural systems operate in a single county or a community; one of four systems operate in more than one county. Six out of ten of the rural transit systems are public organizations, three out of ten are nonprofit organizations, and the rest are private companies or trial operations. Many of the rural systems are funded by the Federal Transit Act, a federal grant program that provides both capital for equipment and facilities and operating grants to areas with fewer than 50,000 residents.

The DOT carries out its transit mission through the activities of the Federal Transit Administration (FTA). The FTA works with public and private mass transit organizations to develop transportation facilities, equipment, techniques, and operating methods. The agency also coordinates transit funding and operations with state and local organizations in forming mass transportation systems; helps state and local governments finance systems; and provides financial aid to state and local governments to increase mobility for aged, disabled, and economically disadvantaged citizens. The FTA administers federal funding to support a variety of locally planned, constructed, and operated public transportation systems throughout the United States. These include bus systems, subways, light rail, commuter rail, streetcars, monorail, passenger ferry boats, inclined railways, and people movers (FTA 2008).

This large scope of the activities of the transit administration and its counterparts and partners at the state and local levels makes this a rich area for case research. However, for some reason, only limited published case research has appeared in the mainstream public administration and management academic literature. It may be that much of the research in this area is directed toward professional journals, which were not reviewed for this text.

Recent Legislation Affecting Public Transit

Two important pieces of federal legislation affecting public transit were introduced or adopted in the second term of President George W. Bush. The first
was the Safe, Accountable, Flexible, and Efficient Transportation Equity Act:
A Legacy for Users (SAFETEA-LU), which was signed into law on August 10,
2005. The second was the Saving Energy Through Public Transportation Act of
2008 (H.R. 6052), which was passed by the U.S. House of Representatives on
June 26, 2008, by a vote of 322 to 98. The bill was sent to the Senate on June
27, where it was read twice and referred to the Senate Committee on Banking,
Housing, and Urban Affairs. The act was not passed by the Senate during the
110th session of Congress, however.

SAFETEA-LU did pass and was signed into law. This act provided $244.1
billion for highway construction safety and public transportation; at that time it
represented the largest surface transportation investment in U.S. history (DOT
2005). The key programs addressed in the 2005 legislation with selected high
points include the following:

- Safety: A new core highway safety-improvement program to cut highway
  fatalities almost doubled the funds for infrastructure safety and highway
  planning.
- Equity: Improvements were made in states' returned share of contributions
  to the highway trust fund; states were guaranteed a rate of growth in funding
  levels, regardless of fund contributions.
- Innovative finance: It is easier for the private sector to participate in highway
  infrastructure projects.
- Congestion relief: The act gives states more flexibility to use road pricing to
  manage congestion, promotes real-time traffic management, and provides
  better information to travelers and emergency responders.
- Mobility and productivity: Funds are provided for core federal-aid programs,
  as well as programs to improve interregional and international transportation,
  address regional needs, and fund critical high-cost transportation infrastructure
  projects of regional and national significance.
- Efficiency: The act advances longer-lasting highways using innovative
  technologies and practices and speeds up construction of efficient and safe
  highways and bridges.
- Environmental stewardship: Funding is retained and increased for environmental programs and new programs added that focus on the environment,
  including a pilot program for nonmotorized transportation and safe routes to
  school.
- Environmental streamlining: The act streamlines the environmental process
  for transportation projects while adding some important steps and requirements for transportation agencies.

The 2008 Saving Energy Through Public Transportation Act would have authorized appropriations for fiscal years 2008 and 2009 for public transportation grants for urbanized and other areas. As introduced, the act would have enhanced local transit services in five major ways (Govtrack.us 2008).

Transit Services Enhanced Five Ways

First, the secretary of transportation would be authorized to supply grants for (1) operating costs of equipment and facilities used for public transportation that recipients would no longer pay because of reduced fares (to enhance citizens' mobility) and (2) operating and capital costs of equipment and facilities used to provide transportation services the recipient would incur by expanding such services. The federal government would provide a 100 percent share of the costs for these two types of grants.

Second, transit systems would be eligible for a fiscal year 2008–2009 grant for up to 100 percent of the cost for acquiring clean fuel or alternative fuel vehicle-related equipment or facilities for complying with Clean Air Act provisions.

Third, the new bill would amend the SAFETEA-LU Act to require (1) to offer qualified federal employees in urban areas of the United States served by public transportation transit passes as fringe benefits and (2) issuance of guidelines on national implementation of a transportation fringe benefit program.

Fourth, the act would require establishment of a pilot program for carpool demonstration projects in no more than three urban areas and no more than two other areas.

Fifth, grants of up to 100 percent of the net cost would be available for a capital project that involves the purchase of real property, or for the design, engineering, or construction of additional parking facilities at an end-of-the-line fixed station.

The status of public transportation in the United States is certainly on the rise. Major public management problems such as already heavy and growing traffic congestion, environmental degradation from the use of fossil fuels and their high costs, and the need to find alternative ways of maintaining mobility for large groups of citizens help ensure that the transportation systems will remain a rich source of research opportunities for decades to come. Some of the case research in this field is reviewed in the following sections.

Multicase Studies of Transportation Systems

Public authorities are special organizations formed outside of established government systems to manage one or a small number of related public services. Many authorities are multijurisdictional in scope, providing their services beyond a single central geographic entity. Because of this, they must often develop strong, collaborative working conditions with elected and appointed leaders in a wide variety of formal governments.

A reoccurring problem in all such voluntary, cross-jurisdictional organizations is the delicate balance that must be maintained to give the organizations the authority to effectively manage the system with the degree of accountability public agencies are expected to display. There is always the potential for one or more of the smaller jurisdictional partners opting out of the system and starting their own local bus systems if they feel they are not being treated fairly. The first multicase study in this section looks at how five regional transportation authorities handled this issue. The second looks at how some state transportation departments are implementing strategic management practices.

Urban and Suburban Managing Authorities

Smith (1987) examined five urban and suburban transportation authorities in a multicase study of how the managing authorities deal with the issue of constituent balance. He examined public transportation authorities in five regions of the country: Chicago, Minneapolis–St. Paul, Los Angeles, New York, and Boston.

Northeastern Illinois

The Northeastern Illinois Regional Transportation Authority (RTA) had just been forced to undergo an organizational transformation from an operating transportation provider to an oversight organization with operations turned over to three service boards: the seven-member Chicago Transit Authority, the twelve-member Suburban Bus Board, and the seven-member Commuter Rail Board.

The revised regional RTA board focuses on planning reviews and operational oversight. The transformation took place in response to demands by suburban regions for more power in regional transport decisions. Originally, the system was structured to provide an almost even balance of power between the city of Chicago and the six counties in the system. A small majority of the revised RTA thirteen-member board is held by jurisdictions outside of Chicago.

Minneapolis–St. Paul

The twin cities area of Minneapolis–St. Paul has also separated planning and operations in its transit authority, but in a different manner than that used by the Chicago RTA. The Metropolitan Council of the Twin Cities turned its Metropolitan Transit Commission (MTC) into an operating agency and then formed a comprehensive planning unit, the Regional Transit Board, with authority for transportation planning, liaison with the state legislature, and approval of the operating unit's budget. As in Chicago, the change came about after pressure for retrenchment from local government partners. Believing they were being ignored, several partners were asking to opt out of the system.

Los Angeles County

Los Angeles County had returned to the roots of the special district model by placing distribution of transit funds in the hands of an organization representing the general-purpose governments of Los Angeles and suburban communities. The Los Angeles County Transportation Commission (LACTC) sets policies and priorities and develops transportation system programs. Bus operators such as the Southern California Rapid Transit District, and all other transit operators in the county, interact with LACTC planners. In 1980, a 1 percent additional sales tax passed, and in 1985, 35 percent of it was earmarked for the regional rail transit systems, alienating many communities that did not benefit from the system. LACTC countered the disaffection by earmarking 40 percent of the sales tax discretionary funds to communities to subsidize local bus fares.

New York MTA

In March 1986, Governor Mario Cuomo of New York introduced legislation to allow three counties to withdraw from the New York Metropolitan Transportation Authority (MTA). The three had the smallest populations of the twelve counties in the MTA. In addition to rider fares, each of the twelve counties paid special taxes for transit (such as a sales tax, corporate profit tax, or transfer of proper tax). State approval was needed because when it was formed, the enabling legislation made no provisions for withdrawal. The new law made it possible for any of the counties to withdraw, but also gave those that elected to remain in the system a greater voice by increasing suburban membership on the governing board.

Massachusetts Bay

The Massachusetts Bay Transportation Authority (MBTA), with headquarters in Boston, suffered such poor city-suburb relations that in 1980 it very nearly had to shut down its bus and rail service entirely. The authority's board refused to appropriate funds greater than the annual budget unless the power of the unions was slashed and political patronage eliminated.

When the money ran out, first the governor took control of the system, but when state courts declared his decision illegal, the state legislature passed legislation that established an advisory board and completely revamped the system's governance and funding. The state would pay half of the system's operating costs, and member communities would pay the other half. However, the legislature also required significant changes in labor practices, productivity standards, and management responsibilities.

Reforms included the Advisory Board, which gave the governor the right to appoint a member who would have the same voting percentage as Boston, the city with the largest number of votes. If the governor and mayor of Boston disagreed on an issue, their votes would thus cancel out. Two additional members, appointed by the governor to give greater representation to surrounding communities, were named to the MBTA. The state secretary of transportation was to be the chair of the MBTA board, and a general manager was hired to run authority operations.

The five special-purpose governments analyzed in this case were all regional, and all were involved in public transportation. Beyond that, they differed substantially. A lesson to learn from this is that anyone researching special authorities must realize that great diversity exists in their structure and responsibilities; they cannot be treated as a monolithic group. The issue is, therefore, a complicated one, and one that makes it difficult to identify common features or develop theory. Thus, the case method is particularly appropriate for research on this organization.

Transportation Infrastructure and Urban Development

Aspa Gospodini of the University of Thessaly, Greece, reported on a 2005 multicase research study of the urban development and redevelopment roles of transportation infrastructure projects in twelve European cities. Urban transport infrastructure projects included metro systems and regional rail and tram projects. The cases selected were funded by the European Commission (EC). Table 19.1 lists the locations and types of case projects and the scope of the system investments.

The objective of this multicase study was to determine whether urban transport infrastructure investments have had any effect on the development, redevelopment, or regeneration of urban areas in Europe. These types of investments are known to require large sums of public and/or private investment capital.

The stated primary purposes for developing these new urban transport systems are to (1) improve the speed, reliability, and effectiveness of public urban transportation; (2) improve access to urban areas; (3) reduce automobile use in urban areas; and (4) improve environmental conditions. Although not discussed in this case, Alesina and Giavazzi (2006) identified another purpose for making these large infrastructure investments: spending on public infrastructure projects for Keynesian pump-priming during periods of slow economic growth.

Whatever the objective for such investments in Europe, Gospodini (2005) concluded that spending on transport infrastructure had only played a limited role in urban socioeconomic and regional planning policies. His multicase study was funded by the EC to examine the possible indirect effects and impacts upon urban areas. Selected findings are presented in Table 19.2.

The research study examined the twelve case projects from two broad points of view. The first was to evaluate the impact that the twelve transport infrastructure projects have had on urban development, redevelopment, and/or regeneration of urban areas. The second was to evaluate urban transport on five economic scales: land-use patterns, development and renewal investments in the urban areas, development and renewal investments in public spaces, real estate prices, and economic rents.

Table 19.1

Location and Scope of Urban Transport Case Studies

Case Study Cities	Transport Project Type	Status	Scope of the Transport System Project
Athens, Greece	Metro system	New	Extension of network with new lines and connections
Bratislava, Slovakia	Tramway and trolley bus	New	Extension of existing line
Brussels, Belgium	Metro system	New	Extension of existing line
Helsinki, Finland	Metro system	New	Extension of network with new lines and connections
Lyon, France	Metro system	New	Extension of network with new lines and connections
Madrid, Spain	Metro system	New	Extension of existing line
Manchester, U.K.	Hybrid tram and suburban-train system	Part new and part existing	Extension of network with new lines and connections and improvements to existing lines
Stuttgart, Germany	Suburban-train	Existing	Improvements of existing lines and connections
Tyne and Wear, U.K.	Hybrid metro and suburban-train	Part new and part existing	Improvements of existing lines, new lines and connections
Valencia, Spain	Tram	Part new and part existing	Improvements of existing lines and connections
Vienna, Austria	Metro system	New	Improvements of existing lines and connections
Zurich, Switzerland	Suburban-train	Part new and part existing	Improvements of existing lines and connections

Source: Gospodini (2005).

Strategic Management in Transportation Departments

The purpose of the second case study report in this section was to explore approaches to strategic management taken in a selected group of state departments of transportation (DOTs). Setting the scene for their subsequent analysis, Poister and Van Slyke (2002) asserted that state transportation departments have been operating in a period of "unprecedented change." They then identified these seven important "drivers" of the changes facing managers in state DOTs:

Table 19.2

Selected Findings from a Twelve-City Transport Investment Case Study

Case Study City	Selected Findings
Athens, Greece	A strong impact was found on the central corridor areas in terms of urban development and regeneration and a weak impact on urban development and redevelopment in peripheral areas.
Bratislava, Slovakia	Hard data revealed not clear effect on the new transport infrastructure, but a dramatic increase of construction and reconstruction after the new tram began operations.
Brussels, Belgium	Analysis suggested that the new metro line had a significant impact on urban redevelopment and regeneration in some areas.
Helsinki, Finland	No clear positive impact was found on urban development or regeneration from extension of the metro line. There was some decline in commercial/retail and mixed residence/office land use in the corridor regions.
Lyon, France	Construction of the new line had a significant impact on urban development and redevelopment in the central corridor area, with new and/or renovated residential buildings and urban open space.
Madrid, Spain	With no hard data available, anecdotal evidence suggested that the line resulted in increases in property values in the corridor.
Manchester, U.K.	No clear urban development or regeneration effect occurred from the infrastructure improvement. Real estate prices remained constant (rising in all areas of the region).
Stuttgart, Germany	Both hard and soft data indicated that the new infrastructure had a strong impact on development in the southwest sector of the city.
Tyne and Wear, U.K.	Soft data suggested significant regeneration had occurred in the central corridor, with some decline in less affected areas.
Valencia, Spain	Urban regeneration in all corridor areas has been positively affected by the new tram line. Significant changes were found in land use patterns, including redevelopment of residential and commercial uses.
Vienna, Austria	Land use patterns have enjoyed significant improvements, with considerable growth in residential and commercial facilities.
Zurich, Switzerland	Urban regeneration has occurred in corridor areas, with changes and improvements in land use taking place.

Source: Gospodini (2005).

- The need to find multimodal solutions to transportation problems
- Mandates to support economic development and sustainable environmental goals
- Spectacular advances in available technologies
- Big changes in federal, state, and local responsibilities for planning and programming
- An aging workforce and trouble finding and keeping qualified people
- Pressures to be more "customer oriented"
- Growing demands from the public for accountability

In reacting to these pressures, many DOTs have applied a variety of strategic management tools. They have also transformed their organizations and management and decision systems in efforts to improve efficiency and effectiveness. Poister and Van Slyke (2002) conducted twenty-one in-depth interviews of DOT chief executives and department personnel to learn what strategic management tools and practices were being adopted. They also conducted a content analysis of reports and other documents supplied by the departments; these included strategic plans, business and action plans, performance measures and other performance data, budgets, survey results, marketing studies, annual reports, and program evaluations.

States Have Strategic Plans in Place

All of the twenty-one state DOTs examined had strategic plans in place. In developing their plans, most had completed what have become standard strategic planning processes: mission and value statements, a future vision for the agency, environmental analysis and strengths and weaknesses, analysis of the agency's capabilities and past performance, and identification of strategic objectives and the strategies to achieve them. Innovative performance measurement systems were also in place. Some additional key points of this case study include the following:

- Top management took responsibility for strategic planning and involved a group made up of the CEO and from ten to twenty-five key executives in the process.
- Some states also involved external stakeholder groups in the planning process.
- State DOT strategic planning is more oriented toward customer needs and expectations than it was in the recent past. Agencies collect stakeholder data using focus groups, advisory boards, and customer surveys.
- Strategic plans are typically linked to strategic objectives, and many cut across all divisions and units in the department.
- New generation performance measurements are tied to overall strategy, and many states use performance measurements as proactive management tools.
- Monitoring performance indicators tied to strategic goals and objectives is common among the DOTs. The Florida DOT was singled out as one of the

most ambitious efforts to forge a comprehensive set of transportation outcome measurements.

- The DOTs use high-visibility progress reports to help build employee ownership of the program. Engaging many managers and staff members in the planning process also helps to build ownership.
- Many DOTs tie budgets to strategic plans and target resources to strategic initiatives. Results-based budgeting is increasingly being applied.

Differences Found in Planning Approaches

While all of the state DOTs examined engaged in the strategic management process, their approaches and efforts differed significantly. The authors of this case report came to the following conclusion:

> This exploratory research reveals that state DOTs are spread out over the "management capacity curve" regarding strategic management capabilities. Although a few DOTs have been engaged in strategic planning for many years and may have completed several rounds of strategic plans, other have just recently initiated strategic planning processes. Many of those departments with more experience in this area have taken more opportunities to strengthen their strategic management capacity along the way. . . . Not surprisingly, this is an area in which "one size does not fit all." (Poister and Van Slyke 2002, 71)

They were quick to add, however, that many of the innovative practices and tools they identified in the research can be modified and used in a number of other public agencies about to embark on implementation of the strategic management approach. However, the practices should not be considered a panacea for other agencies taking a future focus; rather, they contribute to the understanding of how governments can improve their effectiveness by forging strategies, plan programs to accomplish those objectives, build staff ownership in the plan and programs, and target resources to specific goals and objectives.

A Case of Sustainable Urban Transportation

The rapidly rising costs of fuels, urban congestion—more often urban gridlock—and pollution, and the need to maintain efficient means of transporting large numbers of people and goods in order to achieve and maintain strong economic growth have forced urban governments to show considerable interest in developing an efficient and sustainable transportation sector (Black, Paez, and Suthanaya 2002).

An example of a case study in which performance indicators and appropriate means of analyzing performance in urban transportation focused on the case of Sidney, Australia. The study was conducted to augment the recommendations of the Ecologically Sustainable Development Transport Group (ESDTG), which included goals, objectives, and altering citizens' value systems. Analytical tools and metrics, including sustainability indicators, were absent from the ESDTG report. Accordingly, Black, Paez, and Suthanaya elected to do case research in order to rectify the problems of the early study.

The Sidney case study began with a review of the literature on urban sustainable transportation. The goals of the review were (1) to organize the data by geographic scale, (2) to propose a framework that linked definitions and objectives for sustainability with performance indicators and techniques for analysis, and (3) to demonstrate the appropriateness of their recommended indicators and analytical techniques with a case example.

Because the focus of the study was sustainability, the research began by referring to an unpublished study by the EC's Environment and Sustainability Development Program to establish what it is that makes an urban transport and land-use system "sustainable." From their review of the literature, they first determined that a sustainable urban transport system is one that

- ensures efficient access to goods and services for all inhabitants of the service area;
- protects the environment, ecosystems, and cultural heritage of the areas served for the present generation; and
- does not limit the opportunities of future generations to achieve the same welfare level as the current generation, including the benefits they derive from the natural environment and their cultural heritage.

In addition to this definitional proposition, the EC researchers added a list of six subobjectives for a sustainable transport system that included economic efficiency, livable streets and neighborhoods, protection of the environment, equity and social inclusion for all citizens, safety, and ability to contribute to economic growth. These were approved by the six European cities (the "core cities") taking part in the EC study: Edinburgh, Helsinki, Madrid, Oslo, Stockholm, and Vienna.

Three Key Issues

From their analysis of the literature, Black, Paez, and Suthanaya concluded that globally, sustainable transportation objectives focus on three issues: environmental sustainability, economic efficiency, and social equity. The team then focused their study of the first of these three issues, environmental sustainability, grouping objectives into two levels: (1) global and (2) local and regional. Global sustainability objectives are to reduce fuel consumption and reduce pollution by minimizing greenhouse gases. A major local and regional objective is to reduce pollutants, and environmental subobjectives include cutting noise and reducing accidents and congestion.

Sidney was considered a good, general study case that because of its physical characteristics (a large, sprawling city with considerable growth and relocation of economic areas) make it similar to many Australian and North American cities. The core of the research was to apply metrics available from Sidney and New South Wales to an analytical structure that included the following:

1. Exploratory and graphic methods for descriptive statistics
2. Spatial mapping (using geographic information system [GIS] hardware and software)
3. Spatial statistics (using GIS hardware and software)
4. Citizens' travel preference functions (including linear programming and other methods)
5. Regression analysis

Black, Paez, and Suthanaya concluded that to achieve and maintain sustainable transportation requires indicators to show progress against targets. Their analytical model was tested to determine whether it was possible to identify appropriate indicators from broad goals and objectives, as well as provide measures for determining whether alternative policies will allow meeting strategic targets.

A Multicase Transportation Planning Organization Study

Goetz, Dempsey, and Larson (2002) published a multicase study in which the phenomenon of interest was the institution of metropolitan planning organizations (MPOs). They compared the experiences of MPOs in four fast-growing metropolitan areas: Dallas–Fort Worth, Texas; Denver, Colorado; Phoenix, Arizona; and Seattle, Washington.

The purpose of the study was an assessment of the success of the MPOs in meeting regional transportation needs. Success was to be measured on such issues as need satisfaction, funding location, and the quality and effectiveness of the decision process. The data were gathered through a process of personal interviews with 378 participants in their local area MPOs.

Participants in the study included transportation providers (roadway and rail), engineers, planners, citizens, and elected and appointed federal, state, and local government officials. Other success criteria were established from reviews of federal and state statutory and regulatory frameworks, MPO short- and long-range plans, state-funding provisions, federal certifications of the MPOs, and the literature on MPOs and transportation planning and intergovernmental relations.

Success Factors Identified

The study also identified the success factors that distinguish between MPOs with greater success and those that have been less successful. They included effective leadership, staff competence and credibility, level and quality of public involvement, and development of a regional ethos. Additional factors included the existence of streamlined and efficient planning processes, cooperative relationships with state departments of transportation (DOTs), land-use coordination, and accountability to members.

Prior to passage of the federal Intermodal Surface Transportation Efficiency Act of 1991 (ISTEA), agencies other than the local MPO played a larger role in local transportation planning. In many situations, the agency with greatest responsibility for transportation planning and provision was the local state department of transportation. Congress enacted the ISTEA legislation in the belief that local responsibility for metropolitan transportation planning would improve the quality of planning, as well as speed up the process. As a result, state and local governments became equal partners in the planning process.

3-C Planning

The first federal requirement that transportation planning be a condition of states receiving federal funds occurred in 1962. At the same time, the planning was to be continuous, comprehensive, and cooperative—what was to be known as "3-C planning." The cooperative component referred to cooperation between federal, state, and local governments, and between multiple agencies across local governments. At the time, the 43,000-mile Interstate Highway System was nearing completion. Congressional leaders were looking for ways to shift transportation from single-occupancy vehicles to modes that would prevent the transportation gridlocks that were beginning to occur or would soon do so. Roadway congestion, urban sprawl, and pollution—all problems that crossed jurisdictional boundaries—were emerging as political issues.

Enactment of ISTEA in 1991 was a product of those concerns. One of the most significant steps in its development and passage was removal of the word "highway" from its title; all earlier highway legislation contained the word. The other key component was to greatly expand the role of MPOs in transportation planning and give them authority with the state in transportation infrastructure project selection.

ISTEA gave large MPOs the power to allocate Surface Transportation Program–Metro funds. In some states, they administered Congestion Mitigation and Air Quality and Enhancement (bicycle and pedestrian) funds in consultation with the state DOT.

Not everyone welcomed the changes resulting from the new act, however. Some DOTs rebelled at what they conceived as a dilution of their decision-making authority. Local pro-highway and road-building coalitions also reacted negatively, believing that the MPOs would result in less friendly attitudes and decisions toward highways than the state agencies had held. Interestingly, for most of their existence, state DOTs have been Departments of Highways (DOHs), with the broader "transportation" label and responsibility only a more recent development.

ISTEA Provisions Sustained

Reassuringly, the 1998 Transportation Equity Act for the 21st Century (TERA-21) reaffirmed many of ISTEA's provisions. It also added to the importance of MPOs by continuing to specify finds over which they have allocation responsibility. The authors concluded that

> All this gave transportation planning a new perspective. The interstate and interregional "top-down" highway planning process of the federal and state governments, respectively, and the localized "bottom-up" street and road planning process of the cities and counties, were coupled with a third process—the regional one. This regional process extends beyond highways, streets, and roads into a comprehensive transportation planning process that takes into account all modes, as well as a number of related social, economic, and environmental issues. (Goetz, Dempsey, and Larson 2002, 90)

During the study, the four regional MPOs were rated on thirteen quality and effectiveness criteria, using a six-point scale, with 1 representing the lowest scores and 6 the highest. The summary in Table 19.3 thus serves as a shorthand tool for comparing the four case organizations on these attributes.

Clearly, the respondents showed a moderately positive assessment of the MPOs in their communities, although the results also reveal a wide range in the scores across the four MPOs. The Dallas–Fort Worth MPO was consistently rated higher than all of the other cases.

Qualitative assessments (open-ended questions or voluntary comments in personal interviews) highlighted a number of possible success factors that other MPOs might wish to consider in their planning and implementation processes. First, the most successful MPOs appeared to have strong leaders with the ability to gain and maintain collaboration and consensus building. Strong leadership was present in the Dallas–Fort Worth and Seattle MPOs, and these two organizations were rated higher than the other two community organizations. It is impossible to overstate the importance of maintaining a collaborative atmosphere throughout the planning and implementation of regional transportation systems. The authors of this study emphasized this point in this way:

> MPOs are collaborative structures. They were created to promote collaborative problem solving on issues of common concern that transcend parochial, short-term interests. Successful collaboration requires a different set of leadership skills and capacities than those associated with traditional politics and positional authority. The right combination of leadership attitudes, skills, and capacities can be the most important determinant of whether successful collaboration, or effective regional transportation planning, can occur. (Goetz, Dempsey, and Larson 2002, 100)

Summary

Case research in the area of public transportation tends to focus on issues associated with the planning, construction, operation, or management of bus, light rail and trolley (tram), and commuter train systems, as well as water- and airborne trans-

Table 19.3

MPO Ratings on Quality and Effectiveness Variables

	Factor	Dallas	Denver	Phoenix	Seattle
1.	Quality of process	4.51	3.98	3.73	4.35
2.	Regional needs met	5.11	4.25	3.96	4.37
3.	Rapidly changing needs met	5.01	3.54	3.73	3.93
4.	Works well with transit agencies	5.09	4.09	4.55	4.35
5.	Works well with state DOT	5.03	4.00	3.93	4.46
6.	Satisfies capacity needs	4.48	3.29	3.59	3.92
7.	Satisfies road construction needs	4.52	3.46	3.65	3.93
8.	Satisfies operational/safety needs	4.65	3.78	3.73	3.92
9.	Satisfies investment in bus service	4.62	3.46	3.27	3.92
10.	Satisfies investment in bike/pedestrian facilities	4.39	3.74	3.69	4.04
11.	MPO meets long-term needs	5.02	3.83	3.63	4.15
12.	Transportation improvement programs (TIP) criteria are fair (1–8 scoring)	6.34	5.55	4.84	5.31
13.	MPO process is fair (1–8 scoring)	6.71	5.43	4.76	4.15

Source: Goetz, Dempsey, and Larson (2002, 93).

portation. As with much of the public management case research, projects can be focused on issues at the federal, state, county, and/or municipal government level, and can involve a mix of public and private financing, planning, and operating issues. Its importance at the federal level is exemplified by the existence of a major cabinet post and department, the U.S. Department of Transportation. As followed in each of the chapters in which examples of case research are included, this chapter included both single-case and multicase research designs.

Note

1. At the time of this statement, Gambaccini was vice president and general manager of the Port Authority Trans-Hudson Corporation (PATH), an underground rapid transit railroad operated by the Port Authority of New York and New Jersey, linking Manhattan with New Jersey.

➤ 20 ◄

Case Research in the Work of Government

Transforming existing governance structures is a theme that's especially important [in managing the work of government]. . . . As the pace of change accelerates in every aspect of life, national [and state and local] governments face new and more complex challenges that they cannot address alone. If we're to meet the public's wants and needs in light of these long-term trends, governance systems in America and most other countries must be revised. In the twenty-first century, an effective governance structure recognizes that more and more policy challenges require multilateral action.
—David M. Walker (2007)

A recurring theme in case research in public management has been an emphasis on internal and external administrative reform and improvements in the way government operations are carried out by government workers (deLeon and Denhardt 2000; Fallows 1992; Kamensky 1996). Cases on change management in organizations represent one of the most visible components of the movement to bring the delivery of government services closer to a performance-oriented model.

Two important areas of research into internal operations improvements focus first on finding ways to improve worker productivity in the public sector and second on making government agencies and workers more accountable for their actions. The process organizations go through to make these changes is referred to as *transformation,* and it involves the following issues:

- *Productivity.* For many legislators and administrators, the issue of increasing government productivity is a central concern. Governments must attempt to do more with fewer financial and other resources. Limits on local tax increases, tax cuts at the highest level, and rapidly rising costs place government managers in the unenviable position of deciding which services to retain, which to increase, and which to cut—all in the face of continued public demand for services.

- *Accountability.* This refers to the drive to make government managers accountable for the successes and failures of their agencies. It includes such activities as performance measurement and benchmarking to achieve continuous
  improvements in the delivery of government services.
- *Transformation.* This is the process of achieving a fundamental change in the
  way an organization functions. True transformation of a public agency is a
  process of change in external form or inner nature, or conversion to a new state
  (Geri and McNabb 2008). It transcends simple reorganization and requires a
  comprehensive analysis of an organization and its various strategies. This is
  a relatively rare phenomenon. Audits, evaluations, and investigations enable
  agencies to correct most ongoing difficulties with their programs and systems,
  while webs of interest groups act to reinforce organizational inertia.

Case Research on Improving Productivity

Economists define productivity as the relationship between the amount of work
accomplished by a given application of financial, human, and/or technology
resources—output divided by input. As work (output) increases and resources (inputs) stay the same or decline, productivity increases. Input refers to the resources
invested in order for individuals to carry out their work activities. It includes money,
physical resources—including technology—and human capital. Throughputs refer
to the work activities that process and convert resources to outputs. Outcomes are
the effects that outputs have on the particular environment.

Other authors have concluded that the input-output model does not fully explain
productivity in public organizations. What is needed beyond measuring productivity in output is measuring productivity in the *outcomes* of government services—a
much more difficult process (Bouchaert 1990, 75). Uphoff (1994) considered the
economics definition too mechanistic for understanding and measuring productivity
gains or losses in government organizations. He believed that the chief problem
with relying exclusively on the input-output model was its inability to explain such
paradoxes as why changes in government outputs are not more clearly and reliably
proportional to changes in inputs:

> There is little correlation between *resources* expended through a unit of bureaucracy
> and the *results* produced, as should occur with mechanical processes [emphasis
> in the original]. The accomplishments of bureaucracies are supposed to be greater
> than the cost of operating them . . . this is sadly not the rule. (Uphoff 1994, 9)

Despite his rejection of the input-output mechanistic model, Uphoff (1994)
believed that lapses in performance are the result of "friction" in the system. By
friction, he was referring to the barriers that impede improvements in productivity.
The search for answers to why public organizations fail to meet plans and expectations given the resources devoted to them has long been a research question behind
much case research in government productivity.

History of the Productivity Movement

Bouchaert (1990) traced the history and development of the productivity move-ment in his extensive article in *Public Productivity and Management Review*. He divided the movement into four distinct eras. From a research point of view, it is important to recognize that traces of all programs still influence some aspects of productivity improvement initiatives.

The first phase, from 1900 to 1940, was characterized by efforts to apply scien-tific management principles to the public sector. The goal was to make government more efficient and thereby *better*. The way to do that was to separate politics and administration in order to create a nonpartisan, administrative state where policy was set by elected politicians, and actions were executed by neutral administrators.

The second period of productivity reform ran from 1940 to 1970. A key char-acteristic of this period was two ways of determining what should be the role of public administration. One equated public administration with political science; the second saw public administration as an administrative science. This set the stage for the new public management (NPM) movement that soon followed. In general, however, the main objective for efforts to improve productivity shifted from ef-forts to produce better government to one of controlling government spending. Productivity was equated to efforts to do more with less.

The third phase of productivity improvement, from 1970 to 1980, saw a decline of interest in productivity along with the global emergence of the NPM movement. Public administration was giving way to public management; this included a broadly based introduction of private-sector management methods into the opera-tions of government. Productivity improvement in this era focused on ways to get more value (i.e., quality) from expenditure of tax dollars—to "get more bang for the buck." Government agencies at all levels and in many countries designed and implemented comprehensive programs for improving the quality of their services, just as American industry had been forced to do to meet competition from German and Japanese manufacturers (Rago 1996).

Bouchaert saw the change affecting both the political and administrative side of government:

> The public administrator became a public manager. This metamorphosis promoted an atmosphere and environment of professionalism, creativity, innovation, and combativity that was supposed to be typical of the private sector. But as the ad-ministrative part is not always restricted to administration, the management part is not always confined to management. Politics remained an interfering factor. This resulted in administrative and political managers. (Bouchaert 1990, 55)

A fourth phase followed after 1980 with the surfacing of a renewed interest in productivity improvement. Two trends characterized the period. One was a con-tinuation of the focus on improving the yield of government performance; this was achieved by forcing deep budget cuts on government agencies.

The second was an emphasis that promoted a private-sector approach to productivity. This was achieved by reducing government spending through privatization of many government services. This approach came to dominate productivity improvement efforts and has continued to do so into the early years of the new century. It became crystallized in the 2002 management agenda policy of President George W. Bush.

Barriers to Productivity Improvement

In an era of fewer resources available to government agencies, improving productivity has become increasingly important to public managers. Achieving improvements in productivity occurs by either producing more and/or better program output (work) with the same level of resources, or by using a smaller amount of resources to achieve the same or a higher level or quality of output.

Achieving improvements in government productivity is not a simple task, however. Federal, state, and local governments do not have the same profit motive to invest in operations improvements that exists in the private sector. In addition to lacking this incentive, a number of barriers prevent or limit productivity improvement initiatives in government agencies. Many researchers have come up with lists of barriers to improvements in productivity. Possibly the shortest list consists of the three barriers identified by the Government Accountability Office (GAO) in 1978. GAO named internal resistance to change (inertia), agencies' inability to budget large initial investments needed to begin an improvement program, and the work capacity limitations of most government organizations.

Caudle came up with a list of ten barriers to productivity improvements in the federal government (1987, 40):

1. Fear that productivity measures will be misused for political reasons
2. Changes in work or new technology that make productivity measurements over time problematic
3. Lack of appreciation by managers of how measures might help managers' work and/or cut through internal resistance
4. Strict human resources procedures, wage rules, and management regulations
5. Budget limitations, resource controls, and short-term appropriations
6. Complex organizational structures
7. Poor management skills and high turnover of appointed and elected officials
8. Assumptions of poor government worker performance and better private-sector results
9. Pressure for rapid results for new programs and pressure to retain old programs
10. Poor productivity improvement program implementation

Productivity Problems in Local Governments

Productivity improvements in local governments have been, apparently, even more problematic. Ammons (1984) came up with a list of thirty-four barriers to productivity improvements in a study of productivity in cities. By 1985, he had found another three, bringing his list to thirty-seven barriers; some barriers were technical, but most were political. Leading the longer list were political factors that override public managers' rational decisions. Failure to demolish unneeded or ramshackle city-owned, unsafe buildings because of pressures by local community groups is an example. Thus, rational recommendations that offer potential gains in productivity lose out to political decisions.

Second on the lengthy list compiled by Ammons is the lack of political appeal inherent in many laborious, time-consuming efforts to improve productivity. While political candidates often promise to cut taxes, reduce red tape, and improve services, once in office they put aside the frustrating effort needed to achieve productivity growth and turn instead to other local problems or opportunities with more political glamour.

Case Research in Accountability

Government accountability means that elected officials and public employees have an obligation to explain their decisions and actions to the people they serve. Government accountability is exercised through a variety of means, including political, legal, and administrative processes. The underlying purpose of all such accountability processes is to prevent corruption and ensure that public officials are answerable and accessible to the people they serve. When such accountability processes are not available, corruption and malfeasance often appear (U.S. Department of State, 2004). This is clearly exemplified in the high levels of corruption that exist in Russia, where accountability mechanisms disintegrated with the breakup of the Soviet Union.

Accountability has become increasingly important since the spread of the NPM revolution that began in the 1970s. With this popularity have come problems. One of the major trends in this movement has been the decentralization of governance and collaborative government, private-sector, and nonprofit agreements. These activities are part and parcel of the NPM movement.

Scott (2000) identified some of the problems that could spring from maintaining traditional government accountability programs in light of transformational changes occurring from the NPM approach to government:

> The problems of accountability have been made manifest by the transformations wrought on public administration by the NPM revolution which have further fragmented the public sector. . . . The central problem of accountability arises from the delegation of authority to a wide range of public and some private actors, through legislation, contracts or other mechanisms. Debates over accountability have to grapple with the uncomfortable dilemma of how to give sufficient autonomy to these actors for them to be able to achieve their tasks, while at the same time ensuring an adequate degree of control. (Scott 2000, 38–39)

The most problematic of the NPM features may be implementation of market-based competition into management of government services. Related to this is the trend toward greater government decentralization, which includes greater collaborative delivery and management of services through networks and partnerships.

Accountability Processes

At least five types of accountability processes and procedures exist across all levels of government: political loyalties and commitments to citizens, traditional bureaucratic or hierarchical relationships, legally binding agreements and obligations, personal professional standards, and moral or ethical standards (Romzek and Dubnick 1994; Dicke and Ott 1999; Barker 2000).

Political Accountability

Political accountability may be the most important mechanism for holding government accountable. It is founded on the right of citizens to control their government through free and fair elections. Political accountability is further manifested by participating in the provision of government services through voluntary service on civic boards and commissions.

Bureaucratic Accountability

Bureaucratic accountability processes involve traditional hierarchical structures that formalize relationships between superiors and subordinates, the close supervision of workers, and clearly defined operating procedures. These processes are exercised through such means as establishment of internal offices within government organizations to make sure that the actions and decisions of government officials are just and in the interest of the public. They include such operations as agency ombudsmen, independent auditors, administrative courts, inspectors general, and procedures to protect whistle-blowers from retribution.

Legal Accountability

Legal accountability is based on relationships between government organizations and outside parties that have the power to force compliance with contract obligations. Bases for legal accountability include constitutions, laws, decrees and findings, rules, performance requirements, disclosure laws, judicial review, and other legal instruments that specify actions that public officials can and cannot take. These mechanisms also identify what actions citizens can take against officials found guilty of unseemly or illegal conduct.

Personal Accountability

Personal or professional accountability is based on the relationships that experts, advisors, counselors, consultants, and similar professionals have with their client agencies and organizations. The service providers can be held answerable for their decisions, recommendations, and actions.

Ethical Accountability

Ethical or moral accountability is based upon standards of behavior that are agreed upon by society. *Ethics* is the study of the moral behavior of humans in society; it is the set of principles that governs the conduct of an individual or a group of persons; in short, it is the study of morality or moral behavior (Velasquez 1998).

Morality refers to the standards that people in and out of government have about what is right, what is wrong, what is good, or what is evil; these standards are the behavior norms of a society. *Moral behavior* is acting in ways that follow the moral standards that exist in society.

Moral standards are the rules by which a society functions; they tell us what behavior is acceptable, what is "right," what is "good" in society, and their opposites. Moral standards vary from society to society; there are few absolutes in ethics. However, the fundamental standards of behavior tend to be quite similar throughout the industrialized nations of the world.

Methods for Exercising Accountability

Dicke and Ott (1999) identified ten methods or techniques by which government managers, legislative and executive policymakers, and private and public stakeholders exercise accountability in human services delivered by contract with nonprofit and business-sector organizations. Their list is equally appropriate for most if not all other government collaborative activities (Table 20.1). Case research has been conducted in all of these accountability options.

Case Research on Enterprise Transformation

Transformation refers to the fundamental changes in internal and external operations in order to achieve improvements in productivity and accountability. Strategic transformation requires a process that includes establishing or reviewing the vision and mission for the organization; analyzing internal and external environmental factors; forming both long-term and short-term objectives; and selecting, implementing, and evaluating a strategy to accomplish those objectives.

Public-sector leaders typically operate under severe constraints and lack the

Table 20.1

Methods for Exercising Accountability

	Method	Description
1.	Auditing	The systematic process of after-the-fact assessment of the gap between standards and an existing situation. In financial audits, it involves a formal verification of financial records. In program audits, auditors determine whether program goals are being met.
2.	Monitoring	Ongoing oversight inspection for compliance with contract provisions. It involves on-site observation, interviewing, reviews of provider records, progress reports, and follow-up on citizen complaints.
3.	Licensure	Official or legal permission to practice a profession or operate a service. A public agency may revoke a license for noncompliance with requirements or standards.
4.	Markets	An NPM mechanism that assumes efficient operation can best be achieved through competition for contracts and citizen/customer choice.
5.	Contracts	Formal, binding agreements between two or more parties. They include an agreement to do or not do something, specifications for performance, and financial consideration.
6.	Registries	Centralized databases that permit tracking of professionals in a field. They are designed to prevent false certification, abuse of privilege, and other incorrect or improper actions.
7.	Courts	Venue for the exercise of legal justice, suit for breach of contract or dereliction of duty, etc.
8.	Whistle-blowing	Disclosure of violations, mismanagement, gross waste of funds, abuse of authority, danger to public health or welfare, sexual abuse, and other corruption. Whistle-blowers may or may not be members of the organization.
9.	Codes of ethics	Statements of professional standards of conduct that are not usually legally binding but serve to identify unacceptable behavior.
10.	Outcomes-based assessment (OBA)	OBA is a program evaluation tool that attempts to verify accountability by measuring and evaluating end results of government programs.

Source: Dicke and Ott (1999).

formal power to bring about change based on narratives sketchily supported by sparse data, no matter how compelling. Despite these constraints, a number of transformation initiatives have been successful; case studies of successful examples include the transformation at the Veterans Health Administration from 1995 to 1999 and at the Bonneville Power Administration in the mid-1990s.

Transformation at the Veterans Health Administration

The Veterans Health Administration (VHA), one of the largest agencies in the federal government, underwent a far-reaching transformation over a five-year period beginning in 1995. The VHA administers the nation's health care system for veterans. In 2000, it served 3.6 million veterans in its 172 hospitals, 132 nursing homes, 73 home health care programs, 40 residential care programs, and more than 600 outpatient clinics. The VHA sponsors extensive research and teaching activities, and has academic affiliations with many university medical schools and schools of other health-related professions. It had more than 180,000 employees and an annual operating budget that exceeded $17 billion.

When the VHA began its transformation in 1995, it was rapidly falling behind the prevailing trends in the delivery of health care services. The VHA still devoted much of its resources and equipment to inpatient care, while the health care industry was shifting delivery of health care from inpatient tertiary care to outpatient primary care.

The VHA's hospitals were large, technology-intensive, and often underused facilities. Medical staffs at those hospitals were largely composed of medical specialists with little experience or interest in providing primary care. Its primary service market was made up of veterans with military service–related injuries and low-income veterans.

In addition to these forces for change at VHA, Congress indicated it would freeze the VHA's budgets, despite rising costs of serving an aging client base that required more and longer care. The VHA was described as "gradually becoming a health care dinosaur in danger of extinction" (Young 2000, 68).

The VHA recognized that it needed to make significant changes in the way it operated if it was to survive into the new century. However, revitalizing the VHA was not going to be easy, as this description reveals:

> Like many large, established organizations, the VHA was not oriented to flexibility and innovation. The agency's management systems and culture were deeply rooted in a command-and-control, military-style mind set. Decision making was highly centralized and bureaucratic. VHA headquarters tended to micro-manage many of the decisions and activities of the agency's hospitals and other operating units. This decision-making structure impeded operating units from adapting to local circumstances in a timely manner. Additionally, the VHA's system for allocating resources to operating units . . . did not provide incentives for the efficient delivery of health care services to the patient population. (Young 2000, 69)

Transformation Progress

Significant progress was achieved during the five-year program of transformation at the VHA. Performance metrics were developed and agreed upon in many different operational areas. Chief among the areas targeted for improvements were

(1) outpatient-oriented primary care, (2) convenience and accessibility of care, (3) operational efficiency, and (4) patient satisfaction. After the shift from inpatient to outpatient care, the following improvements were reported:

- Yearly inpatient admissions declined by more than 32 percent; ambulatory care visits increased by more than 45 percent.
- Surgeries performed on an outpatient basis increased from about 35 percent to more than 70 percent.
- Nearly 60 percent of hospital beds were eliminated.
- Percentage of patients receiving early cancer screening increased from 34 to 74 percent.
- Percentage of patients receiving treatment for preventing or controlling disease has increased from 74 to nearly 100 percent.

Indicators of progress in the other three performance measurement categories were the following:

- In convenience and accessibility: More than 300 new community-based outpatient clinics were established, and telephone-linked care was established at all hospitals.
- In operational efficiency: The number of full-time employees was reduced by more than 14 percent, while the number of patients served increased by more than 25 percent.
- In patient satisfaction: Scores on outpatient care satisfaction surveys improved by more than 15 percent.

Lessons Learned During the VHA Transformation

By 1999, in spite of these and other problems, the transformation effort at the VHA was considered a success. The shift from inpatient to outpatient care was largely completed; substantial improvements in the efficiency and quality of care were reported; and the VHA became a national leader in efforts to improve patient safety. The VHA's experiences provided a number of lessons that other government agencies might find useful in managing their own organizational change initiatives (Table 20.2).

Change at the Bonneville Power Administration

Relative to other developed countries, the United States has relatively few public enterprises at the national level. Major exceptions include the U.S. Postal Service and federal power marketing administrations (PMAs) within the U.S. Department of Energy. These PMAs are responsible for marketing power from federally owned dams. PMAs provide goods and services to the public; they are generally self-

Table 20.2

Lessons Learned During a Five-year Transformation Effort at the VHA

Lesson 1	Appoint leaders whose backgrounds and experiences are appropriate for the transformation.
Lesson 2	Follow a focused and coherent transformation plan:
	• Create a clear and comprehensive vision for the agency.
	• Adopt a new organizational structure.
	• Establish an accountability system linked to performance goals.
	• Modify agency rules and regulations that hinder change.
Lesson 3	Persevere despite imperfection, controversy, and criticism; make mid-course corrections to address technical problems as they occur.
Lesson 4	Match changes in the external environment with changes in the internal environment; changes that capitalize on the interdependencies between the two may contribute substantially to a successful transformation.
Lesson 5	Develop and manage communication channels from highest to lowest levels of the organization; keep frontline employees informed.
Lesson 6	Do not overlook training and education; these tools can improve workers' ability to adapt to the new structure, organization, rules, and procedures.
Lesson 7	Balance systemwide unity with operating unit flexibility. Determining how much decision-making authority to give to operating units and how much should be retained at headquarters is often central to transformations.

Source: Young (2000).

supporting, with earned revenues providing most of their budget (McNabb 2005). The U.S. Postal Service has even been mandated to earn a profit to cover future changes and improvements (Geri 1996; Geri and McNabb 2008).

The largest of the PMAs is the Bonneville Power Administration (BPA), which markets power from a system of dams and other generating facilities in the Pacific Northwest. The BPA coordinates the Northwest power supply, including three-fourths of the region's major transmission lines. With yearly revenues of over $2 billion, the BPA has long attracted attention thanks to its size, complexity, and impact on its region of the country.

The low-cost hydro power the BPA markets is the backbone of the region's power supply, and it must establish rules for the operation of the federal Columbia River Power System that meet stringent environmental and fisheries standards. Dams in the Northwest have decimated salmon and steelhead trout runs; as a result of new regulations, the BPA must provide power while trying to preserve the fish that are left.

Management Challenges

Managing the BPA's operations is challenging. It has multiple, politically powerful stakeholders, including over 100 utilities and major users, the aluminum industry, the federal agencies managing the dams, plus advocates for fish and wildlife and renewable energy. Also, the power supplies available for the agency to sell are dependent on annual precipitation. A year with less than average snowfall in the Cascade Mountains will mean less cheap hydropower is available; any gap in demand must be met by purchasing much more expensive energy generated by coal, gas, or nuclear power. Only recently have wind and geothermal generation of electricity become significant, accounting for something like 1 percent of all power generated in the United States.

By the mid-1990s, changes in the national electricity market left the BPA's business model badly out of step with its customers and overall operating environment. The organization had long operated as a specialized federal agency. This approach was effective as long as the electric utility industry was a relatively cozy world of monopoly service providers within fixed geographic areas. However, when changes in technology and the regulatory environment led to deregulation of the industry in the 1990s, it enabled competition in power production and, to a lesser extent, in transmission and distribution. These changes offered real alternatives to large users of power, particularly in industry. The BPA was faced with the possibility of mass defections to other suppliers. This possible loss of revenues threatened its ability to meet its responsibility for annual payments to the U.S. Treasury.

Top-to-Bottom Changes Needed

As the BPA's top management team watched this process develop, they began to believe that top-to-bottom changes in the organization were required to keep it competitive. In 1993 they initiated the Competitiveness Project, which included a comprehensive analysis of its structure, mission, and operations. Largely a top-down process, it also included substantive discussions with stakeholders and employees.

Many of these discussions focused on how difficult it was to work with Bonneville. Teams of agency officials and stakeholders reviewed its products, pricing, and efforts to support renewable energy and protect fish and wildlife. The project resulted in a series of proposals, including a Strategic Business Plan and a Marketing Plan, intended to change the culture and practices of the organization to emphasize a market-driven model.

A 1995 Energy Information Service (EIS) documented the decision processes that led to the selection of the "market-driven" business plan model (Geri 1996).

In the judgment of the BPA's leadership, this model was the only one that would enable it to meet its challenging goals within the new competitive environment. The new business model included a focus on customer types rather than geographic regions, account executives with clear responsibilities and authority, unbundled power products more attractive to customers, and simplified contract processes. The BPA also downsized dramatically, slashing over 1,000 federal and contractor positions.

These changes reduced its overall budget by about $250 million per year and improved the BPA's ability to listen to its customers and clients. Although in the short run, this improved its financial position and overall competitiveness, vagaries of the weather (notably a drought in 2001) and an unstable electricity market in the western United States drove the BPA into the red again by 2001. Arguably, however, its strategic transformation enabled the BPA to avoid more extreme alternatives, including privatization, and kept the overall power market in the region more stable—despite subsequent market shenanigans by Enron and the state of California—than it would have been otherwise.

Implementing Change in Local Government

Denhardt and Denhardt included three case studies in their 1999 analysis of the role of leadership in initiating change in local government. The authors profiled two city managers and one county executive who were held up as examples of leading successful transformations. From interviews with the managers and a number of their administrators, Denhardt and Denhardt were able to distill a series of steps that other public managers might find useful when implementing change initiatives in their jurisdictions.

Change in Fairfax County, Virginia

The first case profiled Robert O'Neill, the newly appointed executive manager of Fairfax County, a county of more than one million people located in the greater Washington, DC, metropolitan area. An elected board of nine supervisors elected from separate districts plus a board chairman elected at large governed Fairfax County. O'Neill was hired after a term as a successful change leader as the city manager of Hampton, Virginia.

O'Neill took office during a period of low morale among county employees and low confidence in county government among its citizens. The county had just suffered through a fiscal crisis. Workers were highly change-adverse. The government operated in a traditional top-down hierarchical organization with little cross-functional communication or cooperation between departments.

O'Neill began his change program by holding a series of intensive conversations, meetings, and brown-bag luncheons with employees in all departments and levels to find out what they had to say about the county's problems and what should or could be done about them. From these internal interactions, he began to involve staff in major decisions facing the county. He then met with local civic leaders and members of local organizations, including business leaders and other community groups. Citizens and members of local civic groups were also enlisted in volunteer advisory groups.

Most of the workers and citizens involved liked what they saw happening; a new culture of openness to change was emerging. The message that employees were getting was that everyone should communicate with one another, across departments and up and down the organization. Local citizens saw that people in the county government were not only receptive to their opinions, they also eagerly sought people's contributions and suggestions.

Although at the time of the case study, O'Neill was still early in his tenure as county executive, Denhardt and Denhardt concluded that he was successful in his efforts to achieve the needed changes in organizational culture from hierarchical, bureaucratic administration to one of openness, widespread involvement, and open communication.

Change in Altamonte Springs, Florida

Altamonte Springs is a suburban community of a little more than 50,000 residents in the Orlando, Florida, metropolitan area. Phil Penland had been city manager for sixteen years at the time of the Denhardt and Denhardt (1999) study. During that period, Penland and the city had gained a reputation for innovation, creativity, and excellence in governance.

Beginning with a comprehensive revitalization of the downtown central business district, Penland and his team of dedicated staff led Altamonte Springs to become one of the first cities in Florida to adopt a program of total quality improvement in all city departments. Employees were encouraged to participate in what resembled quality circles, which addressed issues from work process improvements to enhancing the quality of work life. Penland also led a strong commitment to professional ethics among city managers and workers. This and other, related efforts to bring about a new organizational culture of strong, dedicated public service resulted in the following new way of functioning:

> Perhaps more important than the individual efforts in quality services [was] the fact that Penland and his top management team seem to have created a "culture" of innovation within the city, a culture that is accepted and indeed applauded by citizens, [city] commissioners, [department] managers, and staff throughout the city. People are encouraged to look for innovative ways to approach their work; they are encouraged to try out new ideas (knowing they will be supported even if their good faith efforts fall short), and they are rewarded for their contributions to improve the quality and productivity of city government. (Denhardt and Denhardt 1999, 12)

Transforming City Government in Fremont, California

Jan Perkins became assistant city manager of Fremont, California, in 1992 after serving as city manager of Morgan Hill, California. Ten months after taking the job in Fremont, the city manager was fired, and Perkins became acting city manager and then city manager shortly afterward. In the early 1990s, Fremont was undergoing financial difficulties as the state of California was moving to reduce city governments' reliance on property taxes. Deep cuts in city employment and city services were taking place, while at the same time citizen demand for quality services was high and growing. As a result, both citizens and city employees had lost confidence in the ability of city government to carry out its mission (Denhardt and Denhardt 1999).

After rejecting a suggestion that the city hire a consultant (for a half-million dollar fee) Perkins began working with all parties to see how the quality and quantity of city government could be improved. After meetings and workshops with elected and appointed officials, workers and citizens were invited to produce the changes needed to bring the city to the point where it would become a fast, flexible, customer-oriented organization that focused on results, partnerships, and collaborations internally and externally.

During the first five years of Perkins's tenure as city manager, the Fremont city government became known for delivering high-quality services to its citizens, made possible by the creation of an organizational culture based on continuous, employee-led improvement; a collaborative approach to decision making and problem solving; and a variety of partnerships that were formed within the city and with nearby communities.

Relationships with citizens were particularly well served. All employees were encouraged to consider themselves as representatives of the city and do whatever was necessary to help citizens with their questions or issues. Also, they no longer simply informed citizens about what the city planned to do. Instead, they asked citizens what services they wanted and got citizens involved in the design of the solution. Department managers balance the needs and wants of citizens with the needs of the entire city, while making sure that those affected are fully informed about the decision.

Conclusion: Successful Change Managers Follow the Same Steps

From these and other case studies in the art and practices of public sector leadership, Denhardt and Denhardt were able to identify a series of steps that all public managers interested in change should follow:

- Evaluate the environment that is shaping the need for change.
- Each of the three managers studied began their involvement by gathering information about three factors: (1) the role and attitudes of the governing

body (elected members of the county or city council), (2) the city government, and (3) the community. This became a continuous process.

- Plan for the long term (strategically) and for the immediate situation.
- The three administrators were particularly respected for their ability to keep the long-term path of the region in mind while devoting extensive efforts to solving the immediate problems facing the city.
- Build support for change by involving everyone possible while ensuring that the change process reflects their behaviors.
- Support for change was achieved through the many meetings, conferences, and information-gathering activities led by each of the three administrators, followed by involving employees in every step of the design of the change as well as in its implementation.
- Implement changes, and at the same time reinforce an organizational culture that embraces change and innovation.
- Leading an organization through a process of transformational change is not a one-shot activity. The real goal of the leader should be the acceptance of the fact that change is absolutely necessary for survival.
- Make the change an accepted part of the organization; make it the normal way of operating.

Denhardt and Denhardt emphasized that the change must become the organization's idea, not the administrators. Workers accepting the ideas as their own is often referred to as "buying into the program." After about five years of successful organizational development, the changes should be in place strongly enough so that if the administrator leaves, the changes will be likely to remain in place. "Once ideas such as involvement and communication, quality and innovation, collaboration and engagement become embedded in the culture of the organization, people will begin to automatically look for ways to extend these values" (Denhardt and Denhardt 1999, 21).

This case research report on leadership in local government concludes with the conviction that the most important factor that makes it possible to achieve change in government is a *manager's ability to learn*. These four areas of learning that may be most critical for transformational change to occur are: (1) understanding yourself and your values, and remaining committed to them in the face of required sacrifice in one's personal life; (2) knowing the community and what makes the community what it is; (3) knowing the organization, from the highest administrator to the newest worker (developing the skills of existing workers is usually better than replacing existing personnel); and (4) knowing the governing body. In addition, a critical success criterion is to have an elected board engaged in the change—or at least neutral to it.

Summary

This chapter looked at elements in government's efforts to transform its internal operations for greater productivity and accountability through the process of organizational transformation. Two important standards of case research into operational improvements were discussed: focus on finding ways to improve worker productivity and making government agencies and workers more accountable. Organizations are undergoing significant transformations to make these changes.

Seven important lessons on how to achieve a successful transformation learned during case studies examined in the chapter include (1) appoint a leader with the background and experience appropriate for the sought organizational change; (2) follow a transformation plan, beginning with a clear vision and including a new structure, accountability system, and changes in rules; (3) do not let imperfection kill the effort; (4) make changes in the external and internal environments; (5) establish a communication system to ensure all employees know about the program and its goals and objectives; (6) be sure to include training and education; and (7) balance systemwide unity with operating unit flexibility.

References

Adler, Patricia A. and Peter Adler. 1998. "Observational Techniques." In Norman K. Denzin and Yvonna S. Lincoln, eds. *Collecting and Interpreting Qualitative Materials,* 79–109. Thousand Oaks, CA: Sage.

Agranoff, Robert and Michael McGuire. 2003. *Collaborative Public Management.* Washington, DC: Georgetown University Press.

Agyeman, Julian and Tom Evans. 2003. "Toward Just Sustainability in Urban Communities: Building Equity Rights with Sustainable Solutions." *Annals of the American Academy of Political and Social Science,* 590 (November): 35–53.

Alejandro, Roberto. 1993. *Hermeneutics, Citizenship, and the Public Sphere.* Albany: State University of New York Press.

Alesina, Alberto and Francesco Giavazzi. 2006. *The Future of Europe: Reform of Decline.* Cambridge, MA: MIT University Press.

Alford, Steve. 2002. "Transforming Public Administration: Realizing the Benefits of Technology for Government." Retrieved October 10, 2008, from http://unpan1.un.org/intradoc/groups/public/documents/APCITY/UNPAN011279.pdf.

Ammons, David N. 1984. *Municipal Productivity: A Comparison of Fourteen High-Quality Service Cities.* New York: Praeger.

———. 1985. "Common Barriers to Productivity Improvement in Local Government." *Public Productivity Review,* 9(4): 293–310.

Ammons, David N., Charles Coe and Michael Lombardo. 2001. "Performance-Comparison Projects in Local Government: Participants' Perspectives." *Public Administration Review,* 61(1): 100–110.

Ammons, David N. and William C. Riverbank. 2008. "Factors Influencing the Use of Performance Data to Improve Municipal Services: Evidence from the North Carolina Benchmarking Project." *Public Administration Review,* 68(2): 304–18.

Argyris, Chris, Robert Putnam and Diana M. Smith. 1985. *Action Science.* San Francisco, CA: Jossey-Bass.

Arneson, Pat. 1993. "Situating Three Contemporary Qualitative Methods in Applied Organizational Communication Research: Historical Documentation Techniques, the Case Study Method, and the Critical Approach to Organizational Analysis." In Sandra L. Herndon and Gary L. Kreps, eds. *Qualitative Research: Applications in Organizational Communications,* 159–73. Cresskill, NJ: Hampton Press.

Ash, Amin and Patrick Cohendet. 2004. *Architecture of Knowledge: Firms, Capabilities, and Communities.* Oxford, UK: Oxford University Press.

Astleithner, Florentina and Alexander Hamedinger. 2003. "Urban Sustainability as a New Form of Governance: Obstacles and Potentials in the Case of Vienna." *Innovation: The European Journal of Social Science Research,* 16(1): 51–75.

Bacot, Hunter and Jack Christine. 2006. "What's So 'Special' About Airport Authorities? Assessing the Administrative Structure of U.S. Airports." *Public Administration Review*, 66(2): 241–51.

Bailey, Mary T. 1994. "Do Physicists Use Case Studies?" In Jay B. White and Guy B. Adams, eds. *Research in Public Administration: Reflections on Theory and Practice*, 183–96. Thousand Oaks, CA: Sage.

Ball, Billy. 2006. "Rebuilding Electrical Infrastructure along the Gulf Coast: A Case Study." Retrieved August 10, 2008, from www.nae.edu/NAE/bridgecom.nsf/BridgePrintView/MKEZ-6MYS3U?OpenDocument.

Bangert-Drowns, Robert L. and Lawrence M. Rudner. 1991. "Meta-Analysis in Educational Research." *Practical Assessment, Research & Evaluation*, 2(8). Retrieved May 15, 2008, from http://PAREonline.net/getvn.asp?v=2&n=8.

Barker, Robert S. 2000. "Government Accountability and Its Limits." *Issues of Democracy*, 5(2). Washington, DC: U.S. Department of State, International Information Programs. Retrieved March 21, 2008, from http://italy.usembassy.gov/pdf/ej/ijde0800.pdf.

Barnes, Louis B., C. Roland Christensen and Abby J. Hansen. 1994. *Teaching and the Case Method,* 3rd ed. Cambridge, MA: Harvard Business School Press.

Bauman, Zygmunt. 1992. *Hermeneutics and the Social Sciences.* Aldershot, UK: Gregg Revivals.

Becker, Howard S., Herbert J. Gans, Katherine S. Newman and Diane Vaughan. 2004. "On the Value of Ethnography: Sociology and Public Policy." *Annals of the American Academy of Political and Social Science*, 595 (September): 264–76.

Behn, Robert D. 2007. *What All Mayors Would Like to Know About Baltimore's CitiStat Performance Strategy.* Washington, DC: IBM Center for the Business of Government.

Benbasat, Izak, David K. Goldstein and Melissa Mead. 1987. "The Case Research Strategy in Studies of Information Systems." *MIS Quarterly,* 11(3): 367–86.

Bengtsson, Lars, Rikard Larsson, Andrew Griffiths and Damian Hine. 2007. "Case and iCase: Facilitating Case Survey Methods for Creating Research and Teaching Synergies in Innovation and Enterprise." In Damian Hine and David Carson, eds. *Innovative Methodologies in Enterprise Research,* 101–23. Cheltenham, UK: Edward Elgar.

Bernard, Harvey R. 1995. *Research Methods in Anthropology,* 2nd ed. Walnut Creek, CA: AltaMira Press.

Black, John A., Antonio Paez and Putu A. Suthanaya. 2002. "Sustainable Urban Transportation: Performance Indicators and Some Analytical Approaches." *Journal of Urban Planning and Development*, 128(4): 184–209.

Blampied, Neville M. 2000. "Single-Case Research Designs: A Neglected Alternative." *American Psychologist*, 55(8): 960.

Blau, Sheridan, Peter Elbow and Don Killgallon. (1992). *The Writer's Craft: Ideas to Expression.* Evanston, IL: McDougal, Little.

Blyler, Nancy. 1998. "Taking a Political Turn: The Critical Perspective and Research in Professional Communications." *Technical Communications Quarterly*, 7(1). Retrieved January 10, 2009, from www.attw.org/TQCarticles/7.1/7.1Blyler/pdf.

Bogenschneider, Karen. 1995. "Roles for Professionals in Building Family Policy." *Family Relations,* 44(1): 5–12.

Bonoma, Thomas V. 1995. "Case Research in Marketing: Opportunities, Problems, and a Process." *Journal of Marketing Research,* 22(2): 199–208.

Borins, Sandford. 2001. "Innovation, Success and Failure in Public Management Research." *Public Management Review*, 3(1): 3–17.

Bouchaert, Geert. 1990. "The History of the Productivity Movement." *Public Productivity and Management Review,* 14(1): 53–89.

Bovens, Mark and Stravros Zouridis. 2002. "From Street-Level to System-Level Bureaucracies: How Information and Communications Technology Is Transforming

Administrative Discretion and Constitutional Control." *Public Administration Review*, 62(2): 174–84.

Bovitz, Gregory L. 2002. "Electoral Consequences of Porkbusting in the U.S. House of Representatives." *Political Science Quarterly*, 117(3): 455–77.

Breaux, David A., Christopher M. Duncan, C. Denise Keller and John C. Morris. 2002. "Welfare Reform, Mississippi Style: Temporary Assistance for Needy Families and the Search for Accountability." *Public Administration Review*, 62(1): 92–103.

Brinkerhoff, Jennifer M. 2002. "Global Public Policy, Partnership, and the Case of the World Commission on Dams." *Public Administration Review*, 62(3): 324–36.

Brown, Dennis M. 2004. "Public Transportation on the Move in Rural America." Rural Information Center, National Agricultural Library, U.S. Department of Agriculture. Retrieved July 30, 2008, from www.nal.usda.gov/ric/ricpubs/publictrans.htm.

Bruegmann, Robert. 1993. "Infrastructure Reconstructed." *Design Quarterly*, 158 (Winter): 7–13.

Bryman, Alan and R.G. Burgess, 1999. *Qualitative Research*. London: Sage.

Bushe, Gervase R. and Aniq F. Kassam. 2005. "When Is Appreciative Inquiry Transformational? A Meta-Case Analysis." *Journal of Applied Behavior Science*, 42(2): 161–81. Retrieved November 2, 2008, from www.gervasebushe.ca/aimeta.htm.

Camp, Robert C. 1989. *Benchmarking: The Search for Industry Best Practices That Lead to Superior Performance.* New York: ASQC Quality Press.

Campbell, Mary. 2004. "Improving Agency Performance and Service Delivery." *Journal for Quality and Participation*, 27(4): 43–49.

Caudle, Sharon L. 1987. "Productivity Politics: Gilding the Farthing." *Public Productivity Review,* 11(2): 39–51.

Chapman, Jeffrey I. 2008. "State and Local Fiscal Sustainability: The Challenges." *Public Administration Review*, 68 (Supplement): S115–31.

Charan, Ram. 2008. "A Goal We Can Believe In." *Fortune*, 158(10): 92–93.

Choi, Sang Ok. 2004. "Emergency Management Growth in the State of Florida." *State and Local Government Review*, 36(3): 212–26.

City of Chicago. 2006. *Office of Emergency Management and Communication.* Retrieved August 19, 2009, from http://webapps.cityofchicago.org.ChicagoAlertWeb/index .jsp?content=aboutOEMC.

City of Houston. 2009. *Office of Public Safety and Homeland Security.* Retrieved August 19, 2009, from http://houstontx.gov/publicsafety/index.html.

City of San Francisco. 2009. *Department of Emergency Management.* Retrieved August 19, 2009, from http://www.sfgov.org/site/dem_index.asp?id=95931.

Cohen, Steven, William Eimicke and Jessica Horan. 2002. "Catastrophe and the Public Service: A Case Study of the Government Response to the Destruction of the World Trade Center." *Public Administration Review,* 62 (September Special Issue): 24–32.

Comfort, Louise K. 1985. "Integrating Organizational Action in Emergency Management: Strategies for Change." *Public Administration Review,* 45 (Special Issue): 155–64.

Comstock, Donald E. and Russell Fox. 1993. "Participatory Research as Critical Theory: The North Bonneville, USA, Experience." In Peter Park, Mary Brydon-Miller, Budd Hall and Ted Jackson, eds. *Voices of Change: Participatory Research in the United States and Canada,* 103–24. Wesport, CT: Bergin & Garvey.

Cooper, Randolph B. 2000. "Information Technology Development Creativity: A Case Study of Attempted Radical Change." *MIS Quarterly,* 24(2): 245–76.

Crain, W. Mark and Lisa K. Oakley. 1995. "The Politics of Infrastructure." *Journal of Law and Economics,* 38(1): 1–17.

Czerwinski, Stanley J. 2008. *State and Local Fiscal Challenges: Rising Health Care Costs Drive Long-Term and Immediate Pressures.* Washington, DC: U.S. General Accountability Office. Report GAO-09-210T.

Dearstyne, Bruce W. 1993. *The Archival Enterprise.* Chicago: American Library Association.

deLeon, Linda and Robert B. Denhardt. 2000. "The Political Theory of Reinvention." *Public Administration Review,* 60(2): 89–97.

Denhardt, Kathryn and Eugene Miller. 2000. "Managing a City's Health Benefits." *Public Performance & Management Review,* 24(2): 195–99.

Denhardt, Robert B. and Janet V. Denhardt. 1999. *Leadership for Change: Case Studies in American Local Government.* Washington, DC: The PricewaterhouseCoopers Endowment for the Business of Government.

Denscombe, Martyn. 1998. *The Good Research Guide.* Buckingham, UK: Open University.

Devaraj, Sarv and Rajiv Kohli. 2003. "Performance Impacts of Information Technology: Is Actual Usage the Missing Link?" *Management Science,* 49(3): 273–89.

Denzin Norman K. and Yvonna S. Lincoln. 1998. *Collecting and Interpreting Qualitative Materials.* Thousand Oaks, CA: Sage.

DHS. See U.S. Department of Homeland Security.

Dicke, Lisa A. and J. Stephen Ott. 1999. "Public Agency Accountability in Human Services Contracting." *Public Productivity and Management Review,* 22(4): 502–16.

Dixon, Jill and Joan Buhrman. 2005. "America's Crumbling Infrastructure Eroding Quality of Life." American Society of Civil Engineers press release, March 9, 2005. Retrieved August 5, 2008, from www.asce.org/reportcard/2005/page.cfm?id=108.

DOT. See U.S. Department of Transportation.

Dubé, Line and Guy Paré. 2003. "Rigor in Information Systems Positivist Case Research: Current Practices, Trends and Recommendations." *MIS Quarterly,* 27(4): 597–635.

Dutton, William H. 1981. "The Rejection of an Innovation: The Political Environment of a Computer-Based Model." *Systems, Objectives, Solutions,* 1(4): 179–201.

Duveen, Gerard. 2000. "Piaget Ethnographer." *Social Science Information,* 39(1): 79–97.

Dysard, J.A. II. 2001. "How Competition Is Changing the Face of the Public Water Resources Industry—Trends in Privatization, Management Competition, and Other Alternative Delivery Systems." In W.C. Lauer, ed. *Excellence in Action: Water Utility Management in the 21st Century,* 85–90. Denver: American Water Works Association.

Eckstein, Harry. 2002. "Case Study and Theory in Political Science." In Roger Gomm, Martyn Hammersley and Peter Foster, eds. *Case Study Method: Key Issues, Key Texts,* 119–64. London: Sage.

Economist. 2008. "The Cracks Are Showing." The Economist.com (June 26). Retrieved August 5, 2008, from www.economist.com/world/unitedstates/PrinterFriendly.cfm?stpry _id=1136517.

Ellet, William. 2007. *The Case Study Handbook.* Cambridge, MA: Harvard Business School Press.

Eisenhardt, Kathleen M. 1999. "Building Theories from Case Study Research." In Alan Bryman and Robert G. Burgess, eds. *Qualitative Research,* 135–59. London: Sage.

Epstein, Paul D. 1982. "The Value of Measuring and Improving Performance." *Public Productivity Review,* 6(3): 157–66.

Este, David, Jackie Sieppert and Allan Barsky. 1998. "Teaching and Learning Qualitative Research with and without Qualitative Data Analysis Software." *Journal of Research on Computing in Education,* 31(2): 138–55.

Falleti, Tulia G. 2005. "A Sequential Theory of Decentralization: Latin American Cases in Comparative Perspective." *American Political Science Review,* 99(3): 327–46.

Fallows, James. 1992. "A Case for Reform." *Atlantic Monthly,* 270(2): 119–23.

Farmer, Paul. 2008. "Crumbling Bridges, Oil Imports, Rising VMT, More Roads . . . Oh My!" *Planning,* 74(3): 5.

Federal Emergency Management Administration (FEMA). 2008. *FEMA History.* Washing-

ton, DC: Federal Emergency Management Agency. Retrieved May 12, 2008, from www
.fema.gov/about/history.shtm.

Federal Transit Administration (FTA). 2008. *Welcome to the Federal Transit Administration.*
Retrieved July 30, 2008, from www.fta.dot.gov.

FEMA. See Federal Emergency Management Administration.

Fernandez, Sergio and Ross Fabricant. 2000. "Methodological Pitfalls in Privatization
Research: Two Cases from Florida's Child Support Enforcement Program." *Public
Performance & Management Review,* 24(2): 133–44.

Fetterman, David M. 1989. *Ethnography Step by Step.* Newbury Park, CA: Sage.

Fink, Arlene. 1998. *Conducting Research Literature Reviews.* Thousand Oaks, CA:
Sage.

Fischler, Raphaël. 2000. "Case Studies of Planners at Work." *Journal of Planning Literature,*
15(2): 184–95.

Flick, Ewe. 1999. "Qualitative Research in Sociology in Germany and the U.S.—State of the
Art, Differences and Developments." *Forum: Qualitative Social Research-Online,* 6(3):
1–19. Retrieved May 13, 2008, from www.qualitative-research.net/fqs-texte/3–05/05–
3–23-e_p.html.

Fontana, Andrea and James H. Frey. 1998. "Interviewing: The Art of Science." In Norman
K. Denzin and Yvonna S. Lincoln, eds. *Collecting and Interpreting Qualitative Materials,* 47–78. Thousand Oaks, CA: Sage.

Fox, Elaine R. and Lisa Roth. 1989. "Homeless Children: Philadelphia as a Case Study."
Annals of the American Academy of Political and Social Science, 506 (November):
141–51.

Fox-Penner, Peter S. and Gregory Basheda. 2001. "A Short Honeymoon for Utility Regulation." *Issues in Science and Technology,* 17 (Spring), 51–57.

Franklin, Ronald D., David B. Allison and Bernard S. Gorman, eds. 1997. *Design and
Analysis of Single-Case Research.* Mahwah, NJ: Erlbaum.

Frates, Stephen B. 2004. "Improving Government Efficiency and Effectiveness and Rein-
vigorating Citizen Involvement." *Perspectives on Political Science,* 33(2): 98–103.

Gadamer, Hans-Georg. 1990. *Truth and Method,* 2nd ed. New York: Crossroads.

Gais, Thomas and Lucy Dadayan. 2008. "The New Retrenchment: Social Welfare Spending,
1977–2006." Albany: State University of New York, Nelson A. Rockefeller Institute of
Government. www.rockinst.org.pdf/workforce_welfare_and_social_services/2008–
09–15-the_new_retrenchment_social_welfare_spending_1977–2007.pdf.

Gambaccini, Louis J. 1977. "University Research Programs." *Passenger Transport,* 35
(March): center spread.

GAO. See U.S. Government Accountability Office.

Gardiner, Kathryn L. 2003. "Fighting Terrorism the FATF Way." *Global Governance,*
13(2007): 325–45.

Garson, F. David. 2008. "Case Studies." North Carolina State University. Retrieved November 2, 2008, from http://faculty.chass.ncsu.edu/garson/PA765/cases.htm.

George, Alexander L. and Andrew Bennett. 2005. *Case Studies and Theory Development
in the Social Sciences.* Cambridge, MA: MIT Press.

George, Anu. 2006. "Disaster Management in the Cuddalore District." In Rijiv Mishra,
Vasudha Mishra and Chiranjiv Choudhary, eds. *Readings and Case Studies on Disaster
Management, Vol. 1.,* 1–37. Mussoori, India: Center for Disaster Management, Lal Ba-
hadur Shastri National Academy of Administration.

Geri, Laurance R. 1996. The impacts of user fees on U.S. government agencies. PhD diss.,
University of Southern California.

Geri, Laurance R. and David E. McNabb. 2008. "Strategic Management for Public Sector
Transformation: A Model Approach." Paper presented at the Annual Meeting of the
American Society for Public Administration, Dallas, TX, March 2008.

Gerring, John. 2004. "What Is a Case Study and What Is It Good For?" *American Political Science Review*, 98(2): 341–54.

Gerston, Larry N. 1983. *Making Public Policy: From Conflict to Resolution*. Glenview, IL: Scott Foresman.

Gibson, Robert B. 2006. "Sustainability Assessment: Basic Components of a Practical Approach." *Impact Assessment and Project Appraisal*, 24(3): 170–82.

Gillham, Bill. 2000. *Case Study Research Methods*. London: Continuum.

Glass, Gene V. 1976. "Primary, Secondary, and Meta-Analysis of Research." *Educational Researcher*, 11(18): 3–8.

———. 2000. "Meta-Analysis at 25." Retrieved December 22, 2008, from http://glass.ed.asu.edu/gene/papers/meta25.html.

Glick, Doris F., Bonnie Jerome-D'Emilia, Mary Anne Nolan and Pamela Burke. 2004. "Emergency Preparedness: One Community's Response." *Farm Community Health*, 27(3): 266–73.

Goetz, Andrew R., Paul S. Dempsey and Carl Larson. 2002. "Metropolitan Planning Organizations: Findings and Recommendations for Improving Transportation Planning." *Publius: Journal of Federalism*, 32(1): 87–105.

Golat, Mike. 2005. Series of personal interviews with David E. McNabb. Shelton, WA.

Gomm, Roger, Peter Foster and Martyn Hammersley, eds. 2000. *Case Study Method: Key Issues, Key Texts*. Thousand Oaks, CA: Sage.

Gomm, Roger, Martyn Hammersley and Peter Foster, eds. 2002. *Case Study Method: Key Issues, Key Texts*. London: Sage.

Goodale, James G. 1982. *The Fine Art of Interviewing*. Englewood Cliffs, NJ: Prentice-Hall.

Gordon, Greg. 2007. "Bridge Tragedy Sparks Scrutiny of Federal Inspection Program." McClatchy Newspapers Washington Bureau. Retrieved August 5, 2008, from www.mcclatchydc.com/homepage/v-print/story/18675.html.

Gordon, Jennifer and Franklin C. Shontz. 1990. "Representative Case Research: A Way of Knowing." *Journal of Counseling & Development,* 69(5): 62–69.

Gospodini, Aspa. 2005. "Urban Development, Redevelopment and Regeneration Encouraged by Transport Infrastructure Projects: The Case Study of 12 European Cities." *European Planning Studies*, 13(7): 1083–1122.

Govtrack.us. 2008. "H.R. 6052: Saving Energy Through Public Transportation Act of 2008." Retrieved July 30, 2008, from www.govtrack.us/congress/bill.xpd?tab=main&bill=h110–6052.

Greenwald, Abe. 2008. "Shameful Schumer." *Commentary Magazine, Contentions* (June 3), 63(6).

Grigg, Neil L. 2005. "Institutional Analysis of Infrastructure Problems: Case Study of Water Quality in Distribution Systems." *Journal of Management in Engineering*, 21(4): 152–58.

Gummesson, Evert. 1987. *Qualitative Methods in Management Research*. Newbury Park, CA: Sage.

Hall, Thad. 2008. "Steering Agencies with Short-Term Authorizations." *Public Administration Review,* 68(2): 366–79.

Hamel, Jacque, Stéphane Dufour and Dominic Fortin. 1993. *Case Study Methods*. Newbury Park, CA: Sage.

Handley, Donna M. 2008. "Strengthening the Intergovernmental Grant System: Long-Term Lessons for the Federal-Local Relationship." *Public Administration Review,* 68(1): 126–36.

Hansen, Philip and Alicja Muszyaki. 1990. "Crisis in Rural Life and Crisis in Thinking: Directions for Critical Research." *Canadian Review of Sociology and Anthropology*, 27(2): 1–23.

Hanson, Norwood R. 1958. *Patterns of Discovery: An Inquiry into the Conceptual Foundations of Science.* Cambridge, UK: Cambridge University Press.

Hartley, Jean F. 1994. "Case Studies in Organizational Research." In Catherine Cassell and Gillian Symon, eds. *Qualitative Methods in Organizational Research,* 208–47. London: Sage.

He, Xu, Liu Xiaoqin, Zhang Lei and Jin Guoping. 2006. "The Challenge of Managing Groundwater Sustainabily [*sic*]." *International Review for Environmental Strategies,* 6(2): 387–402.

Heimburger, Angela, Claudia Gras and Allessandra Guedes. 2003. "Expanding Access to Emergency Contraception: The Case of Brazil and Colombia." *Reproductive Health Matters,* 11(21): 150–60.

Heinrich, Carolyn J. 2003. "Outcomes-Based Performance Management in the Public Sector: Implications for Government Accountability and Effectiveness." *Public Administration Review,* 62(6): 712–25.

Heller, M., E.W. Von Sacken, and R.L. Gertsberger. 2001. "Water Utilities as Integrated Businesses." In W.C. Lauer, ed. *Excellence in Action: Water Utility Management in the 21st Century,* 274–300. Denver: American Water Works Association.

Henderson, Lenneal J. 2003. *The Baltimore CitiStat Program: Performance and Accountability.* Washington, DC: IBM Center for the Business of Government.

Hendrick, Rebecca. 2000. "Comprehensive Management and Budgeting Reform in Local Government: The Case of Milwaukee." *Public Productivity and Management Review,* 23(3): 312–37.

Hersen, Michel and David H. Barlow. 1976. *Single-case Experimental Designs: Strategies for Studying Behavior Change.* New York: Pergamon Press.

Hesse-Biber, Sharlene, Paul Dupuis and T. Scott Kinder. 1991. "HyperRESEARCH: A Computer Program for the Analysis of Qualitative Data with an Emphasis on Hypothesis Testing and Multimedia Analysis." *Qualitative Sociology,* 14(4): 289–306.

HHS. See U.S. Department of Health and Human Services.

Hill, Charles W.L. and Gareth R. Jones. 2001. *Strategic Management.* Boston: Houghton Mifflin.

Hodder, Ian. 1998. "The Interpretation of Documents and Material Culture." In Norman K. Denzin and Yvonna S. Lincoln, eds. *Collecting and Interpreting Qualitative Materials,* 110–29. Thousand Oaks, CA: Sage.

Holsti, Ole R. 1969. *Content Analysis for the Social Sciences and Humanities.* Menlo Park, CA: Addison-Wesley.

Holzer, Marc and Seop-Hwan Lee, eds. 2004. *Public Productivity Handbook,* 2nd ed. New York: Marcel Dekker.

Huber, Günter L. and Carlos M. Garcia. 1991. "Computer Assistance for Testing Hypotheses about Qualitative Data: The Software Package AQUAD 3.0." *Qualitative Sociology,* 14(4): 325–47.

ICMA. See International City/County Management Association.

International City/County Management Association (ICMA). 2008. *ICMA Center for Performance Management.* Washington, DC: International City/County Management Association. Retrieved July 28, 2008, from http://icma.org/main/bcv.asp?bcid=107&hs id=1*ssid1+50&ssid2=220&ssid3=297&t=0.

International Union for the Conservation of Nature (IUCN). 1991. *Caring for the Earth.* Gland, Switzerland: International Union for the Conservation of Nature.

IUCN. See International Union for the Conservation of Nature.

Jacques, Elliott. 1951. *The Changing Culture of a Factory: A Study of Authority and Participation in an Industrial Setting.* London: Tavistock Institute.

Jain, Abhijit, Munir Mandviwalla and Rajiv D. Banker. 2007. "Government as Catalyst: Can It Work Again with Wireless Internet Access?" *Public Administration Review,* 67(6): 993–1005.

Joas, Marko and Björn Grönholm. 2004. "A Comparative Perspective of Self-Assessment of Local Agenda 21 in European Cities." *Boreal Environment Research*, 9 (December): 499–507.

Johnson, Janet B., Richard A. Joslyn and H.T. Reynolds. 2001. *Political Science Research Methods*, 4th ed. Washington, DC: CQ Press.

Johnston, Jocelyn M. and Barbara S. Romzek. 2000. *Implementing State Contracts for Social Services: An Assessment of the Kansas Experience.* Washington, DC: PricewaterhouseCoopers Endowment for the Business of Government.

Jones, Russell A. 1996. *Research Methods in the Social and Behavioral Sciences,* 2nd ed. Sunderland, MA: Sinuar Associates.

Jun, Jong S. 1976. "Reviewing the Study of Comparative Administration: Some Reflections on the Current Possibilities." *Public Administration Review,* 36(1): 141–47.

———. 2000. "Transcending the Limits of Comparative Administration: A New Internationalism in the Making." *Administrative Theory and Praxis,* 22(2): 273–86.

Kaarbo, Juliet and Ryan K. Beasley. 1999. "A Practical Guide to the Comparative Case Study Method in Political Psychology." *Political Psychology*, 20(2): 369–91.

Kamensky, John M. 1996. "The Role of the Reinventing Government Movement in Federal Management Reform." *Public Administration Review*, 56(3): 247–55.

——— and Thomas J. Burlin, eds. 2004. *Collaboration: Using Networks and Partnerships.* Lanham, MD: Rowman and Littlefield.

———, Thomas J. Burlin and Mark A. Abramson. 2004. "Networks and Partnerships: Collaborating to Achieve Results No One Can Achieve Alone." In John M. Kamensky and Thomas J. Burlin, eds. *Collaboration: Using Networks and Partnerships,* 3–20. Lanham, MD: Rowman and Littlefield.

Kaplan, Robert S. and David P. Norton. 1996. *The Balanced Scorecard: Translating Strategy into Action.* Boston: Harvard Business School Press.

Katz, Bruce. 2007. "America's Infrastructure: Ramping Up or Crashing Down." Third Bernard L. Schwartz Forum on Competiveness, October 10, 2007, Washington, DC. In Bernard Katz, Robert Puentes and Christopher Geissier, eds. *Brooking Institution Conference Report 21*. Retrieved January 3, 2009, from www.brookings.edu/~/media/Files/rc/papers/2008/01_infrastructure_katz_puentes/01_infrastructure_katz_puentes.pdf.

Kaufman, Herbert. 1960. *The Forest Ranger: A Study in Administrative Behavior.* Baltimore: Johns Hopkins University Press.

Kawulich, Barbara B. 2005. "Participant Observation as a Data Collection Method." *Forum: Qualitative Social Research,* 6(43). Retrieved February 16, 2008, from www.qualitative_research.net/fqs-texte/2–05/05–2–43.pdf.

Kearnes, David T. 1986. "Quality Improvement Begins at the Top." *World*, 20(5)(May): 21.

Kelly, Janet M. and William C. Rivenbark. 2003. *Performance Budgeting for State and Local Government.* Armonk, NY: M.E. Sharpe.

Keohane, Robert O. and Joseph Nye. 2000. "Governance." In Robert O. Keohane and John D. Donahue, eds. *Governance in a Globalizing World.* Washington, DC: Brookings Institution Press.

Kettl, Donald F. 2005. *The Global Public Management Revolution.* Washington, DC: Brookings Institution Press.

Kettl, Donald F. and H. Brinton Milward, eds. 1996. *The State of Public Management.* Baltimore, MD: Johns Hopkins University Press.

Kim, Pan Suk 2000. "Administrative Reform in the Korean Central Government: A Case Study of the Dae Jung Kim Administration." *Public Performance & Management Review,* 24(2): 145–60.

Kincheloe, Joe L. and Peter L. McLaren. 1984. "Rethinking Critical Theory and Qualitative Research." In Norman K. Denzin and Yvonna S. Lincoln, eds. *Handbook of Qualitative Research*, 138–57. Thousand Oaks, CA: Sage.

King, Gundar J. and David E. McNabb. 2009. "Crossroads Dynamics in Foreign Policy: The Case of Latvia. *Problems of Post-Communism*, 56(3): 1–13.

Klein, Hans E., ed. 1992. *Forging New Partnerships*. Needham, MA: World Association for Case Method Research and Application.

Klein, Heinz K. and Michael D. Meyers. 1999. "A Set of Principles for Conducting and Evaluating Interpretive Field Studies in Information Systems." *MIS Quarterly*, 23(2): 67–98.

Klitgaard, Robert and Gregory F. Trenton. 2004. "Assessing Partnerships: New Forms of Collaboration." In John M. Kamensky and Thomas J. Burlin, eds. *Collaboration: Using Networks and Partnerships*, 21–59. Lanham, MD: Rowman and Littlefield.

Kornblum, William. 1996. "Introduction." In Carolyn D. Smith and William Kornblum, eds. *In the Field: Readings on the Field Research Experience*, 2nd ed., 1–7. Wesport, CT: Praeger.

Kull, Donald C. 1978. "Productivity Programs in the Federal Government." *Public Administration Review*, 38(1): 5–9.

Kydd, Sally A. 1999. A case study of program planning and evaluation in assisting Montserratian evacuees and British government officials in natural disaster planning. PhD diss., Rutgers University.

Lan, Zhiyong and Kathleen K. Anders. 2000. "A Paradigmatic View of Contemporary Public Administration Research." *Administration and Society*, 32 (May): 138–66.

Lane, Jan-Erik. 2000. *New Public Management*. London: Routledge.

Lang, Gerhard and George D. Heiss. 1994. *A Practical Guide to Research Methods*, 2nd ed. Lanham, MD: University Press of America.

Laws, Glenda. 1988. "Privatization and the Local Welfare State: The Case of Toronto's Social Services." *Transactions of the Institute of British Geographers, New Series*, 13(4): 433–48.

Lee, Allen S. 1989. "A Scientific Methodology for MIS Case Studies." *MIS Quarterly*, 13(1): 33–50.

Lee, Robert D. Jr. and Paul S. Greenlaw. 2000. "Employer Liability for Employee Sexual Harassmant: A Judicial Policy-Making Study." *Public Administration Review*, 60(2): 123–33.

Lee, Thomas W. 1999. *Using Qualitative Methods in Organizational Research*. Thousand Oaks, CA: Sage.

Lehti, Marko (2007). "Protege or Go-Between? The Role of the Baltic States after 9/11 in EU-US Relations." *Journal of Baltic Studies*, 38(2): 127–51.

Liebowitz, Jay. 2004. *Addressing the Human Capital Crisis in the Federal Government*. Amsterdam: Butterworth-Heinemann.

Linden, Russell M. 2002. *Working Across Boundaries: Making Collaboration Work in Government and Nongovernment Organizations*. San Francisco: Jossey-Bass.

Lipsey, Mark W. and David B. Wilson, 2001. *Practical Meta-Analysis*. Thousand Oaks, CA: Sage.

Lipsky, Michael. 1980. *Street-Level Bureaucracy*. New York: Russell Sage.

Los Angeles Sheriff's Department. 2009. *Homeland Security: Special Enforcement Bureau*. Retrieved August 19, 2009, from http://www.lasd.org/divisions/homeland_sec/seb/functn_ovrview.html.

Lucas, Edward (2008). *The New Cold War: Putin's Russia and the Threat to the West*. New York: Palgrave Macmillan.

Lundberg, Craig C., Peter Rainsford, Jeff P. Shay and Cheri A. Young. 2001. "Case Writing Reconsidered." *Journal of Management Education*, 25(4): 450–63.

Mahoney, James and Gary Goertz. 2004. "The Possibility Principle: Choosing Negative Cases in Comparative Research." *American Political Science Review*, 98(4): 653–69.

Manicom, Ann and Marie Campbell, eds. 2005. "Module 2: Participant Observation." In *Qualitative Research Methods: A Data Collector's Field Guide.* San Francisco: Family Health International, 13–27. Retrieved February 16, 2007, from http://www.fhi.org/en/index.htm.

Markman, Roberta H., Peter T. Markman and Marie L. Waddell. 1989. *10 Steps in Writing the Research Paper,* 4th ed. New York: Barron's Educational Series.

Markus, M. Lynn. 1981. "Implementation Politics: Top Management Support and User Involvement." *Systems, Objectives, Solutions,* 1(4): 203–15.

———. 1983. "Power, Politics, and MIS Implementation." *Communications of the ACM,* 26(6): 430–44.

Marshall, Catherine and Gretchen B. Rossman. 1999. *Designing Qualitative Research,* 3rd ed. Thousand Oaks, CA: Sage.

Marshment, Richard. 2007. "Benchmarking Transit Research in the United States." *Journal of Public Transportation,* 10(3): 95–118.

Masoner, Michael. 1988. *An Audit of the Case Study Method.* Westport, CT: Greenwood.

Matouq, Mohammed. 2000. "A Case Study of ISO 14001–Based Environmental Management System Implementation in the People's Republic of China." *Local Environment,* 5(4): 415–33.

McEntire, David A., Christopher Fuller, Chad W. Johnston and Richard Weber. 2002. "A Comparison of Disaster Paradigms: The Search for a Holistic Policy Guide." *Public Management Review,* 62(3): 267–81.

McLaughlin, Paul. 1992. *How to Interview.* Vancouver, Canada: Self-Counsel Press.

McMillan, James H. and Sally Schumacher. 1997. *Research in Education.* New York: Longman.

McNabb, David E. 2005. *Public Utilities: Management Challenges for the 21st Century.* London: Edward Elgar.

———. 2008. *Research Methods in Public Administration and Nonprofit Organization Management,* 2nd. ed. Armonk, NY: M.E. Sharpe.

McNabb, David E. and J. Thad Barnowe. 2008. "Innovations in Collaborative Governance of Public Utilities: Models for Interorganizational Relationship-Building." Paper presented at the IAM conference, Kauai, HI, November 2008.

McNabb, David E., Linda K. Gibson and Bruce W. Finnie. 2006. "The Case of the Vanishing Workforce." *Public Performance & Management Review* 29(3): 358–68.

McNabb, David E. and F. Thomas Sepic. 1995. "Culture, Climate and Total Quality Management: Measuring Readiness for Change." *Public Productivity and Management Review,* 18(4): 369–85.

Meacham, Shuaib J. 1998. "Threads of a New Language: A Response to Eisenhart's 'On the Subject of Interpretive Review.'" *Review of Educational Research,* 68 (Winter): 401–7.

Meier, Kenneth J. 1979. *Politics and the Bureaucracy.* North Scituate, MA: Duxbury.

Merriam, Sharan B. 1998. *Qualitative Research and Case Study Applications in Education.* San Francisco: Jossey-Bass.

Mertens, Donna M. 1998. *Research Methods in Education and Psychology.* Thousand Oaks, CA: Sage.

MetaStat. 2008. "The Meta Analysis of Research Studies." College Park: University of Maryland, Department of Measurement, Statistics and Evaluation. Retrieved December 22, 2008, from http://echo.edres.org:8080/meta/.

Miles, Matthew B. and A. Michael Huberman. 1994. *Qualitative Data Analysis: A Sourcebook of New Methods.* Beverly Hills, CA: Sage.

Milward, H. Brinton. 1996. "Conclusion: What Is Public Management?" In Donald F. Kettl and H. Brinton Milward, eds. *The State of Public Management,* 307–12. Baltimore: Johns Hopkins University Press.

Mohr, Lawrence B. 1992. "Causation and the Case Study." In Hans E. Klein, ed. *Forging Partnerships with Cases, Simulations, Games and Other Interactive Methods,* 79–90. Needham, MA: World Association for Case Method Research and Application.

Monopoli, John and Lori L. Alworth. 2000. "The Use of the Thematic Apperception Test in the Study of Native American Psychological Characteristics: A Review and Archival Study of Navaho Men." *Genetic, Social and General Psychology Monographs,* 126(1): 43–79.

Mühr, Thomas. 1991. "ATLAS/ti—A Prototype for the Support of Text Interpretation." *Qualitative Sociology,* 14(4): 349–71.

Mycoo, Michelle. 2005. "Shifting Paradigms in Water Provisioning Policies: A Trinidad Case Study." *Water Resources Development,* 21(3): 509–23.

NOAA. 2009. "Billion Dollar U.S. Weather Disasters." *National Oceanographic and Atmospheric Administration Satellite and Information Services, National Climatic Center, U.S. Department of Commerce.* Retrieved August 15, 2009, from http:www.ncdc,noaa.gov/oa/reports/billionz.html.

Nesterczuk, George. 1996. "Reviewing the National Performance Review." *Regulation: The Cato Review of Business and Government,* 19(3). Retrieved July 27, 2008, from www.cato.org/pubs/regulation/reg19n3b.html.

Neuman, W. Lawrence. 2000. *Social Research Methods: Qualitative and Quantitative Methods,* 4th ed. Boston: Allyn and Bacon.

Nevada Department of Health and Human Services. 2006. "From Director Mike Wilden." Retrieved March 30, 2008, from http://dhhs.nv.gov/.

Ni, Anna Ya and Alfred Tat-Kei Ho. 2008. "A Quiet Revolution or a Flashy Blip? The Real ID Act and U.S. National Identification System Reform." *Public Administration Review,* 68(6): 1063–78.

Nigro, Lloyd G. and J. Edward Kellough. 2008. "Personnel Reform in the States: A Look at Progress Fifteen Years after the Winter Commission." *Public Administration Review,* 68 (Supplement): S50–S57.

Norris, Donald F., Marvin B. Mandell and William E. Hathaway. 1993. "Volunteers in Emergency Medical Service: A Case Study from Rural America." *Public Productivity and Management Review,* 16(23): 257–69.

North Carolina Department of Health and Human Services. 2008. "NCDHHS: Who We Are." Retrieved March 30, 2008, from www.dhhs.state.nc.us/whoweare.htm.

North Dakota Department of Human Services. 2007. "About the Department of Human Services." Retrieved April 1, 2008, from www.nd.gov/dhs/about/.

O'Connell, Paul E. 2001. *Using Performance Data for Accountability.* Washington, DC: IBM Center for the Business of Government.

OECD. See Organisation for Economic Co-operation and Development.

Olson, Margrethe. 1981. "User Involvement and Decentralization of the Development Function: A Comparison of Two Case Studies." *Systems, Objectives, Solutions,* 1(2): 59–69.

Oosterman, Bas J. 2001. "Introduction to the research problem." In Improving product development projects by matching product architecture and organization. PhD diss., University of Groningen, Netherlands. Retrieved January 13, 2009, from http://dissertations.ub/rug.nl/FILES/faculties/management/2001/b.j.oosterman/ci.pdf.

Organ, Dennis W. and Thomas S. Bateman. 1991. *Organizational Behavior,* 4th ed. Homewood, IL: Richard D. Irwin.

Organisation for Economic Co-operation and Development (OECD). 2004a. "European Union Sustainable Development Indicators." OECD Statistics, Knowledge and Policy. OECD World Forum on Key Indicators. Retrieved November 8, 2008, from www.oecd.org/documentprint/0,3455,en-21571361_31834434_33637186_1_1_1_1_00.html.

———. 2004b. "OECD Check-List of Criteria to Define Terrorism for the Purpose of Compensation: Recommendation of the Council." Paris: OECD Directorate for Financial and Enterprise Affairs. Retrieved August 9, 2008, from www.oecd.org/dataoecd/55/2/34065606.pdf.

Orlikowski, Wanda J. 1991. "Integrated Information Environment or Matrix of Control? The Contradictory Implications of Information Technology." *Accounting, Management and Information Technology,* 1(1): 9–42.

———. 2000. "Using Technology and Constituting Structures: A Practical Lens for Studying Technology in Organizations." *Organizational Science,* 11(4): 404–28.

Osborne, David and Ted Gaebler. 1992. *Reinventing Government: How the Entrepreneurial Sprit Is Transforming the Public Sector.* Reading, MA: Addison-Wesley.

Ozoliņa, Žaneta and Airis Rikveilis. 2006. "Latvian and Russian Foreign Policy: Bound by a Post-Soviet Heritage." In Nils Muižnieks, ed. *Latvian and Russian Foreign Policy: Domestic and International Dimensions,* 87–97. Riga: University of Latvia Press.

Pagano, Michael A. and David Perry. 2008. "Financing Infrastructure in the 21st Century City." *Public Works Management & Policy,* 13(1): 22–38.

Pascal, Gerald R. 1983. *The Practical Art of Diagnostic Interviewing.* Homewood, IL: Dow Jones-Irwin.

PA Times. 2008. "Transportation Infrastructure Needs Overhaul." *American Society for Public Administration,* (September): 7.

Patton, Michael Q. 1980. *Qualitative Evaluation Methods.* Beverly Hills, CA: Sage.

Patusky, Christopher, Leigh Botwinik and Mary Shelley. 2007. *The Philadelphia SchoolStat Model.* Washington, DC: IBM Center for the Business of Government.

Pearson, Christine M. and Judith A. Clair. 1998. "Reframing Crisis Management." *Academy of Management Review,* 23(1): 59–76.

Pelfrey, William V. Jr. 2007. "Local Law Enforcement Terrorism Prevention Efforts: A State Level Case Study." *Journal of Criminal Justice,* 35(3): 313–21.

Pennings, Paul, Hans Keman and Jan Kleinnijenhuis. 1999. *Doing Research in Political Science.* London: Sage.

Perlich, Martin. 2007. *The Art of the Interview.* Los Angeles: Silman-James Press.

Perrow, Charles. 2006. "Using Organizations: The Case of FEMA." Retrieved November 27, 2008, from http://understandingkatrina.ssrc.org/Perrow/.

Phillips, Denis C. 1987. *Philosophy, Science and Social Inquiry.* Oxford, UK: Pergamon.

Piantanida, Maria and Noreen B. Garman. 1999. *The Qualitative Dissertation.* Thousand Oaks, CA: Sage.

Pina, Jamie. 2006. "Using Participant Observation for Organizational Discovery and Systems Analysis: Global AIDS Program Uganda." Paper presented at the symposium of American Medical Informatics Association. Washington, DC, November 11–22, 2006. AMIA 2006 Symposium Proceedings: 1064.

Platt, J. 1999. "What Can Case Studies Do?" In Alan Bryman and Robert G. Burgess, eds. *Qualitative Research,* 160–79. London: Sage.

Poister, Theodore H. and Richard H. Harris Jr. 2000. "Building Quality Improvement Over the Long Run: Approaches, Results, and Lessons Learned from the PennDOT Experience." *Public Productivity and Management Review,* 24(2): 161–76.

Poister, Theodore H. and David M. Van Slyke. 2002. "Strategic Management Innovations in State Transportation Departments." *Public Performance & Management Review,* 26(1): 58–74.

Prager, Jonas. 2008. "Contract City Redux: Weston, Florida as the Ultimate New Public Management Model City." *Public Administration Review,* 68(1): 167–80.

Pyburn, Philip J. 1983. "Linking the MIS Plan with Corporate Strategy: An Exploratory Study." *MIS Quarterly* 7(2): 1–14.

Ragin, Charles C. 1987. *The Comparative Method: Moving Beyond Qualitative and Quantitative Strategies.* Berkeley: University of California Press.

Rago, William V. 1996. "Struggles in Transformation: A Study in TQM, Leadership, and

Organizational Culture in a Government Agency." *Public Administration Review*, 56(3): 227–34.

Reid, Robert L. 2008. "Infrastructure 'Conversion' Focus on Investment Plan for Water, Energy, Transportation." *Civil Engineering*, (August): 35–39.

Rhode Island Department of Human Services. 2005. "Secretariat of Health and Human Services Will Target Coordination Among Agencies." Retrieved April 1, 2008, from www.ri.gov/press/view.php?id=539.

Richards, Thomas J. and Lyn Richards. 1998. "Using Computers in Qualitative Research." In Norman K. Denzin and Yvonna S. Lincoln, eds. *Collecting and Interpreting Qualitative Materials,* 211–45. Thousand Oaks, CA: Sage.

Risher, Howard and Charles H. Fay. 2007. *Managing for Better Performance: Enhancing Federal Performance Management Practices*: Washington, DC: IBM Center for the Business of Government.

Rist, Ray C. 1998. "Influencing the Policy Process with Qualitative Research." In Norman K. Denzin and Yvonna S. Lincoln, eds. *Collecting and Interpreting Qualitative Materials,* 400–24. Thousand Oaks, CA: Sage.

Rizzuto, Tracey E. and Laura K. Maloney. 2008. "Organizing Chaos: Crisis Management in the Wake of Hurricane Katrina." *Professional Psychology: Research and Practice,* 39(1): 77–85.

Roberts, Celia. 2005. "Case Studies." *Reflect Magazine Online,* 3 (June). London: National Research and Development Centre for Adult Literacy and Numeracy. Retrieved May 10, 2008, from http://www.nrdc.org.uk/content.asp?CategoryID=771.

Romzek Barbara S. and Melvin J. Dubnick. 1994. "Issues of Accountability in Flexible Personnel Systems." In Patricia W. Ingrahm and Barbara S. Romzek, eds. *New Paradigms for Government,* 263–94. San Francisco: Jossey-Bass.

Rosenwald, George C. 1988. "A Theory of Multiple-Case Research." *Journal of Personality,* 56(1): 249–64.

Sahely, Halla R., Christopher A. Kennedy and Barry J. Adams. 2005. "Developing Sustainability Criteria for Urban Infrastructure Systems." *Canadian Journal of Civil Engineering,* 32(1): 72–85.

Salkind, Neil J. 2000. *Exploring Research,* 4th ed. Upper Saddle River, NJ: Prentice Hall.

Savas, E. S. 2002. "Competition and Choice in New York City Social Services." *Public Administration Review,* 62(1): 82–91.

Schachter, Hindy L. 2008. "Lillian Borrone: Weaving a Web to Revitalize Port Commerce in New York and New Jersey." *Public Administration Review,* 68(1): 61–67.

Schaeffer, Peter V. and Scott Loveridge. 2002. "Toward an Understanding of Types of Public-Private Cooperation." *Public Performance and Management Review,* 26(2): 169–89.

Schneider, Kirk J. 1999. "Multiple-Case Depth Research: Bringing Experience-Near Closer." *Journal of Clinical Psychology,* 55(12): 1531–40.

Schwandt, Thomas A. 1997. *Qualitative Inquiry: A Dictionary of Terms.* Thousand Oaks, CA: Sage.

Scott, Colin. 2000. "Accountability in the Regulatory State." *Journal of Law and Society,* 27(1): 38–60.

Secret, Mary and Jennifer Swanberg. 2008. "Work-Family Experience and the Insights of Municipal Employees: A Case Study." *Public Personnel Management,* 37(2): 199–221.

Segal, Lydia. 2002. "Roadblocks in Reforming Corrupt Agencies: The Case of the New York City School Custodians." *Public Administration Review* 62(4): 445–60.

Seifert, Jeffrey W. 2008. *Federal Enterprise Architecture and E-Government: Issues for Information Technology Management.* Washington, DC: Congressional Research Service. Form RL33417. Retrieved November 27, 2008, from www.ipmall.info/hosted_resources/crs/RL33417_080410.pdf.

Sekhon, Jasjeet. 2004. "Quality Meets Quantity: Case Studies, Conditional Probability, and Counterfactuals." *Perspectives on Politics,* 2(2): 281–93.

Selznick, Philip. 1949. *TVA and the Grass Roots: A Study in the Sociology of Formal Organization.* Berkeley: University of California Press.

Shapiro, Benson P. 2007. *Hints for Case Teaching.* Cambridge, MA: Harvard Business School Press.

Shapiro, Jacob N. and Dara Kay Cohen. 2007. "Color Blind: Lessons from the Failed Homeland Security Advisory System." *International Security,* 32(2): 121–54.

Sindico, Francesco. 2005. "Ex-post and Ex-ante (Legal) Approaches to Climate Change Treats to the International Community." *New Zealand Journal for Environmental Law,* 9: 209–38.

Smith, Robert G. 1987. "Regionalization of Regional Transportation Authorities to Maintain Urban/Suburban Constituency Balance." *Public Administration Review,* 47(2): 171–79.

Smith, Wally and John Dowell. 2000. "A Case Study of Coordinative Decision-Making in Disaster Management." *Ergonomics,* 43(8): 1153–66.

Snyder, William M. and Xavier de Souza Briggs. 2004. "Communities of Practice: A New Tool for Government Managers." In John M. Kamensky and Thomas J. Burlin, eds. *Collaboration: Using Networks and Partnerships,* 171–272. Lanham, MD: Rowman and Littlefield.

Social Scientists Working Group (SSWG). 2000. "Learning About a Drug Use Problem: Session Guide." In Qualitative Methods to Learn About Drug Use. Retrieved August 19, 2009, from http://archives.who.int/PRDUC2004/RDUCD_2000_DROM/PRDU_course/session_Guides/5_LearningSG.doc.

Sociology Guide. 2006. "Design of Sociological Research." Retrieved January 14, 2009, from www.sociologyguide.com/research-methods&statistics/research-design.php.

Soni, Vidu. 2000. "A Twenty-First Century Reception for Diversity in the Public Sector: A Case Study." *Public Administration Review,* 60(5): 395–408.

Sorrels, Bobbye D. 1984. *Business Communications Fundamentals.* New York: Macmillan.

Sproull, Natalie L. 1988. *Handbook of Research Methods.* Metuchen, NJ: Scarecrow Press.

SSWG. See Social Scientists Working Group.

Stake, Robert E. 1994. "Case Studies." In N. K. Denzin and Y. S. Lincoln, eds. *Handbook of Qualitative Research,* 236–47. Thousand Oaks, CA: Sage.

———. 1995. *The Art of Case Study Research.* Thousand Oaks, CA: Sage.

———. 2006. *Multiple Case Study Analysis.* New York: Guilford Press.

State of Alabama. 2003. "Alabama Homeland Security: About the Alabama Department of Homeland Security." Retrieved March 29, 2008, from http://www.homelandsecurity.alabama.gov/department.htm.

State of Alaska. 2008. "Division of Homeland Security and Emergency Management: Welcome to the Office of Homeland Security Website." Retrieved March 29, 2008, from www.ak-prepared.com/homelandsecurity/.

State of Oklahoma. 2008. "Oklahoma Office of Homeland Security: OKOHS Objectives and Duties." Retrieved March 29, 2008, from http://ok-gov/homeland/About_Us/index.html.

State of Pennsylvania. 2007. "Pennsylvania Homeland Security: Mission." Retrieved March 29, 2008, from www.homelandsecurity.state.pa.us/homelandsecurity/cwp/view.asp?a=378&q=1752.

State of Tennessee. 2008. "The Office of Homeland Security Has Merged with the Department of Safety. Preserving Freedom, Protecting Tennessee." Tennessee Office of Homeland Security. Retrieved March 29, 2008, from www.state.tn.us/homelandsecurity/.

Stein, Harold, ed. 1952. *Public Administration and Policy Development: A Case Book.* New York: Harcourt Brace.

Stokes, Robyn and Chad Perry. 2007. "Case Research about Enterprises." In Damian Hine and David Carson, eds. *Innovative Methodologies in Enterprise Research,* 137–51. Cheltenham, UK: Edward Elgar.

Strauss, Anselm and Juliet M. Corbin. 1998. *Basics of Qualitative Research,* 2nd ed. Thousand Oaks, CA: Sage.

Streib, Gregory, Bert J. Slotkin and Mark Rivera. 2001. "Public Administration Research from a Practitioner Perspective." *Public Administration Review,* 61(5): 515–25.

Stringer, Ernie, ed. 1997. *Community-Based Ethnography: Breaking Traditional Boundaries of Research, Teaching, and Learning.* Mahwah, NJ: Erlbaum.

Tabuns, Aivars. 2006. "Attitudes Towards the State and Latvian Foreign Policy." In Muižnieks, Nils, ed. *Latvian-Russian Relations: Domestic and International Dimensions.* Riga: University of Latvia Press.

Tak, Sunghee H., Margaret Nield and Heather Becker. 1999. "Use of a Computer Software Program for Qualitative Analyses—Part 1: Introduction to NUD*IST (N1)." *Western Journal of Nursing Research,* 31(1): 111–18.

Taylor, Jeannette. 2006. "Performance Measurement in Australian and Hong Kong Government Departments." *Public Performance & Management Review,* 29(3): 334–57.

Taylor, Steven J. and Robert Bogdan. 1998. *Introduction to Qualitative Research Methods,* 3rd ed. New York: Wiley.

Thompson, James R. 2000. "Reinvention as Reform: Assessing the National Performance Review." *Public Administration Review,* 60(6): 508–21.

Tirasirichai, Chakkaphan and David Enke. 2007. "Case Study: Applying a Regional CGE Model for Estimation of Indirect Economic Losses Due to Damaged Highway Bridges." *The Engineering Economist,* 52(4): 367–401.

Treņins, Dimitrij. (1998). "Krievija un Baltijas valstis: drošības aspekti." In Jundzis, Tālavs, ed. *Baltijas valstis liktengriežos.* Riga: Latvijas Zinātņu Akademija.

Trethanya, Suparb and L. A. S. Ranjith Perera. 2008. "Environmental Assessment for Non-Prescribed Infrastructure Development Projects: A Case Study in Bangkok Metropolitan." *Impact Assessment and Project Appraisal,* 26(2): 127–38.

Ulhöi, John P. 2004. "Policies for Sustainable Development: The Case of Government Agency." *Problems and Perspectives in Management,* 2(2004): 109–20.

Uphoff, Norman, ed. 1994. *Puzzles of Productivity.* San Francisco: Contemporary Studies Press.

U.S. Census Bureau. 2004. "Census of Governments: 2002 Public Employment Data, State and Local Governments, United States Total." Revised October 2004. Retrieved March 27, 2008, from http://ftp2.census.gov/govs/apes/02stlus.txt.

———. 2007. "Federal Government Civilian Employment by Function: December 2006." Retrieved March 27, 2008, from www.census.gov/govs/apes/06fedfun.pdf.

———. 2008a. "Federal Civilian Employment and Annual Payroll by Branch: 1970–2006." Retrieved March 27, 2008, from http://www.allcountries.org/uscensus/558_federal_civilian_employment_and_annual_payroll.html.

———. 2008b. "Federal, State and Local Governments: 2007 Census of Governments." Retrieved March 27, 2008, from www.census.gov/govs/www/cog2007.html.

U.S. Chamber of Commerce. 2008. "Fixing America's Crumbling Infrastructure." U.S. Chamber of Commerce Magazine (July). Retrieved August 5, 2008, from www.uschambermagazine.com/content/print.htm?page=0807_6.

U.S. Department of Health and Human Services (DHHS). 2008. "U.S. Department of Health and Human Services: What We Do." Retrieved March 30, 2008, from www.hhs.gov/about/whatwedo.html/.

U.S. Department of Homeland Security (DHS). 2008. "The United States Government's

National Threat Level Is Elevated or Yellow." Press release, August 25, 2008. Retrieved August 27, 2008, from www.dhs.gov/xinfoshare/programs/Copy_of_press_release_0046 .shtm.

U.S. Department of State. 2004. *Principles of Democracy: Government Accountability.* Washington, DC: U.S. Department of State. Retrieved March 21, 2008, from http:// usinfor.state.gov/products/pubs/principles/government.htm.

U.S. Department of Transportation (DOT). 2003. *Strategic Plan, 2003–2008.* Washington, DC: Department of Transportation.

———. 2005. "A Summary of Highway Provisions in SAFETEA-LU." Washington DC: U.S. Department of Transportation, Federal Highway Administration. Retrieved July 30, 2008, from www.fhwa.dot.gov/safetealu/summary.htm.

U.S. Government Accountability Office (GAO). 2007. "The Forces That Will Shape America's Future: Themes from GAO's Strategic Plan, 2007–2012." Washington, DC: U.S. Government Accountability Office. Report GAO-07–467SP.

———. 2008a. "Department of Homeland Security: Progress Made in Implementation of Management and Mission Functions, but More Work Remains." Testimony of Controller General David M. Walker before the U.S. House of Representatives Subcommittee on Homeland Security, Committee on Appropriations. Washington, DC: U.S. Government Accountability Office. Report GAO-08–457T.

———. 2008b. "Homeland Security: DHS Improved Its Risk-Based Grant Programs' Allocation and Management Methods, but Measuring Programs' Impact on National Capabilities Remains a Challenge." Testimony of William O. Jenkins Jr., Director of Homeland Security and Justice Issues, before the U.S. House of Representatives Subcommittee on Homeland Security, Committee on Appropriations. Washington, DC: U.S. Government Accountability Office. Report GAO-08–488T.

———. 2008c. "Strengthening Preparedness for Large-Scale Public Health Emergencies. GAO Key Reports: What Needs to Be Done." Retrieved November 9, 2008, from www .gao.gov/transition_2009/urgent/public-health.php.

Van Evera, Stephen. 1997. *Guide to Methods for Students of Political Science.* Ithaca, NY: Cornell University Press.

Velasquez, Manuel. 1998. *Business Ethics: Concepts and Cases,* 4th ed. Upper Saddle River, NJ: Prentice Hall.

Wachterhauser, Brice. 1986. "History and Language in Understanding." In Brice Wachterhauser, ed. *Hermeneutics and Modern Philosophy,* 5–61. Albany: State University of New York Press.

Walker, David M. 2007. "Foresight for Government." *The Futurist,* 41(2): 18–22.

Ward, Robert, Gary Wamsley, Aaron Schroeder and David B. Robins. 2000. "Network Organizational Development in the Public Sector: A Case Study of the Federal Emergency Management Administration (FEMA)." *Journal of the American Society for Information Science,* 5(11): 1018–32.

Wasko, Molly M. and Samer Faraj. 2005. "Why Should I Share? Examining Social Capital and Knowledge Contribution in Electronic Networks of Practice." *MIS Quarterly,* 29(2): 35–57.

Waugh, William L. 1994. "Regionalizing Emergency Management: Counties as State and Local Government." *Public Administration Review,* 54(3): 253–58.

WCED. See World Commission on Environment and Development.

Webb, Eugene J., Donald T. Campbell, Richard D. Swartz and Lee Sechrest. 2000. *Unobtrusive Measures.* Rev. ed. Thousand Oaks, CA: Sage.

Weiss, Robert S. 1994. *Learning from Strangers: The Art and Method of Qualitative Interview Studies.* New York: The Free Press.

Weitzman, E. and Michael Miles, 1995. *Computer Programs for Qualitative Data Analysis: A Software Sourcebook.* Thousand Oaks: Sage.

Westgren, Randall and Kelly Zering. 1998. "Case Study Research Methods for Firm and Market Research." *Agribusiness*, 14(5): 415-23.

Wheeler, Edward T. 1993. *Government That Works: Innovation in State and Local Government*. Jefferson, NC: McFarland.

Whelan, Robert K. 1989. "Data Administration and Research Methods in Public Administration." In J. Rabin, W.B. Hildreth and G.J. Miller, eds. *Handbook of Public Administration*, 657–82. New York: Marcel Dekker.

White, Jay D. 1999. *The Narrative Foundations of Public Administration Research*. Washington, DC: Georgetown University Press.

White, Jay D. and Guy B. Adams, eds. 1994. *Research in Public Administration*. Thousand Oaks, CA: Sage.

Whiting, Beatrice and John Whiting. 1973. "Methods for Observing and Recording Behavior." In Raoul Naroll and Ronald Cohen, eds. *A Handbook of Method in Cultural Anthropology*. 282-315. New York: Columbia University Press.

Wineburg, Robert J. 1994. "A Longitudinal Case Study of Religious Congregations in Local Human Services." *Nonprofit and Voluntary Sector Quarterly*, 23(2): 159–69.

Wise, Lois R. 2002. "Public Management Reform: Competing Drivers of Change." *Public Management Review*, 62(5): 555–67.

World Commission on Environment and Development (WCED). 1987. *Our Common Future*. Oxford, UK: Oxford University Press.

Yager, William F. 1992. "The Use of Structured Comparative Case Studies as a Research Methodology in International Technology Transfer." In Hans E. Klein, ed. *Forging Partnerships with Cases, Simulations, Games and Other Interactive Methods*, 43–52. Needham, MA: World Association for Case Method Research and Application.

Yeager, Samuel J. 1989. "Classic Methods in Public Administration Research." In Jack Rabin, W.B. Hildreth and G.J. Miller, eds. *Handbook of Public Administration*, 683–793. New York: Marcel Dekker.

Yin, Robert K. 1994. *Case Study Research: Design and Methods*, 2nd ed. Thousand Oaks, CA: Sage.

Young, Gary J. 2000. "Managing Organizational Transformations: Lessons from the Veterans Health Administration." *California Management Review*, 43(1): 66–82.

Index

About the Author

David E. McNabb, Pacific Lutheran University professor emeritus, is the author of two comprehensive research methods texts, both of which are now in their second edition. The first edition of his *Research Methods in Public Administration and Nonprofit Organizations* was awarded the 2004 John Grenzebach Research Award for Research in Philanthropy. He continues to teach at colleges and universities in the United States and internationally. He has been an adjunct professor in the master's degree program in Public Administration at The Evergreen State College (TESC) in Olympia, Washington, the European master's degree program of the University of Maryland–University College, and an adjunct professor at the University of Washington–Tacoma. He is currently teaching at a branch campus of Olympic College, Bremerton, Washington.

Professor McNabb periodically serves as a visiting professor at the Riga, Latvia, campus of the Stockholm School of Economics. He was a visiting professor at the American University in Bulgaria in 1992 and a Fulbright Senior Specialist in Latvia in 2007. He earned a B.A. in 1965 at California State University–Fullerton, an M.A. in 1968 at the University of Washington, and a Ph.D. in 1980 at Oregon State University. He is the author of nearly ninety articles and conference papers and six books.

Professor McNabb is a member of the American Society for Public Administration and the American Political Science Association, and a past member of the Academy of Management, the American Marketing Association, and Rotary International.